MODELS OF NARRATIVE

THEORY AND PRACTICE

DAVID K. DANOW

ST. MARTIN'S PRESS
NEW YORK

ISBN 0–312–16388–6

Library of Congress Cataloging-in-Publication Data

Danow, David K. (David Keevin), 1944–
    Models of narrative : theory and practice / David K. Danow.
        p. cm.
    Includes bibliographical references and index.
    ISBN 0–312–16388–6
    1. Literature—History and criticism—Theory, etc. 2. Narration
(Rhetoric) I. Title.
PN81.D36 1997
809—dc20   96-34402
                                                                CIP

Interior design by Harry Katz

First Edition: January 1997
10   9   8   7   6   5   4   3   2   1

Several chapters of this book have been published previously in an earlier form.
Chapter 1 originally appeared as "Temporal Strategies and Constraints in
Narrative" in *Semiotica,* 1986, 58:3-4; Chapter 2 as "Epiphany in *Doctor Zhivago*"
in *The Modern Language Review,* 1981, 76:4; and Chapter 8 as "A Poetics of
Inversion: The Non-Dialogic Aspect in Isaac Babel's *Red Calvary,*" in *The
Modern Language Review,* 1991, 86:4.

For Victor Terras,
esteemed teacher, valued friend

CONTENTS

Literary Models: Theoretical Considerations 1

PART I.   TEMPORAL RELATIONS 13
1. Linear Perspectives (Dostoevsky and Tolstoy) 23

2. The Moment of Revelation:
Epiphany in *Doctor Zhivago* (Pasternak) 39

3. Memory as Duration: *Love in the Time of Cholera*
(García Márquez) 57

PART II.   SPATIAL RELATIONS 69
4. Convergence in *The Master and Margarita* (Bulgakov) 77

5. Divergence in "The Minister's Black Veil" (Hawthorne) 91

6. The Figural Labyrinth in *The General in His Labyrinth*
(García Márquez) 101

PART III.   DIALOGIC RELATIONS 113
7. A Poetics of Silence (Dostoevsky, O'Connor, Endo) 119

8. The Nondialogic Encounter: *Red Cavalry* (Babel) 133

9. Supradialogue: *Doctor Zhivago* (Pasternak) 153

Literary Models: Practical Conclusions 173

Notes 181

Works Cited 195

Index 201

LITERARY MODELS:
THEORETICAL CONSIDERATIONS

■ □ ■

As readers and critics, we look for certain ideal concepts, or models of order, to coalesce into patterns of coherence that permit us to understand. In analogous, complementary fashion, we routinely create certain models as the means for presenting our own ideas in accessible and engaging terms. This book is designed to take considered account of this common practice. The concept of literary modeling is not new. There have been untold isolated attempts to apply elementary ad hoc models to individual narrative texts. More concerted efforts to employ fully elaborated modeling systems to the study of entire literary genres have also been attempted. There is indeed much to be gained by examining a hermeneutic tool that has proven itself eminently productive in both the humanities and sciences. Yet no extensive treatment of literary modeling currently exists. Designed to outline the bare lineaments of this seminal but largely ignored topic, this study explores what amounts to not only a common mode of approach in both scientific and humanistic endeavor but a highly productive mode of human conceptualization, deserving far greater attention.

To define briefly my central term, a model may be conceived as a predetermined configuration of ideas that serve as an explanatory or heuristic device. Comprising a certain abstract schema, it is a useful speculative instrument intended to reveal structural detail belonging to a given original to which it stands as a meaningful analogue. Most important, a model focuses the critical project and contains it within a cohesive conceptual framework. Models thus set forth a corresponding set of determinate relations, designed to illustrate the principles by which the subject at hand had been generated and may later be explicated. They represent "patterns of coherence that we expect to find, and seek to find, in discourse" (Dillon 53), including, of course, the critical enterprise. Broadly conceived as a set of exemplifying schemata, ideally affording wide applicability, the concept of *model* is treated here at the outset in abstract terms, and in relation to common understandings in the sciences, addressing particular theoretical underpinnings. Virtually all that follows represents critical practice in light of the fact that this book intends to present a series of practical methodologies rather than to set out more dogma related to yet another theory.

Inherently disposed toward an intrinsic approach to the literary work, the use of a model need not imply, or advocate, one critical method over another. Rather, it simply acknowledges the basic utility of a certain designated "frame" or mode of approach as a viable heuristic technique in the concrete endeavor of literary criticism. Within that frame "the model prescribes a context" and thus "sets a limit to what can be said" (Hutten 295). Models circumscribe and encompass their subjects. Yet they need not be entirely neutral or be perceived as such. For our choice of terminology or nomenclature, how as critics and analysts we cast our terms and project our models, always goes some distance toward determining our findings. In going a certain distance in this study toward acknowledging this incomparable resource, a model may be understood in terms of overlapping capacities that I will refer to as interpretive, definitive, or generative. Yet the sense of hard and fast categories is here meant to be immediately eschewed in favor of a kind of spectrum of interrelated functions.

As preliminary considerations within that spectrum, a model may be construed in the most rudimentary terms, first, as representing a basic definition designed to encompass a given subject. "A mode of managing or transforming material. . . . [It] should be understood as a working concept rather than a real entity, as an ideal construct created by the researcher" (Shukman 19, 24), or as a certain continuum, providing a delimited range of possibility. From another perspective it may be derived from a single binary opposition or series of such oppositions, according to that common structuralist ploy. It may be either descriptive or prescriptive in its general orientation, predicated upon either a complex or relatively simple proposition. This book will be characterized by ventures more closely aligned with the latter, in accord with a common-sense dictum enunciated by Tzvetan Todorov, asserting that "one of the criteria for choosing between two equally faithful descriptions is that of simplicity" (Chatman 91). This same dictum, I feel, holds in choosing between any number of presumably faithful descriptions or systems, where the more that one claims for itself the less likely it is to deliver.

Essentially, that same view applies to the sciences. Thus, from a scientific viewpoint it is argued that "models play an essential role in reducing the multiplicity of phenomena to conceptually amenable systems" (Leatherdale 55). That emphasis correlates directly with the present endeavor. In fact, there are a number of parallels between the concept of model in the sciences and how I propose for it to be understood in relation to the humanities in general and literature in particular. Concerning its use in science, several features are of immediate interest. First, "as a matter of historical fact models have played a key role in the development of science" (83), especially in physics. This may be explained in terms of their explanatory functions and in light of the view that models "are almost essential heuristically for scientific discovery" (48). In response to (the several) detractors of this position, a philosopher contends: "Those who see a model as a mere crutch are like those who consider metaphor a mere decoration or ornament. . . . Metaphorical thought is a distinctive mode of achieving insight, not to be construed as an ornamental substitute for plain thought" (Black 236-37). This same perspective holds that "the severest critic of the method will have to concede that recourse to models yields results. . . . [Models] play a distinctive and irreplaceable part in scientific investigation" (231, 236). It is precisely this compelling sense of a model's essential, intuitional aspect that has inspired the present inquiry within the literary domain and remains central throughout its pages, whose overall intent is perhaps only to make explicit what has generally been taken as implicit—that is, to foreground what amounts to common practice, if not exactly common knowledge.

Oddly, the terms *model, theory, analogue,* and perhaps most significant, *metaphor,* have been used interchangeably in the sciences. The topic of this interchangeability, or confusion, is beyond the scope of this study, yet the binding relationship between *model* and *theory* can be explained by the compelling notion that "theory construction is primarily model building" (Harré 46). Further, in light of their common reliance on analogy, the confounding of *model* and *metaphor* may be readily explained thus: "A model for something . . . can be described in the language of simile as a thing or process analogous to that of which it is a model" (47). Which is to say, from the standpoint of the literary critic: "We tend to describe the nature of something in similes and metaphors, and the vehicles of these recurrent figures, when analyzed, often turn out to be the attributes of an implicit analogue through which we are viewing the object we describe" (Abrams 32), as when a model is employed. Hence the seemingly inevitable and clearly evident intertwining of these several closely related concepts. Beyond the inevitability, however, or underlying it, is the need to establish a convincing relationship between an explanatory device, or model, and the subject under investigation. This is both fundamental to concrete scientific exploration and yet paradoxically situated in figurative expression, which is itself a consideration, indeed a problem, for certain theorists, who perceive a danger in a "system of metaphors" that are "picturesque" but may ultimately appear as only "the terminological debris of a dead model" (Harré 47).

Of related concern is the "unfortunate" fact that "the literature on 'models' displays a bewildering lack of agreement about what exactly is meant by the word 'model' in relation to science" (Leatherdale 41). As a result, "items called models in the sciences" appear an unqualified "varied lot" (Achinstein 209), including representational, theoretical, and imaginary types and their various subsets, as one theorist (among numerous others, operating with different taxonomic principles) sees fit to categorize them. Understood as a "simplified approximation" (214), utilizing "idealized relationships" (217), the concept of a theoretical model, based on a certain "*analogy* between the object or system described in the model and some different object or system" (216), as the literary work has been termed (in Formalist thinking), comes closest to our understanding and use of the term. Yet the relative proliferation of the use of models in the sciences has confounded rather than clarified the related issues of terminology and utility, which find their place in occasionally contentious discussion within the scientific literature.

For our purposes, and in accord with common understandings in the sciences, a model displays an analogy, or establishes a certain analogue, between the known and the unknown, between what is generally comprehended and what is not. In this important regard "the model is a useful and indeed inescapable tool of thought, in that it enables us to think about the unfamiliar in terms of the familiar" (Bridgman 53), "to use the better known to elucidate the less known, to discuss the intangible in terms of the tangible" (Abrams 31-32). Part of such thinking clearly implies the ability to apply considerable intuition, even imagination, as it does in like humanistic endeavors. If, on the one hand, "a promising model is one with implications rich enough to suggest novel hypotheses," then, it is reasonably argued, "to make good use of a model, we usually need intuitive grasp . . . of its capacities" (Black 232-33). "To find the right model," in other words, "is a matter of imagination and skill" (Hutten 299). Thus a student of what might be termed "modeling theory" (an expression clearly lacking common currency) emphatically acknowledges the significant role played by "the *creative act* involved in analogical thinking" (Leatherdale 62; emphasis added).

Indeed, it is precisely this mode of conceptualizing—analogically, in the "language of simile"—that permits the analyst to be articulate and convincing, virtues that correlate with the simplifying, summarizing aspects of models, resulting, ideally, in a shared conviction among researchers.

Further implied in this understanding is the use of an underlying, commonly understood "metalanguage," which grounds, in effect, a potentially convincing argument. It does so by creating certain (logical) links, or simply by allowing us "to *see new connections*" (Black 237) between theory and object. Such newly found vision may be attained in part by recognizing that "the model functions as a more general kind of *metaphor*" (Hutten 289), to which is attached considerable weight and power. Thus it is argued (with perhaps greater reliance on literary effect than scientific logic): "Perhaps every science must start with metaphor and end with algebra; and perhaps without the metaphor there would never have been any algebra" (Black 242). Such (appealing) argumentation, however, is based on the notion that "perhaps those interested in excavating the presuppositions and latent archetypes of scientists may have something to learn from the industry of literary critics" (243), a view that is perhaps generous to the critic. In the following critical readings, in any case, expressions prominently employed in chapter headings—*convergence* and *divergence*, *epiphany* and *duration*, *nondialogic* and *supradialogue*—serve as instances of metalinguistic terms employed in the job of applying a model as heuristic device to the critical analyses of literary texts.

On other counts relating scientific approaches with present humanistic concerns, it is reasonable to say, first, that an essential part of the meaning and explanation derived from the use of a particular model is potentially inherent to the formulated analogy, which leads to particular findings. The model employed, in other words, may go some way (as noted) toward indicating, if not dictating, the eventual results. In science, where the generic aim is to make empirical discoveries, this represents a distinct problem for those who argue against the use of models as relying too greatly on little more than figurative thinking in the search for concrete results. It may well be argued, however, in more neutral terms, that "there always in practice *are* reasons for examining a hypothetical interpretation, and these reasons are drawn from models" (Hesse 33). Similarly, in literary studies a like application of "analogical thinking" can lead only to additional, perhaps new and meaningful understandings. Just as the canon is subject to welcome expansion, so are attendant critical responses likewise enriching in their often varied readings.

Second, in science a model may be conceived "as a set of proposi-
tions or statements connected together in a deductive system" (Hesse
43). For present purposes, essentially this same view is held—namely,
that in applying a model to a literary work, the goal is to deduce certain
understandings pertaining to that work rather than attempt to work
inductively toward the elaboration of entire theories based on specific
models. An alternative view holds that "one of the chief functions of a
model [is] to supply a descriptive terminology for theories" (48). That
perspective finds its place here in the various distinctions that are made
later in the present chapter among several types of model. Further, the
definitions, oppositions, and analogies that underlie our subsequent
readings and discussions are meant to be seen as other than sui generis
to the respective texts at hand and as being pertinent to the analysis of
other works than those treated here.

Third, it is contended in science that "models are an important part
of theories because . . . they make the theory strongly predictive" (79).
With respect to literary inquiry, where each individual work is unique,
the idea of predictive ability finds little or no place. Ultimately, the literary model is meant to be descriptive rather than prescriptive. Just as
scientific explanation eschews ambiguity in favor of a single, uniform
understanding, literature values multiplicity and the sense of extended,
open-ended possibility beyond any individual reading or any single
model supporting that reading. In literary study multivalent, polysemic
renderings remain paramount as guiding virtues for both writer and
reader, even the reader who favors particular explanatory models in
making critical assumptions.

※　※　※

Affording rich implications, two basic models initially command our
attention. The first is primarily interpretive, the second generative. A
half-century ago, Eric Auerbach proposed the concept of "figural interpretation" as a viable approach to questions of archetypal patterns in literature. According to this view, both fictive characters and events are
shown to signify not only an obvious primary referent but also some
other related, "hidden" meaning or relation, borrowed from another
text. Hence a certain interrelation is established among such representations, preparing the way for its interpretation.

Also more than a half-century ago, Mikhail Bakhtin expounded his
concept of the "chronotope," a time/space model designed to elaborate

the generative mechanisms by which narratives exhibiting common structural elements are produced in a particular culture at a certain historical moment. In this understanding the elaborate temporal and spatial configurations that govern the perception of the actual world (as part of a given culturally ingrained perspective) are those that determine as well the making of a text. As Bakhtin expresses it: "Out of the chronotopes of our world (which serve as the source of representation) emerge the reflected and *created* chronotopes of the world represented in the work" (*Dialogic* 253). But the process also works in reverse, as both the world and the world of the text appropriate what they need from each other, in the fundamental human activity of making sense of the world through art, resulting in a series of potentially infinite progressions. This mutually influenced, dual-directed flow of information may be directly attributed to the merging of two interrelated normative systems: the cultural codes of the actual world with the literary codes that are superimposed upon the represented world in narrative. For it is the concatenation of these two distinctly related systems that affords the literary work its modeling capability in the first place.

From the perspective of the Russian literary theorist, the concept of genre is conceived as "a mode for representing the world" (*Dialogic* 28). Unmistakable in its lineaments, this view is clearly drawn from the veritable tradition that conceives of art as mimesis, as a vast, intricately related modeling system of the world. Similarly, in discussing a properly significant instance in the verbal representation of reality, Auerbach observes: "The Old Testament . . . presents universal history; it begins with the beginning of time, with the creation of the world, and will end with the Last Days . . . with which the world will come to an end. Everything else that happens in the world can only be conceived as an element in this sequence; into it everything that is known about the world . . . must be fitted as an ingredient of the divine plan." As another (lesser) form of "plan," a literary model is conceived and designed to serve as a creative device in the analysis of verbal art. Thus what Auerbach observes concerning the Bible, itself serving as a kind of model in support of his argument, applies as well to the broader generic concept of models and modeling, since such intuitive devices must be able to embrace those "ingredients" properly inherent to them as forms of expansive (and contractive) hermeneutic techniques. As Auerbach remarks further: "The new and strange world which now comes into view and which . . . proves to be wholly unutilizable within the religious frame must be so interpreted that it can find a place there. But this process nearly always reacts upon the frame, which requires enlarging and modifying" (16). This same stricture applies as well to the employment of literary models in general, since each such constituent "frame" would also need to be consistently modified to accommodate the necessarily unique object of study.

Complementary to the mimetic concerns of Auerbach's figural interpretation and Bakhtin's chronotope, similarly compelling observations are espoused by the Russian theorist Yuri Lotman. From the broad theoretical perspective to which we subscribe here, a model's constituent features ideally encompass the subject it is meant to elucidate. In Lotman's view each individual text exists as well on some level as a self-descriptive model immanent to culture in general. As an artifact that uniquely exemplifies the culture in which it is produced, a given text necessarily affords a partially definitive perspective of that culture. Yet no single work is capable of modeling the culture accurately in its entirety. Rather, through the production of individual texts the culture creates an always incomplete, ever-changing model of itself (Danow, "Perfusion" 344). Being a meaningful fragment, therefore, within a virtually infinite configuration of like artifacts, the text mirrors the greater context of which it is a part in necessarily truncated but potentially significant form. As the product of the artist, performing in this related sense a similar reflective function, the aesthetic work may be viewed as the proper, and primary, generic analogue to the elucidative model—itself a complementary, but secondary, creative endeavor—produced by the analyst. Hence, the former, as a cultural manifestation, is designed to reflect the world in some sense, while the latter, as a critical device, is conceived, in turn, to mirror the text.

In a far more rudimentary conception, a literary model finds its immediate realization when the critic provides a hypothetical framework or broadly encompassing definition that affords a clear set of guidelines for description and supposition. Drawing, for instance, upon Joyce's definition of "epiphany" as the sudden recognition of an unexpected truth, I apply (chapter 2) a like understanding of the term to Boris Pasternak's *Doctor Zhivago*, in accounting for that novel's peculiar reliance upon poetic imagery. For *Zhivago* is designed to afford not only the hero a repeated experience of epiphany but, in a certain analogous fashion, the reader as well. In these terms Pasternak's great novel is thus seen to mirror the intended experience of the reader, whose perceptions, ideally, parallel those of the hero. From this critical perspective the concept of epiphany emerges as the crucial feature upon which the entire argument depends. Abstract definition as a comparatively primitive model, in other words, serves as the cohesive force that secures and integrates both the figurative and literal aspects of a given philosophical view, ensuring a unified and convincing argument in the process.

Further, the concept of epiphany, realized and experienced in an instant of time—we might say in "zero time"—relates therefore to the challenging, often (self-)defeating problem of articulating in meaningful fashion temporal models that bear on chosen aspects of temporal relations. Intimately linked to their spatial twins, such models demand much of the innovative critic in the attempt to construe a convincing and productive formulation that will not be devalued by an unforseen text that proclaims its limitations or, worse, proves it all wrong. As *the* two omnipresent aspects of narrative, time and space considerations raise perhaps *the* most challenging problems facing the literary analyst seeking to understand—from the always engaging perspective of temporal and spatial relations—how (as the Formalists put it) the work is made. In encapsulated form Bakhtin situated this fundamental notion in his concept of the chronotope, to which we will return.

Representing an instance of another essentially primitive, very basic formulation analogous in this one respect to the profitable notion of a model emerging as a working definition that actually works, the Russian term for model, *obrazec*, exists in relation to the etymologically related term for image, *obraz*, where the former (as a diminutive form) is clearly derived from the latter. By extension a model may be regarded as a kind of example, designed to afford an inclusive "image" or likeness reflective of some other, more expansive idea, and is thus iconic in this regard. This view is akin to Barthes' conception of what he terms an "organigram" (as opposed to "diagram"), which, according to the French thinker, "enables one to grasp visually the various kinds of relationships that bind together members of a complex, hierarchically structured organization." The concept of a model, in effect, essentially fulfills the criteria set forth by Barthes in this sense, although of course a given concept need not necessarily lend itself to a pictorial or graphic representation, as the preceding consideration of the abstract notion of epiphany clearly demonstrates. On the other hand, it would appear that the role of a model, itself an abstract concept, mirrors essentially that function assigned to Barthes' organigram, designed appropriately to "set forth an abstract set of relations" (269 n. 73).

In shifting from the speculative realm of the ideal to the concrete endeavor of defining the real, our subject inevitably remains "rooted," however paradoxically, precisely in the ideal. For, regardless of the topic of analysis, the critic (wittingly or not) provides within a hypothetical framework a model conceived as an ideal concept or (re)formulation of a given theoretical view. As an aggregate of characteristic elements designed to encompass its subject in concrete or figurative illustrative terms, this incomparable analytic tool functions in interpretive, definitive, or generative fashion, with each aspect in some sense implying the others. But what does it mean to refer to a model in these terms (none of which is meant to represent an inclusive category in any case)? First, let us note that, just as there is no pure sign (one that is exclusively iconic, indexical, or symbolic), a given model will similarly incorporate various functions that overlap.

In recognizing that there are no "pure" models but only an open set of hybrids, a model may be conceived as "interpretive" when it provides a framework for understanding an individual concept ("epiphany") or an individual text *(Doctor Zhivago)*. Yet a more ambitious goal is to argue for the common utilization of models beyond a limited—no matter how worthy—purpose. Thus a more broadly encompassing model, applied, for instance, to the opposition between verbal and nonverbal communication, may be termed "definitive" in recognition of the broad applicability that may be claimed for it. Our point, however, does not reside so much in questions of appropriate terminology as in acknowledging the important distinction between models of limited potential as opposed to those that are more inclusive in their applicability.

In addressing scientific concerns, it is observed: "Part of the great importance of models in science derives from their role as the progenitors of hypothetical mechanisms. It often happens that the antecedents of an effect are well known but the causal mechanism by which the antecedents bring about the effect is not" (Harré 39). Such an understanding applies, mutatis mutandis, to what may be termed a "generative" model (itself a kind of "progenitor"), which attempts to explain, or even itself represent, such a "causal mechanism." As a case in point, Bakhtin's chronotopic model demonstrates a set of "dual-directed" relations, since at issue is both how a given text comes into being at a certain time and place and how it might be explained as a result of these determining factors. So the generative form will function in explanatory fashion, just as interpretive or definitive models may afford a particular sensitivity to generative issues. For all three share the same fundamental heuristic concerns. The way each is weighted, however, differs according to the critical challenge, as defined by the analyst and presented by the subject at hand.

❋ ❋ ❋

In self-reflexive terms, addressing its overall organization, this book's own master model may be derived in effect from Bakhtin's concept of the chronotope, which, within its broad theoretical confines, incorporates both temporal and spatial, as well as dialogic, relations. As Bakhtin puts it, the chronotope specifies the "intrinsic connectedness of temporal and spatial relationships that are artistically expressed in literature" (*Dialogic* 84). In abstract formulation the chronotope permits the artistic realization of every narrated event in time and space. "All the novel's abstract elements . . . gravitate toward the chronotope and through it take on flesh and blood, permitting the imaging power of art to do its work" (250). Conversely, without the governing, originating presence of the chronotope, which situates the artistic image, there would remain only a lifeless abstraction finding no place within the bounds of novelistic conception. The chronotope thus specifies the temporal and spatial coordinates of "any and every literary image" (251), including of course each instance of dialogic relations, conveying to the reader in all cases pertinent social, historical, and cultural dimensions.

My goal in what follows is to transform such dimensions from abstract consideration to concrete understanding in the only way possible: by analytically treating a series of specific texts in the search for necessarily partial solutions to the challenging issues of temporal, spatial, and dialogic relations. Arranged in triadic chapter configurations, each of the following set of relations is composed of distinct but related analyses introduced separately. For the proper consideration of such topics as time, space, and speech lends itself only grudgingly (when properly nudged), if at all, to any semblance of meaningful delimitation. Yet, as always, the profundity of the challenge only enhances the critical engagement, offering the chance for greater rewards.

Part I

Temporal Relations

From the standpoint of the physicist, "it is one of the properties of physical time to flow always forward" (Bridgman 79). Yet the creative writer thinks, projects, and depicts otherwise. Thus, in contemplating "the abysmal problem of time," Borges proclaims in his story "The Garden of Forking Paths": "He believed in an infinite series of times, in a growing, dizzying net of divergent, convergent and parallel times" (*Labyrinths* 27-28). Elsewhere he observes in like figurative and paradoxical spirit: "The one true enigma was time, that seamless chain of past, present, and future, of the ever and the never" (*Sand* 57). Likewise occupied with that very "enigma," Bergson reflects perhaps more from a metaphysical than physical standpoint that, in depicting time, "movement serves as a means of representation" (*Metaphysics* 43), a means, model, or metaphor that is commonly shared by scientist and artist but that does not preclude other visions or representations. Thus we read that "time is not anchored anywhere. It has no front, back or sides. Time does not rise and set. Only to express me the Infinite becomes finite. . . . Time is instantaneous" (Devi 10, 228), which is just another point of view—no better or worse than any other.

Confronting the paradox of commonly shared yet individualized (and individually realized) scientific as well as artistic conceptions of time, the British anthropologist Edmund Leach poses the seemingly arbitrary question: "But if there is nothing in the principle of the thing, or in the nature of our experience, to suggest that time must necessarily flow past at constant speed, we are not required to think of time as a constant flow at all. Why shouldn't time slow down and stop occasionally, or even go into reverse?" (133). Precisely such apparent perversity is not only realized in narrative but is occasionally explored as a constitutive feature. Thus we find the idea of time's "slowing down" or progressing relatively slowly in Allende's *Eva Luna*.

> All ages of history co-exist in this immoderate geography. While in the capital entrepreneurs conduct business affairs by telephone with associates in other cities on the globe, there are regions in the Andes where standards of behavior are those introduced five centuries earlier by the Spanish conquistadors, and in some jungle villages men roam naked through the jungle, like their ancestors in the Stone Age. (178)

> While you and I are speaking here, behind your back Christopher
> Columbus is inventing America, and the same Indians that wel-
> come him in the stained-glass window are still naked in a jungle
> a few hours from this office, and will be there a hundred years
> from now. (300-301)

Time may also "stop occasionally," as in Borges' story "The Secret
Miracle," in which the central ploy depends on time's having been halted
(in response to prayer) for an entire year everywhere, except in the creative mind of a solitary individual standing before a fascist firing squad.
This ostensible stoppage of time allows the condemned man to complete his literary life's work in and for his own consciousness exclusively just prior to the obliteration of that same consciousness.

> He had asked God for a whole year to finish his work; His
> omnipotence had granted it. God had worked a secret miracle
> for him; German lead would kill him at the set hour, but in his
> mind a year would go by between the order and its execution.
> From perplexity he passed to stupor, from stupor to resigna-
> tion, from resignation to sudden gratitude. . . . Meticulously,
> motionlessly, secretly, he wrought in time his lofty, invisible
> labyrinth. . . . He concluded his drama. . . . He opened his
> mouth in a maddened cry, moved his face, dropped under the
> quadruple blast. (Labyrinths 93-94)

Similarly, in Carpentier's *The Lost Steps* there is the sense of time's
having stopped, which appears fantastic but also plausible.

> Some stated that near the mouth of that volcano disappearing
> from sight behind the lower peaks eight members of a scientific
> expedition lay encrusted in ice as in a show window; they had
> succumbed half a century before. They sat in a circle, in a
> state of suspended animation, just as death had transfixed
> them, gazing out from the crystal that covered their faces like
> a transparent death mask. (77)

In contrast, in García Márquez' *The Autumn of the Patriarch* plausi-
bility is diminished in favor of a comparatively augmented sense of the
fantastic.

> We cut through the gloomy streams of the cloister of the con-
> vent of Biscayan nuns, we saw the abandoned cells, we saw the
> harpsichord adrift in the intimate pool of the music room, in
> the depths of the sleeping waters of the refectory we saw the

whole community of virgins drowned in their dinner places at
the long table with the food served on it. (97)

The sense of time's "going into reverse" also finds its place—for
instance, in works chronicling the horror of war and fascist terror. Thus,
in Aharon Appelfeld's *Badenheim 1939* we find the chilling observation:
"[It] seemed that some other time, from some other place, had invaded
the town and was silently establishing itself" (38). In Elie Wiesel's *The
Gates of the Forest* essentially the same point is made even starker:
"The clock was turned back for a thousand years: a police dog was the
animal that now determined the destiny of the world" (52-53).

Leach also points out that "there is nothing intrinsically geometrical
about time as we actually experience it." Moreover, in certain cultures
"time is experienced as something discontinuous, a repetition of
repeated reversal, a sequence of oscillations between polar opposites:
night and day, winter and summer, drought and flood, age and youth, life
and death. In such a scheme the past has no 'depth' to it, all past is
equally past; it is simply the opposite of now" (126). According to such
thinking, time is conceived as moving back and forth, like a pendulum,
in a series of alternations between dissimilar events. In this view time
is determined by (mythological) thinking that relies on a set of binary
oppositions as its underlying principle, whereby all of the past is equally
past, so that there is only now in contrast to what was.

A conception of time's existing only in the present finds its literary
realization in Allende's *The House of the Spirits*, in which a temporal
principle of simultaneity is affirmed: "We believe in the fiction of past,
present, and future, but it may also be true that everything happens
simultaneously" (432). Expressed in narrative, this conception, as well
as those preceding, confirms in turn the following theoretical point of
view. "The deepest layers of our assumptive world are probably those
where we unreflectingly conceive the nature of time and space. . . . people at different times and places have held different unconscious beliefs
about the nature of time and space that are unique to their *own* time and
space" (Holquist 142). Literature, in effect, consistently appropriates
such speculative theoretical views for its own philosophical and aesthetic aims in an ongoing effort to *concretize* within a fictive (paradoxically, figural) framework various cultural and individual
understandings of time and space.

Providing a veritable compendium of possibility for chronicling
the passage of time, García Márquez in *One Hundred Years of Solitude*

conceives of time in multitudinous ways: as capable of reversing itself ("It's as if time had turned around and we were back at the beginning" [185]); as repetitive ("It's as if the world were repeating itself" [276]); as circular ("Time was not passing . . . but . . . was turning in a circle" [310]); as fragmented ("time also stumbled and had accidents and could therefore splinter and leave an eternalized fragment in a room" [322]); as translucent (affirming "the scientific possibility of seeing the future showing through in time as one sees what is written on the back of a sheet of paper through the light" [360]); and as coexistent (having "concentrated a century of daily episodes in such a way that they coexisted in one instant" [382]).

Time is thus conceived, of course, in various contrastive or complementary ways. Diverse cultures envision it as "moving" in either linear, cyclical, or circular fashion, as being inherently dynamic, static, or recurrent, among numerous other possible conceptions. Certain models afford an understanding of time that is dynamic and progressive, teleological or future oriented, in the sense that new goals or higher levels of achievement are immanently linked to its passage. Others suggest that time is fundamentally static or regressive, that a move back in time is essential in order to maintain or reclaim a culturally definitive, basic set of values that identifies a given culture, making it distinctive and viable. Such models seek to maintain a certain status quo, denying, in effect, any notion of either progressivity *or* regressivity in favor of an essential ontology: that is, time is understood to be fixed or static, or, if it is considered to pass, there is no special significance or meaning attached to that passage. This kind of understanding is conceived according to the principle of similarity; that is, every moment, every day, is like any other. Everything that happens in the world is rooted in what happened before. Thus, in speaking of the cosmology of an indigenous Peruvian tribe, Vargas Llosa observes that "history marches neither forward nor backward: it goes around and around in circles, repeats itself" (240). Such an understanding confirms a sense of recurrence within a status quo that is all the same static, affording no possibility for the intrusion of something new and unknown.

Time that is conceived as circular thus adheres to the notion that there is no possibility of attaining any higher knowledge or understanding as a result of its passing. All that need be known is already known. A people survives and flourishes on the basis of that information that has already been (orally) passed down since time immemorial. This is the realm of mythic time, wherein the recognition and acknowledgment of myth, with its attendant certainties, its telling and retelling, allow for time to appear circular or recurrent, seeking nothing beyond what is already known, what is already conceived to be absolute Truth. Hence what we might call the "ultimate" story is understood to be "something primordial, something that the very existence of a people may depend on" (Vargas Llosa 94) and something also that cannot be improved on.

In contrast, a linear model conceives of events as taking place in sequential order. In this understanding time progresses according to the linked principles of consecutiveness and contiguity. One time frame follows another, bearing its own distinctive qualities and features that lead (presumably according to some generative principle) to the next time frame that is likewise inherently unique. Yet it is that very singularity that affords *in potentia* the opportunity to attain new knowledge and discover new truths. Belonging more to modern than to primitive thought, this concept of time allows, then, for the possibility of progress: as time proceeds along a continuum that permits regression only as an alternative path to knowledge, so are human beings or their literary representations seen (accurately or not) to progress and to learn in the process. Yet that understanding, while affirming a clear sense of linearity, need not be all that optimistic, to which the following emblematic temporal image testifies. "The days mingled with one another, and time stretched out in an unbroken flow into the dark abyss" (Appelfeld, *Soul* 93).

In yet greater contrast to a static or circular conception of time are what may be termed cyclical models. Conceived here as rounds of repeated recurrence, events appear iterative, while corresponding ideas are formulated and reformulated, consistently emerging on an advanced, higher plane. Instead of proceeding along a certain continuum, time in this sense may be understood to traverse, as it were, the circumference of a cone, whereby each of its loci corresponds to others in a distinctly upward movement that likewise reflects an inherent sense of progress. The recurrence of an event therefore implies at least the possibility for those witnessing or participating in the event to attain a higher understanding than had been achieved previously. While Frye (150) refers to a "sinister spiral" (and a "sinister circle"), in our configurations we conceive of a more felicitous spiral (and an essentially benign circle), exhibiting an epistemological function at its core. *Before* and *After* thus move beyond the oppositional distinction of primitive thought to become cultural markers that reveal an intended or assumed progression toward the attainment of new understanding and greater knowledge of oneself, the world, and one's place in the world. Here, in this cyclical domain, "improvement" is eminently possible.

Affirming some of the preceding abstract reflections, Aharon Appelfeld's novel *Katerina*, a compelling tale of the spiritual sojourn of a crude peasant woman during the Holocaust in Eastern Europe, explicitly acknowledges its circular construction. The last paragraph begins: "Now, as the proverb says, the water has flowed back into the river, the circle is closed" (7, 212). That pronounced circularity is enhanced by the curious fact that Appelfeld concludes his novel by repeating verbatim its opening paragraphs (hence the preceding dual page citation). Yet the link between circular and cyclical models also becomes evident in this singular instance of novelistic repetition because everything that is repeated at the end bears an *additional* attendant (richer and greater) meaning that could not have been registered by the reader at the beginning. In repeating a significant portion of his first chapter at the close of the novel, the novelist underscores our point that in the cyclical model there is the potential to attain a fuller understanding than might previously have been achieved.

All such intuitive models of time as just sketched all too briefly are explored cognitively by anthropologists who get their data from actual, original sources, and by novelists who utilize such conceptions of time in erecting the fictive scaffoldings that buttress their work and that depend above all else on related principles of time and space, upon which narrative is implicitly predicated. From a literary perspective it may be argued that the difference between the circular and cyclical conceptions of time is that the former may not allow for the possible reception of new information, while the latter does advocate that latent potentiality as even a sure eventuality. With the passage of time, according to the latter model, one learns, as a new, higher level of experience and comprehension is attained. "Sight" may be achieved, in other words, through a flash of insight. At times, then, epiphany, acknowledged or not, wittingly or unwittingly (on the part of the perceiver or "seer"), plays its special role.

As Joyce's famous definition has it: "By an epiphany he meant a sudden spiritual manifestation, whether in the vulgarity of speech or gesture or in a memorable phase of the mind itself. He believed that it was for the man of letters to record these epiphanies with extreme care, seeing that they themselves are the most delicate and evanescent of moments" (211). Epiphany is here understood to emerge from and embrace immediate perceptions and recognitions that may not necessarily be lofty and uplifting but are nonetheless poignant and poetic, eliciting a sometimes painful reality that, through the artist's artifice, participates in and reveals something of Spirit. Such "sudden illuminations," as Appelfeld (*Healer* 95) felicitously refers to these revelatory moments, may thus figure as significant constitutive factors in distinguishing the various models by which we (as representatives of diverse cultures) view both time and ourselves in time. The circular model, for instance, does not recognize the attainment of knowledge through a sudden insight or in any other fashion; mythic time likewise permits no incursions of anything new. Nonetheless, a sudden recognition or unexpected insight may play a significant role in the way the characters within a fictional universe attain their understanding of the complexities inherent therein. In this regard chapter 2 examines how Boris Pasternak presents this "most delicate and evanescent of moments" in *Doctor Zhivago* and, equally important, how they may be received by the reader.

Related to our cyclical model, the concept of synoptic time is understood in terms of a collective memory that is intertwined with the personal, whereby we find "a continuous presence of past events." In this view "collective memory and personal response coalesce into a totality, making the past not a cold historical fact but a vital, ever-present experience" (Ramras-Rauch 9, 13). Such "intertwining" or "coalescing" of the past with the present in both personal and collective memory, as manifested in literature, yields a certain "totality" that emerges with its own peculiar sense of immediacy. In discussing García Márquez' *Love in the Time of Cholera*, chapter 3 explores precisely this sense of the past incorporated within the present as well as the attendant immediacy that is generated by its very incorporation. Conversely, the absence of an acute consciousness of the past would appear to make the present virtually impossible, turning it into a largely empty category devoid of all vitality and vision.

Although literature at large is preoccupied with events that ostensibly take place in the present (including historical novels and historical and biographical reflections within the novel), and although these events are conventionally depicted as taking place "now," that here and now, which might appear as "given," could not be transcribed without the sense of its being at least grounded in a certain past. In García Márquez' splendid novel, however, the past does not simply ground present events but is the very source of nearly everything that takes place within the present. Discussed within the framework of Bergson's notion of duration, chapter 3, devoted to the problem of time past, is designed to show in concrete terms, derived from *Love in the Time of Cholera*, that memory—in its exhaustive duration—serves as a vital source of narrative. It is the past alive in a character's memory, in other words, that gives life to the novel's *present*, which is all there is in the fictional realm just as it is in the actual domain.

Hence all three temporal concepts of linearity, epiphany, and enduring memory are thoroughly interconnected, since every narrative, first of all, is dependent to some degree on sequence and successiveness. The principle of contiguity, that is, will inevitably have its role to play. All narrative requires a forward movement, a sense of the past being absorbed by the present, even as the latter gives way to the future. In related terms the moment of epiphany is likewise dependent upon an enduring memory. Without the latter there would be no point to the former. What value is afforded by a revelatory moment if it is not retained as an insight perceived, an understanding achieved somewhere in the recesses of our memory, where it endures and persists as a guide to the future? Rather, the moment of epiphany resides in memory as a moment of transformation, which in turn serves to transform a necessarily passive past (which is not necessarily finished and done with) into a dynamic present. In this significant sense chapters 2 and 3 represent interior companion studies (as do virtually all subsequent chapters), whereas the book's opening study presents the primary temporal model that is requisite to all narrative, evidenced in every account (literary and otherwise) that purports to relate a series of events in a certain order.

Thus linear progression and sequential relations are explored in chapter 1, which is constructed differently from all that follows in its consolidation of our governing rubrics of theory and practice within a single, comprehensive framework. Devoted to a relatively extensive treatment of linear perspectives in narrative, theoretically formulated, and subsequently grounded in supportive references to the works of Dostoevsky and Tolstoy, the first chapter seeks to provide a synthesis of thought that is otherwise sought within the broader formulations embracing parts 1, 2, and 3, respectively, or within the wider, more inclusive territory encompassed by the book in its entirety. In wrestling with the basic problem of linearity, in other words, the opening chapter is singular in respect to its being driven more by theoretical exegesis than by concrete textual analysis, a mode that is essentially reversed in the entire rest of the book.

1

LINEAR PERSPECTIVES
(DOSTOEVSKY AND TOLSTOY)

■ □ ■

For two of this century's most important literary theorists, Georg Lukács and Mikhail Bakhtin, the epic—as opposed to the novel—represents the genre that most clearly reflects a given order to the world. The epic depicts a world that is ordered and finished; its hero's role is predetermined by his place in that world. The novel reveals a private and public sphere that is contingent and indeterminate; its hero attempts to give meaning to his life in spite of the oppressive uncertainty and indeterminacy. As Lukács formulates it, "The novel is the epic of an age in which the extensive totality of life is no longer given, in which the immanence of meaning in life has become a problem, yet which still thinks in terms of totality. . . . the novel seeks, by giving form, to uncover the concealed totality of life" (56, 60). That form, designed to reveal a "concealed totality," is achieved in large part through the novelist's use of time as a crucial determining factor. Whereas the novel attempts to reflect an ordered world, or one seemingly capable of being ordered according to certain basic precepts, time, in its linear aspect, as a principal constituent element of the novel, is itself arranged according to certain perceptible patterns, which afford the sense of that totality.

In the jointly held view of Lukács and Bakhtin, time defines the genre of the novel in opposition to the timeless quality of the epic. But time is a crucial aspect of all narrative in the sense that no narrative structure can proceed to unfold without recourse to temporal features—their organization and possible subsequent reorganization designed to achieve a certain aesthetic effect. As Ivanov puts it, time is "a category outside of which the artist's intention cannot be realized" (1). Deserved central importance is similarly ascribed to the novel's temporal considerations thus: "In the final analysis, virtually all the techniques and devices of fiction reduce themselves to the treatment accorded to the different time-values and time-series, and to the way one is played off against another" (Mendilow 63). In attempting both to substantiate and expand upon such points of view, I will sketch here in necessarily delimited fashion what Barthes terms "a hypothetical model of description" (239), whose aim in effect is to encompass the architectonics of the conventional nineteenth-century novel of resolution. Among other things, it is assumed that such a "traditional" form not only exists but is still being written today. In a word, our concern is with novelistic time approached exclusively as *order*,[1] where a standard use of chronology is deemed a basic constituent device. Exemplars are drawn from the major novels of Dostoevsky and Tolstoy, whose works provide generally familiar territory and who—in their vast differences as novelists—encompass much of the variety exhibited (at least in its Russian form) by the novel at that stage of its development that is our immediate concern.

To anticipate briefly that concern, let us take as aphoristic an inconspicuous remark made by a Tolstoyan hero conspicuously attempting to arrange his life according to certain tenets designed to give it meaning. "Because a just idea cannot but be fruitful," declares Tolstoy's truth seeker, Konstantin Levin, in *Anna Karenina* (364). The remark clearly amounts to an article of faith. In uttering it, the speaker typifies other such characters in the Tolstoy canon. But such a view is also common to a far larger corpus. What is presupposed by the remark are the linked notions of there being a unifying idea capable of imparting lasting meaning in the personal sphere and of there being some yet-to-be-discovered corresponding principle capable of organizing the larger sphere—the world as such—in which justice is seen eventually, inevitably, to triumph. Perhaps a common point of view when Tolstoy's novel was fresh off the press, such a contention receives far less currency in the face of twentieth-century reality, where meaning has become peripheral and ephemeral in a public domain marked more by the chaos envisioned by Dostoevsky than by the order sought by Tolstoy's seekers intent upon giving meaning to their lives and to their world. I draw upon Levin's brief remark, reflecting an optimism now dimmed and only flickering at best, in order to suggest in decidedly abbreviated form a seemingly evident distinction between a point of view espoused and essentially taken for granted in a representative classic of nineteenth-century literature as opposed to its very likely *not* being espoused at all and surely *not* taken as given within the grim, broad purview of the twentieth-century novel.

The virtue of the linear model that will be outlined here is twofold. First, it embraces a large representative body of narrative fiction within a schema designed to outline the temporal strategies and constraints by which that fiction may be broadly defined. Second, there is acknowledged within that fiction both a view of the world and an approach to it that is encapsulated in Levin's words just cited or that may be expanded in the distinction between epic and novel previously noted. A considerably large corpus, in other words, is characterized by an overall orientation toward that perspective belonging to Tolstoy's seeker or toward that fundamental, metaphysical search for a unifying force that Lukács considers—in relation to the timelessness of the epic—a lost totality. Nonetheless, such an orientation implies a corresponding belief that the world itself, as reflected in the novel, is similarly organizable. One level upon which this bias is clearly reflected is the temporal, where time is organized in such a way as to suggest that the world of the novel is likewise subject to a certain meaningful order. This essentially positive perspective affords an entire body of narrative informed by such an approach a sense of uniformity in its simply attempting to effect a thematic resolution in a way perhaps more difficult to discern in much of today's fiction. It is the burden of our linear model to reveal this uniformity.

In heralding the importance of both temporal and spatial factors as dual, inextricably linked conceptual and structural elements in narrative, Bakhtin defines the "chronotope" as an abstract cohering element that unites these two utterly crucial aspects of the novel. Indispensable and inseparable in narrative constructs, time and space are conceived as a single unit. Yet this theoretical consideration does not amount to a stricture precluding the feasibility of privileging one over the other in critical analysis. In fact, Bakhtin himself credits one feature more strongly when he observes that Dostoevsky "conceived his world primarily in terms of space, not time" (*Poetics* 28). But, as Forster reasonably assures us, time is "far more fatal than place" (29). For present purposes the chronotope, a "dynamic time-shape" that situates a character in terms of moment and place, will be seen to allow for the materialization of time in space. For Bakhtin the novel is perceived as "an image of temporal art; one that represents spatially perceptible phenomena in their movement and development" (*Dialogic* 251). The novel may thus be regarded as "a complex of time values" (Mendilow 63); at the same time we recognize that "in novelistic time people are always remaking values" (Morson 238). In linking these two related observations, we underscore an obvious slippage or

shift from concerns that are largely structural to ones that are broadly
epistemological (axiological). Our focus will remain generally upon the
former but with a certain scrutiny applied to the reception and interpretation of chronotopic information by the receiver situated "outside novelistic time." What the reader and fictional character have in common, in
other words, is that both are problem solvers—the one within, the other
outside the text. As Segre felicitously expresses it, "the adventure
entrusted to the narrative is supplemented by another; the adventure of
reading" (*Structures* 17). In its rich and complex temporal implications,
that adventure in particular will engage us here.

Definitions and distinctions attributed to the Russian Formalists, who
formulated their ideas in the second and third decades of this century,
still have relevance today as broadly applicable contributions to narrative theory, particularly in defining the lineaments of a theory of reading from a time-oriented perspective. Their views suggest that one
method by which the reader's attention and active participation are
maintained is through the writer's reorganization of material, allowing
for information to be withheld or advanced according to the novelist's
strategy for telling the tale. Such strategies always proceed from the
complex utilization of time, made evident in the Formalists' distinction
between *fabula* and *sjuzhet*. The *fabula*, or story, represents the
chronological order of material prior to its aesthetic reorganization. It
is the unaltered temporal sequence of events comprising the narrative
account. The *sjuzet*, or plot, represents the writer's redistribution of
events—that is, the rearrangement of the chronological order according to a narrative plan seeking to achieve a series of calculated effects.
Such discourse emerges as the ultimately realized narrative structure
whose altered temporal sequence is designed to relate the story in a
manner deemed most effective. As Culler says, "there is always a basic
distinction between a sequence of events and a discourse that orders
and presents events" (*Pursuit* 170). It is the job of the reader to register that distinction in the ongoing effort to relate the multifarious
chronotopic features of a work and thus, on the most fundamental
level, to meet the challenge of the text.

For the Formalists plot is a concept that entails both a formal and a
semantic aspect; it is a continuum that interconnects the chronological
ordering of events with the substance of the account, its semantic plane.

Meaning is thus inextricably bound to the moment at which it is revealed. As a related, significant part of the process, matters of causation and their determination become part of the reader's efforts at decipherment. Primary among these is the problem of relating plot, or the "finished" discourse, to story, itself "a constant against which the variables of narrative presentation can be measured" (Culler, *Pursuit* 170).[2]

From the reader's perspective the *fabula* represents an ideal construct or series of (temporal) reference points by which one organizes the heterogeneous material comprising the text. Through careful consideration of the text's formal and semantic aspects, the reader in effect transforms plot into story, thereby reversing the role of the writer. This operation allows the reader to conceive the story in its original temporal order prior to the writer's reorganization of it and consequent imposition of the various deformations that constitute its completed form.[3] Such effort is carried out through a process of segmentation that presupposes the reader's ability to distinguish among episodes—their beginning and end. On a like fundamental level the reader will recognize temporal shifts from the story proper or fictive present[4] to regressive (past-oriented) or progressive (future-oriented) segments. In interpreting all texts governed by what Genette terms "anachrony,"[5] or interruptions of the present narrative, and which by definition therefore do not maintain the temporal sequence of the *fabula*, this dual task assigned the reader is both fundamental and essential.

The least complex narrative structure from a temporal standpoint is one that constitutes a series of episodes presented in ordered, chronological sequence, in which time follows essentially the same linear pattern as in life—but with a single, crucial difference: the conventional work of fiction requires some form of motivation to make the sequence of events comprehensible and credible (whereas life is subject to no such exacting strictures).[6] Thus the Formalist theorist Boris Tomashevsky argues in effect that a rationale *(motivirovka)* for subsequent occurrences is an essential plot component (144-52). Aside from the requisite logic that a certain temporal order be maintained, the series of events must be clearly motivated in order that the plot be generated; a more or less believable rationale for what has already occurred is the prerequisite for what follows. From a purely temporal perspective, then, a work ordered according to chronological sequence may begin with either the purported past or present, but in both instances will follow its own predetermined system by which past yields to present and ultimately to future, with essentially no accommodation for any significant interruption of the prescribed sequence of events. In such narrative, events proceed exclusively in syntagmatic fashion, characterized by a chronology that is linear, presumably logical, and relatively simple.

When a text is ordered according to an inverted chronological system, however, that does not proceed in a direct, uninterrupted progression, it allows for both past and future events to be incorporated within its overall temporal framework in potentially multitudinous forms of anachrony, represented by "the forward and backward movement of the text along the syntagmatic axis" (Stankiewicz, "Poetics" 70).[7] Yet all fictional works, including those exhibiting anachronies as well as those following an uninterrupted chronological sequence, will adhere as a matter of course to certain basic temporal constraints. On the most elementary level there is bound to be some point in narrative time from which the action issues and a moment when it all comes to rest. In addition, there may be numerous references to centuries past, prior to the novel's actual opening temporal frame, or to the dim future, whose events go well beyond the work's closing temporal bounds. Yet all such references are likewise bound to be made within the context of those central events that the plot proper is concerned to depict. There must be some connection or linkage, in other words, between episodes that are part of some other time frame and the novel's fictive present, or "first narrative," which constitutes its main plot.

Within an entire spectrum of possibility repeated references to both past and future may punctuate the fictive present, interrupting it to provide more information, allow for greater anticipation, or generate further action. Related in inverted chronological fashion, the plot may thus be interrupted to allow for a change in perspective *(a)* from present to past, *(b)* from present to the distant (rather than immediate) future,[8] and ultimately, *(c)* from either past or future back to present. Construed within a range of varying complexity and potential interlarding of anachronies, such are the possible displacements embedded within or grafted upon texts governed by inverted chronologies, whose variants may be further conceived as follows.

(a) A work's retrospective views may be expected to eliminate either partially or entirely the lacunae in the reader's knowledge of those past episodes to which the characters and their respective stories are linked. Although structured according to a variety of possibilities, all such retrospective views provide information bearing "regressive relevance," which allows the reader to comprehend more fully what is yet to unfold.

Termed "analepses" by Genette, such past-oriented accounts are realized in three possible ways. The entire retrospective account takes place outside the domain of the first narrative; it is contained within the temporal bounds of the first narrative; it reaches back to a point earlier than the beginning of the first narrative but concludes at a point later than that beginning, and thus falls partially within the main plot line.[9]

(b) In contrast to the preceding forms, references to the future may be either anticipatory or speculative, as occasional prefigurements of what is yet to come. Future-oriented references thus bear a certain corresponding "progressive significance," by which new plot episodes are generated as the result of previous ones. Termed "prolepses" by Genette, such future-directed accounts may also be realized in three ways. The "proleptic tale" takes place entirely outside the bounds of the first narrative, serving essentially as an epilogue to the story proper; it is contained entirely within the bounds of the first narrative, anticipating events and, to a certain extent, perhaps repeating them (but from different perspectives, with different emphases, and with additional details provided); it reaches from the fictive present to some distant moment, at which a single line of the narrative is brought to conclusion, after which the plot is resumed.

(c) Last, any transition from either past or future back to the present implies simply the resumption—for whatever designated period—of the plot proper. Such a transition, in effect, returns the work to the fundamental logical-sequential (or "chrono-logical") order that inevitably governs at least some portion of a given text. Passages (however brief) must exist, in other words, when time in narrative flows sequentially or linearly.

All such time-oriented references, as just noted, may also be conceived as strings of motifs that are primarily indexical in nature. In one sense they reveal the interconnections and linkages that make the intricacies of plot comprehensible and credible. At the same time they are themselves the material from which the story is made. For the various linkages are not simply indicated by indexical signs but are themselves composed of such signs.[10] Conversely, the motif (conventionally understood and defined by Tomashevsky as "irreducible, the smallest particles of thematic material [which] form the thematic bonds of the work" [136-37]) functions as both a basic element of plot and as an indexical sign linked to—and pointing to—further plot developments.[11]

Whether the text be ordered in logical-sequential manner or in inverted chronological fashion, the narrative is realized through a series of time-oriented indexical signs. In the former case, where each event is contiguous with (if not motivated by) the preceding one, the inherent linkage within the text becomes evident once the reader is able to recognize "the logic that is unfolded, exposed, and finally confirmed, in the midst of the sequence" (Barthes 271). In the latter case transitions from present to past, or from present to (other than the immediate) future, bear respectively (as noted) regressive relevance or progressive significance, which jointly represent through the considered manipulation of time an intricate device by which the reader's interest is held and the story is told.

In outlining the basic time-oriented workings of the indexical sign, a model concentrating on the text's temporal strategies, and incorporating three possible narrative planes embracing several distinct interior relations, appears "capable of integrating backtracking and forward leaps" (Barthes 269), among other (a)temporal features, as part of the overall design.

Comprising a hypothetical primary plane, the first narrative is essential to the formation and realization of the entire tale.[12] Recounting those episodes that take place contemporaneously, as it were, with their presentation to the reader, it relates the story's present events. When this single, requisite plane is exclusively evident, and is thus designed to render the entire account in chronological sequence, the narrative exhibits a temporal order equivalent to the *fabula*, conceived (ideally) as the chronologically ordered and linearly displayed uninterrupted series of events composing the tale at hand.

In *Anna Karenina*, for example, there are virtually no references to the past. The novel is almost entirely future directed or sequentially ordered. As Lubbock points out, Tolstoy "unrolls it all as it occurs, illustrating everything in action" (237). An exception is the cursory mention of Karenin's lonely childhood and adolescence, coupled with a brief, cryptic explanation of his mismatch with Anna (532-33). But this is a rare exception, allowing for essentially the entire work to serve as a near pristine exemplar of pure linearity.[13] Similarly composed, Book VIII of *The Brothers Karamazov* represents a like case, as Dmitri frantically runs from one hopeless situation to another in search of funds, with no respite for himself or the reader in his headlong dash, culminating in the dissolute scenes punctuated by his arrest. In contrast to the rest of that work and to Tolstoy's novel, there are present neither the future-oriented, anticipatory elements characteristic of the first half of

The Brothers nor are there evident the retrospective views that constitute the novel's concluding investigation and trial scenes.

When the chronological sequence of events is interrupted, however, by a possible series of anachronies—including both analepses (references to the past) and prolepses (anticipations of the future)—a second narrative plane comes into play. Superimposed upon or embedded within a given text, analepses may constitute one or more nonsequential references to the past (conceivably adjoined to interrelated references to the future). Such past-oriented accounts are thus situated completely outside the temporal bounds of the plot proper, exist partially within those bounds, or belong entirely within them.

The story of Prince Myshkin's convalescing in Switzerland, detailed after the opening scenes in Dostoevsky's *The Idiot* (I:6), illustrates the first case. All of Myshkin's adventures there before his return to Russia take place prior to the opening time frame of the fictive present, which originates on the very first page. So his early experiences abroad interrupt the narrative and take us back to a much earlier time. Similarly, the accounts of the early formative years of the brothers Karamazov (Book I: The History of a Family) provide the necessary background information to their meeting for the first time in the novel's present (Book II: An Unfortunate Gathering). In effect, the first narrative, or plot proper, of Dostoevsky's last great novel begins with Book II; what precedes is prologue and a clear illustration of our first instance of anachrony, which takes place entirely outside the bounds of the novel's fictive present. All such episodes supply the requisite historical or biographical detail designed to inform the reader of what is crucial and necessary prior to the origination of the tale, in the present, or its resumption from that moment when it may have been temporarily interrupted.

In the beginning of *Crime and Punishment*, Marmeladov, a distraught drunkard and failed father, renders an account (I:2) of the past that explains his family's present sorry circumstances. Similarly, the letter received by Raskolnikov from his mother (I:3) provides the motivation that inspires her to visit him in St. Petersburg. In both instances the oral and written records of the past, respectively, provide the necessary information—through a kind of narrative loop that temporarily supersedes the primary account—to bring the reader up to the present. Handsomely illustrating that loop, in the recollection (and repetition) of a single word, is the scene in *War and Peace* when the young Princess Marya sits at her window recollecting the death of her father, which had been depicted previously.

> One after another pictures of the immediate past—her father's
> illness and last moments—rose before her imagination. She
> had a vivid picture of the moment when he was first stricken
> down. And then she recalled with every detail the night at
> Bleak Hills before his stroke. . . . "He was miserable. I heard
> from the door how he lay down groaning on the bed and cried
> out loud. . . . Why didn't I go in then? What could he have done
> to me? What could I have lost? And, perhaps, then he would
> have been comforted, he would have said that word to me."
> And Princess Marya uttered aloud that caressing word he had
> said to her on the day of his death. "Da-ar-ling!" Princess Marya
> repeated the word and broke into sobs that relieved her heart.
> She could see his face before her now. And not the face she had
> known ever since she could remember and had always seen at
> a distance; but the weak and timid face she had seen on the last
> day when, bending to his lips to catch what he said, she had,
> for the first time, looked at it quite close with all its wrinkles.
> "Darling," she repeated. (682-83)

That single endearing epithet, which the princess had waited a whole
lifetime to hear, articulated once by an ungrateful father and *now* by her,
links the recent past with the immediate present.

In the same novel the reader is initially informed in only brief, telegraphic fashion of the rescue from the weakened grip of Napoléon's
forces of one of the novel's main characters: "Among the Russian pris-
oners . . . was Pierre Bezukhov" (986). A half-dozen pages later, however, the rescue scene is presented in full-blown dramatic (rather than
abbreviated diegetic) form.

> "Mates! our own folk! brothers!" the old soldiers cried, weep-
> ing, as they embraced the Cossacks and the hussars. The hus-
> sars and the Cossacks crowded around the prisoners, pressing
> on them clothes, and boots, and bread. Pierre sat sobbing in
> their midst, and could not utter one word; he hugged the first
> soldier who went up to him, and kissed him, weeping. (993)

Framed by the two passages just cited (986-93) are a series of retrospective episodes devoted to an account of Pierre's tribulations while
a prisoner. In contrast to the little tale of Princess Marya, here the
reader is provided new information related to the further development
of the narrative (Pierre's insights gained during his confinement and
march; his talks with the peasant-philosopher Karataev), including its
ideological as well as its plot concerns. Yet both the story of the princess

and her father and of Pierre and his rescue represent the same kind of retrospective structure—all of which is contained and related within the main temporal bounds of the novel at hand.

In contrast, the examples borrowed from *The Idiot* and *The Brothers Karamazov* represent time frames that take place entirely outside the novel's fictive present. Affording further contrast, those derived from *Crime and Punishment* also originate outside the novel's first narrative, or plot proper, but ultimately coincide with it, making for a neat conjoining or "reunion" of the past with the novel's present moment. All such instances, as noted, occur either when the story is interrupted to present a character's biography (or some unrevealed episode in the past destined to have a bearing on the future) or when a "historical," contextual basis for an account that is to follow is first provided to the reader.

Immediately implied by retrospective reference, however, is a hypothetical secondary plane of narrative designed to interrupt the primary in order to anticipate or generate what is yet to come. Characteristic of works ordered according to an inverted chronological plan, a secondary plane of narrative, embracing past-oriented accounts or representing temporal disjunctures within the primary plane, presents either additional information or greater clarification. Further, such retrospective references offer both regressive relevance *and* progressive significance, since all ostensibly past-oriented accounts are essentially future-directed as well. For they refer to the past only to make comprehensible and credible what is to occur in the future. Thus the past-oriented account also bears a future-directed component, making all such indices in effect *dual-directed signs*, designed to allow for the past to be recounted, in order for us to comprehend better the future, which will, in time, emerge as the present.

What had been stated earlier as preliminary considerations regarding the analeptic episode applies as well, mutatis mutandis, to the proleptic account, which may also encompass a narrative segment situated entirely within the temporal bounds of the plot proper, only partially within those bounds, or completely outside them.[14]

In *The Brothers Karamazov* there is a striking lacuna modeled typographically in the text, where the singular inclusion of an additional space between two paragraphs represents iconically the absence of crucial information at the very moment when the murder is perpetrated "in the dark" (VIII:4). Much of what is depicted between the commission of the crime and its resolution is proleptic, since there is an obvious "leap forward" (from what is left blank), requiring that the narrative

return to those fateful moments in order to satisfy the reader's legiti-
mate, long-sustained curiosity as to who killed the elder Karamazov.
This is accomplished during the course of the three interviews between
the "instrument" and the actual author of the crime (XI:6-8). But the first
extended effort to resolve the problem is detailed in Book IX (The
Preliminary Investigation), with its repeated incorrect attempts at
reconstructing the event. Such repeated projections—entirely contained within the temporal bounds of the plot proper—are proleptic in
their efforts to "evoke in advance an event that will take place later":
namely, the murderer's detailed account of the crime, affording its only
accurate depiction (Book XI). Only after that question has been
resolved can the plot proceed to its ironic conclusion (Book XII: A
Judicial Error).

At the conclusion to *War and Peace* there is talk concerning the
formation of a secret society for political reform (Epilogue, I:14). In the
final part of *Anna Karenina* Vronsky sets off to fight and presumably
die in the Serbo-Turkish War (VIII:5). In the epilogue to *The Brothers
Karamazov* there is also talk—of Dmitri's escape plans. All three
instances, exemplifying prolepses that are situated only partially within
the novel's temporal bounds, represent threads within the overall narrative referring in effect to the undepicted future. Originating within
their respective temporal frameworks, these threads extend beyond
their novelistic bounds to an undefined point in time, from which the
narrative quickly returns to its more immediate present concerns. In
contrast, in *Crime and Punishment* and in *The Idiot* the epilogue and
the concluding chapter, respectively, do not allow for a return to the present. In charting the fate of certain characters and in detailing the
course of later events, they nonetheless remain situated outside their
respective novel's temporal bounds.

More likely to appear in diegetic rather than mimetic form, essentially
atemporal aspects of narrative have their role to play within the range
of linear relations that have so far been discussed. These include static
descriptions designed to present a certain image or concept to the
reader, or a report as a kind of "metatext," which, like the reconstructive
analeptic tale, comments upon the primary text. Understood here as representing a tertiary, purely descriptive, philosophical or epistemological
plane, it provides direct explanatory material, interrupting (as does the
novel's secondary plane) the fictive present to do so, causing the (linear)
flow of time also momentarily to be brought to a halt. Characterized by
an absence of dramatic action, its elucidative function distinguishes it

from the first narrative of the primary plane and from the initially elaborated or reconstructed accounts of the secondary. Exemplars include common authorial analyses or discussions of what had previously transpired. The lengthy passages in *War and Peace* devoted to an accounting (rather than a recounting) of the historical events recorded in that novel are a case in point. Characteristic of this generic case, the essay form in effect temporarily intrudes upon the presentation of dramatic events in order to elucidate the work's thematic concerns.[15]

Another critical manifestation of this essentially atemporal form, what is commonly referred to as "interior monologue" (but which might be more appropriately termed "interior dialogue") exhibits its own features, whereby "the boundaries between different periods of [the hero's] life, as well as the boundaries between the real and the imaginary, are erased" (Ivanov 28). As a result of such erasure, the interweaving of real and imaginary events in achronological fashion precludes any possible causal relations among them.[16] At the same time the sense of the passage of time in the fictional world external to the character's mind is obscured.[17] In *Anna Karenina* the carriage ride that Anna takes on the last day of her life, during which "one impression followed rapidly upon another" (792), illustrates the point.[18] Analogous, then, to the "intrusion" of the atemporal essay form within the narrative flow is the like obtrusive presence of such associative, impressionistic, interior modes that periodically but only temporarily put a stop to the linear representation of time.

In sum, a certain logical-sequential order is requisite to the elaboration of at least a part of any narrative, itself composed of a series of indexical signs designed to take the plot in relatively simple fashion directly from beginning to end. Within such chronologically ordered segments of the text, the indexical sign that gives it both substance and direction is itself single directed and future oriented, thus enabling the fictive present to move toward the resolution of plot. In contrast, the inverted chronological system employing anachronies is characterized by reconsiderations of the past (providing regressive relevance) coupled with references to the future (affording progressive significance) that jointly make of their constitutive indices dual-directed signs, derived essentially from their dual temporal orientation.[19] Put differently, the ostensible past orientation of the motif (itself an index) is only the more visible aspect of its corresponding future orientation, serving both as linkage and at times as motivation. "The artistic text is thus marked not only by an anticipatory development, but also by a retroactive impulse which integrates the elements of succession" (Stankiewicz, "Structural" 643). Or, as Mukařovský felicitously expresses it: "There is always something in the work of art which is bound to the past and something which points to the future" (*Aesthetic* 35).[20]

Between the logical-sequential order and the inverted chronological system a clear distinction exists, characterized by a more obvious movement of the plot through a series of simple single-directed indexical signs in the former as opposed to the more complex vagaries attending the dual-directed indices of the latter. In addition to serving as the connective tissue of narrative, however, both indexical forms provide a rationale for new episodes by revealing or generating additional linkages between what has been dramatized for the reader and what has not—between its mimetic and diegetic sequences.[21] The index is thus at once the principal sign and substance of verbal art, pointing to what is either past or future, while itself serving as the object of representation that, at any given moment, is always present.

As one theorist contends, there is "an acute consciousness on the part of writers that literature is a time-art, in which the continuum of the text is apprehended by the reader in a continuum of time and . . . that these conditions may be exploited and manipulated in order to produce various effects on the reader" (Sternberg 34). One of those possibly sought-after effects is to give the sense of a world in which the possibility for rational organization and corresponding meaning is not yet lost. Implicit in our elaboration of an inclusive linear model is the contention that narrative (in its "traditional" form) is governed by certain inherent "belief systems" or fundamental tenets. Among these are several linked features. First, the represented world of the novel is ordered according to a certain pattern or set of (partially) codified principles based on that of the real world it models. "Since authors model whole worlds, they are ineluctably forced to employ the organizing categories of the worlds that they themselves inhabit" (Clark and Holquist 278). Conversely, the real world may either be ordered according to the way it is modeled in the novel or the possibility of it being so is still seen to exist. Further, the dependence of both the represented and the real worlds on some ordering principle (or code) is analogous to a like reliance on those compositional principles governing the linear mode (or model) of narrative that has occupied us here.

If the novel indeed models an ordered, recognizable world, then so should that depicted world reflect back upon the literary form from which it derives, suggesting, first of all, that the novel is itself subject to a related system of organization, of which time considerations are a principal constituent. Again, as Bakhtin argues: "Out of the chronotopes of our world (which serve as the source of representation) emerge the reflected and *created* chronotopes of the world represented in the work" (*Dialogic* 253).

In this view the novel form therefore models a consistent system of organization that, as shown here, is delimitable in its temporal confines, and which in turn affords a certain modicum of meaning by virtue of that clearly evident organization.

In juxtaposing the epic and the novel, Lukács observes: "The immanence of the meaning which the form of the novel requires . . . [affords] a mere glimpse of meaning [as] the highest that life has to offer" (80). In perhaps more sanguine terms Chatman makes essentially the same case when arguing that "in the traditional narrative of resolution, there is a sense of problem solving, of things being worked out in some way, of a kind of ratiocinative or emotional teleology" (48). The idea is reminiscent of Barthes' "hermeneutic" code, "by means of which the narrative raises questions, creates suspense and mystery, before resolving these as it proceeds along its course" (Hawkes 116). But what if that mystery encompasses the world itself? This question has been a part of our present concern, since, as Bakhtin puts it, "however immutable the presence of that categorical boundary line between [the real and the represented world], they are nevertheless indissolubly tied up with each other and find themselves in continual mutual interaction" (*Dialogic* 254). Hence this merging of the cultural codes of the real world with the literary codes superimposed upon the represented world of the novel affords that literary form its modeling capability.

In the traditional narrative of resolution, in particular, there is indeed "a strong sense of temporal order" (Chatman 48). The dimensions of that order, in its linear relations, have been outlined here within a range of all-inclusive possibility intended to encompass the novel form, whose constant endeavor is to provide some resolution to the mystery that is the world, as reflected in verbal art. Thus we may observe with Lukács that "the passage of time alters nothing in the epic," however, "the entire action of the novel is nothing but a struggle against the power of time" (127, 122), as it is in life.

2

THE MOMENT OF REVELATION: EPIPHANY IN *DOCTOR ZHIVAGO* (PASTERNAK)

■ □ ■

The novel form is composed of a configuration of events occurring in novelistic time and appearing as a series of images within its fictive spatial structures. Intricate relations among temporal and spatial elements, interlocked in a fictional universe modeling the real one, allow for the realization of a work of verbal art. Boris Pasternak's *Doctor Zhivago* is a poet's novel about a poet and about how and why poetry is made. Its structure is distinctive in that each individual chapter is itself subdivided into separate sections (occasionally cited as such in what follows). These are in turn governed by a single prominent image. Individual chapters are thus composed of a cluster of related images making for a complex network designed to achieve a singular effect.

The imagery presented in the novel not only engages the reader but presumably serves as a source of poetic inspiration for its hero. Zhivago's reactions to what he senses in the world around him are essentially transmuted into the particular, single-minded endeavor of making poetry. That endeavor, conversely, is inextricably bound to moments of spiritual recognition or epiphany, which both hero and reader recognize as such.[1] In this sense the novel affords the reader the opportunity to participate in the process of creation, born of such immediate recognition and ultimately realized through the mind and eye of the novel's principal protagonist. When for a crucial, brief instant in *Doctor Zhivago* a series of images attains meaning for its hero and are comprehended in turn by the reader, there occurs a moment of ostensibly shared revelation: what was previously concealed is now revealed; for a poetic instant mystery is subsumed by clarity.

Yet the rapid change of scene among the interrelated images of each chapter yields an impression of elaborate fragmentation, achieved in part by the juxtaposition of characteristically brief passages of dialogue, often seemingly having no beginning or end.[2] The snatches of conversation overheard by Zhivago through the slats in the stopped railway car (VII:21) model the fragmented dialogue of the entire novel, exemplifying its governing compositional principle of expansion rather than contraction.[3] Thus even in death Zhivago's words are still heard in the poetry that is his. No conversation or discussion, seemingly, is rendered to completion. Moreover, most appear to begin in medias res. Yet, like a canvas that does not bear viewing at too close range, the work achieves its own singular effect on consideration from a broad, all-encompassing perspective, reminiscent of a highly complex collage exhibiting extraordinary depth and dimension.

Relatively extended, disjointed philosophical statement and generally sketchy background information belonging to the various characters, settings, and events likewise contribute to a sense of fragmentation. For instance, one of the concluding passages of the book is devoted to an abstract discussion of the city as a possible source of inspiration in the making of art (XV:11); the immediately subsequent passage describes in concrete detail the death of the novel's protagonist. Between these two contiguous narrative units there is no evident connection, yet from the perspective of the novel's greater design, one contributes to the further exposition of a well-developed theme, while the other moves the plot toward its end. One passage is thus essentially ontological in nature, the other teleological, with each having its role to play. The first is fundamentally devoid of a temporal component; the second is expressive of nothing if not time—that is, the end of time for one character, apocalypse writ small.

Most commonly the images of the novel are visual; the whiteness of the endless expanses of snow seen from the train heading to the Urals, for example, affords a dazzling effect. Less prominent, aural imagery also plays its role. The persistent sound of the wind hammering at the door (V:9), when Zhivago had hoped it might have been Lara instead, or of the wolves howling at night (XIV:8), as ready in the country to pounce on human prey as are the Bolsheviks in the town, are instances of aural imagery that are equally striking and impressive. Likewise, the deafening sound of the waterfall, heard from the eastbound train, is as intoxicating and heady as the sight of the endless snow. Two of the most prevalent images in the book, however, are of trains and death.

Meant to convey a sense of the perplexing, catastrophic times when both armies and households are constantly on the move, the train recurs as a concrete, realistic detail and as a frequent, symbolic image. With everything in chaotic flux the train figures centrally in Russia's confused, self-perpetuating dance of death. At the very beginning of the novel a train is stopped in the distance; an eccentric millionaire has committed suicide (I:5). In time of war an army train passing in the night inspires a quick resolution to Pasha Antipov's marital problems (IV:6). Later, as the subject of much rumor and talk, an armored train will hurl by in the night to mete out revolutionary justice in the countryside. It is a demonic image: a cold, uncompromising steel projectile, itself the manifestation of a cruel single-mindedness, bent on rending human flesh. At the same time another train moves slowly toward the East, with its cargo of murderous sailors, unfortunate conscripts, and runaways from a new order that defies both their sympathies and comprehension. Early in the novel Zhivago returns home to his family in a near-empty train, after another round of military service on a new front. Later, returning to Lara, his true spiritual home, he makes his way alone in the snowdrifts along the tracks, where the trains are abandoned and immobile in the frozen wasteland—fearful symbols of apocalyptic times.

Even more recurrent are images of death. Providing the dramatic core of the work's principal, philosophical theme, death is the motif with which the novel begins and ends.[4] Opening with a funeral procession, the very first section of the book presents a striking image of the boy clambering onto his mother's newly dug grave. Prayers for a dead mother are intoned, while shortly thereafter, the child's father throws himself under the wheels of a train. Just as the initial suicide forms the backdrop to the early scenes of the novel, so do the more or less "anonymous" deaths at the front, in the forest, and elsewhere serve as the gruesome, historical background to the book's "personal," individualized account. The deaths of such central figures as those of Yury's adoptive mother, of Strelnikov, and of Yury himself all figure strongly as climactic moments. Also contributing to the theme of death are the attempted suicide of Lara's mother and Lara's own attempt on the life of Komarovsky. Yet death in the novel represents not only a concrete event but attains as well to the level of symbolic detail—as an emanation from the realm of darkness and as a source of illumination that heralds at least the possibility of resurrection.

In its corresponding grotesque, meaningless aspect, death finds its most striking manifestation in the misadventure of the unfortunate Gints, who, in making a final, misguided attempt to inspire disillusioned troops by climbing onto a water barrel to deliver a speech, loses first his footing and then his life. Eventually becoming a haunting image for the perpetrator of the crime, the individual death makes the indulgence of mass murder, over a seven-year period, comprehensible in the only terms it can be—through the contemplation of the horror and cruelty of a single instance.

Yet, as the book seeks to make clear, through all of the havoc, disorder, and killing, the struggle continues—not for the making of revolution, or toward the "reshaping of the planet" (Pasternak 502) but "with a view to overcoming death." According to Yury's Uncle Nikolai, the spiritual mentor of all the book's thinkers and philosophers, "Man does not die in a ditch like a dog—but at home in history, while the work toward the conquest of death is in full swing" (10). It is the message of the novel that this struggle is waged on a very quiet, peaceful front, as far from that where war is waged as the realm of art can be. Thus we read of the work's central figure and future poet: "In answer to the desolation brought by death . . . he was drawn, as irresistibly as water funneling downwards, to dream, to think, to work out new forms, to create beauty" (89). Hence the concluding image of the entire work is that of the two friends with the slender volume of poetry in their keeping, which represents a bond between the living and the dead and is itself symbolic of the conquest of death.

Recurrent images of death in the novel are neither solely thematic nor simply a function of murderous times. Death, in the poet-novelist's vision, is symbolic, and both a source for understanding life and an inspiration for the making of art. Early in the novel Anna Ivanovna's initial encounter with death inspires a conception of man and immortality in her young charge: "You in others—this is your soul. This is what you are. This is what your consciousness has breathed and lived on and enjoyed throughout your life—your soul, your immortality, your life in others" (68). At her funeral it is noted with regard to Yury: "More vividly than ever before he realized that art has two constant, two unending concerns: it always meditates on death and thus always creates life" (89-90).[5] Her impending death thus affords one realization, its actual occurrence another. But the two are both interconnected and central to the novel's main philosophical theme, which asserts that life's potential triumph over death is accomplished through love and through art.

❋ ❋ ❋

Doctor Zhivago exhibits a near total absence of any psychological analysis in the development and later dissolution of the book's ultimately fragile relationships. They simply occur of themselves, seemingly according to certain unknown laws, and are eventually fated to be dissolved. When Marina enters Yury's life in its premature twilight, for example, the reader is informed: "One day she stayed with him and did not go back to the lodge. Thus she became Yury Andreyevich's third wife" (479). Similarly, the reader learns no more detail on how Lara, the love of Yury's life, eventually becomes his mistress: "Two months had now elapsed since the day when, instead of going home from Yuryatin, he spent the night at Larisa Fyodorovna's" (302). Clearly, on this occasion it was he who had remained. Yet whatever psychological torment or release might have been experienced remains a consideration about which the reader can only speculate. Further, these two instances correspond in their lack of psychological detail with the depiction of Yury and Tonya's betrothal, in which her mother plays such a crucial role: "If I die, stay together. You're meant for each other. Get married. There now, you're engaged" (71).[6]

Although the novel does not provide detailed psychological exploration of the characters' motivations, the idea of immediate perception is projected throughout the work. From among the novel's characters, it is Zhivago who is inspired by virtue of his immediate recognition and appreciation of images representing all that the world and life have to offer. With regard to the novel's hero, it is remarked early in the book: "He had . . . the gift of taking in everything at a glance and of expressing his thoughts as they first came to him and before they had lost their meaning and vitality" (7), and is thus graced with the gift of the poet.

It is the poet in particular who is challenged to give a name to things—to call by its right name what he encounters in life. The potential to do so is latent in each individual. Thus Yury writes in his Varykino diary: "Every man is born a Faust, with a longing to grasp and experience and express everything in the world" (284). Yet not everyone is gifted or fated to fulfill that potential. Lara, for instance, is destined to leave it to others: "For a moment she discovered the purpose of her life. She was here on earth to grasp the meaning of its wild enchantment and to call each thing by its right name, or, if this were not within her power, to give birth out of love for life to successors who would do it in her place" (75). This in large measure defines her role in her relationship with Zhivago. She is his most constant source of poetic inspiration. But, in contrast to what is said of her, it is observed of the future poet: "Now he was afraid of nothing, neither of life nor of death; everything in the world, all the things in it were words in his vocabulary. He felt he was on an equal footing with the universe" (87). What the passage suggests is that he is gifted not only with the potential but with the ability to fulfill the mission of "Faust."

When the artist finally perceives how to give form and utterance to what he has experienced, the result is poetry. Yet the making of art is inevitably bound up with some inner understanding that comes suddenly and unexpectedly. When the poet has called a thing by its right name, he experiences a moment of revelation, of epiphany. That moment represents an instant in time when certain images from life become associated and bound, when meaning is immediately recognized and retained—either in the mind as a still unrealized (creative) thought or in the world as art.

Such a moment is essentially different from the conventional "climax" to the action or plot, when tensions are relieved or a problem is resolved. An instance of the latter is Zhivago's capture by the Forest Brotherhood at a moment when he is determined to make a decision between the two women in his life. Another such instance occurs when Zhivago receives a letter from Tonya explaining that she and their family are going to be deported (XIII:18). Having been received by Zhivago hopelessly late, it provides, in effect, another abrupt, unhappy resolution to essentially the same dilemma as before, since he no longer needs to decide whether to go to Varykino with Lara or to Moscow to search for his family. But the real analytic substance of the letter, in which Tonya surmises that the nature of their problem is centered in her love being unrequited, is both inaccurate and inadequate. It is, rather, that Lara offers a continual source of revelation to Zhivago's spirit, a feature that is absent in his other love relationship but that is essential to the poet. As the poet-novelist explains: "Their love was great. Most people experience love without becoming aware of the extraordinary nature of this emotion. But to them—and this made them exceptional— the moments when passion visited their doomed human experience like a breath of eternity were moments of revelation, of continually new discoveries about themselves and life" (395). Lara offers the poet, in those moments of revelation, the spiritual essence from which poetry is born. As Lara herself expresses it: "It's a sort of crowning harmony—no limits, no degrees, everything is of equal value, everything is a joy, everything has become spirit" (434-35).

When a certain revelation is made to the spirit, it represents a distinctive high point in the adventure of the mind. Such a moment of epiphany is thus not to be associated with a change in physical or material circumstance. Although this kind of peripeteia is frequent in the novel, neither those bearing on Zhivago's story in particular nor more generally on the Revolution and the cataclysmic events that followed are the main subject of Pasternak's novel. Zhivago may be considered its hero, moreover, not in terms of his accomplishments or critical attitudes but in light of the fact that such moments of spiritual revelation are most consistently and strikingly visited upon him above all other characters. Similarly, Lara represents his most adored love object because she above all others is his most consistent source of spiritual revelation, itself in turn affording poetic inspiration.

At the very beginning of the novel Yury, as a boy, hears the voice of his dead mother calling to him: "The ghost of his mother's voice was hallucinatingly present in the meadows. He heard it in the musical phrases of the birds and the buzzing of the bees. Now and then he imagined with a start that his mother was calling him, asking him to join her somewhere" (11). Later, as an adult and head of a family, Yury hears Lara's voice in a dream (IX:5). Not recognizing at the time to whom it belongs, he will eventually heed her call and go to the woman who is at one point likened to the great expanses of Russia, "his incomparable mother" (391). The imagery of voices thus comes full circle and is complete. One sustaining female image is substituted for another. The voice of the boy's mother permeating all of nature is transformed into that of a woman representing the whole of a ravaged land. For such is Lara to the poet seeking the elemental comfort she alone can offer, during times when life itself appears to be in its final death throes.

Throughout the work such transformations of imagery achieve a transcendent effect. The brief section relating Lara's seduction and degradation, for example, begins with an onomatopoeic description of the late winter thaw: water is dripping everywhere, heralding joyous intimations of spring (II:12). The final note struck, however, is of Lara weeping. Her teardrops become a part of the total scene—and transform it. Nature's thaw is subordinated to and made to contribute to the revelation of Lara's hurt. The drops of melting snow, in effect, make audible the young girl's teardrops, as though the world of nature were itself resonating with her anguish.

Lara's healing, comforting presence is evoked through numerous images during the course of the novel. Representing another transformation—from the peaceful, ordered world of nature to the more restricted, chaotic human realm—one of the most striking images of the novel is that of the rowan tree, to which Lara is likened and equated.

The tree is initially described as being home and shelter to a multitude of birds feeding on its berries: "There seemed to be a living intimacy between the birds and the tree, as if it had watched them for a long time refusing to do anything, but in the end had had pity on them and given in and fed them like a nurse unbuttoning her blouse to give breast to a baby" (353). In this initial depiction the image of the tree evokes that of woman as a source of nourishment and life.

When escaping from the Forest Brotherhood, Yury pauses for a moment in front of the same tree in winter: "It was half in snow, half in frozen leaves and berries, and it held out two white branches toward him. He remembered Lara's strong white arms and seized the branches and pulled them to him. As if in answer, the tree shook snow all over him. He muttered without realizing what he was saying, and completely beside himself: 'I'll find you, my beauty, my love, my rowan tree, my own flesh and blood'" (375). For Yury, inspired by the sight of the tree, the moment represents one of both physical and spiritual release from the stifling bondage of the single-minded, relentless waging of war. Moreover, the woman and the life-giving tree become clearly identified in the mind of the poet. And this identification is strengthened and vitalized at the end, when, hovering over Zhivago's coffin, Lara is portrayed in terms unmistakably reminiscent of Yury's earlier perception of her when he had paused by the tree: "For a moment she stood still and silent, neither thinking nor crying, bowed over the coffin, the flowers, and the body, shielding them with her whole being, her head, her breast, her heart, and her arms, as big as her heart" (500).

In maintaining that posture of helpless, ineffectual protectress, Lara had "wanted, if only for a few moments, to break with Yury's help into the open, out of the sorrows that imprisoned her, to feel again the joy of liberation" (500). Her farewell at the very close of the novel provides just such a moment of revelation when hers and Zhivago's place in the total design of things is both comprehended and felt, while death for an instant represents neither a mystery nor a threat. In both instances, when Yury perceives Lara as reaching out to him, and when she one last time experiences the sense of their union, the moment of understanding and recognition is inspired by the same evocative image—of the tree covered in snow, of the man shrouded in the coffin. The image thus affords a sudden realization, and this is both consistent with and forms a repeated pattern within the overall design of the work.[7]

Through the language of imagery, Pasha, too, is one last time, in death, linked to the only woman in his life: "Strelnikov lay across the path with his head in a snow-drift. He had shot himself. The snow was a red lump under his left temple where he had bled. Drops of spurting blood that had mixed with the snow formed red beads that looked like rowanberries" (464). Although blood is inevitably connected with death, paradoxically, within the special context created by the earlier depiction of the tree, its berries are meant to represent a source of nourishment and are therefore symbolic of life. Thus, in that somber depiction of suicide the victim is associated both with the life-giving tree and, by extension, with the woman identified with it. In a work that proclaims, however, that "there is no such thing as death. Death has nothing to do with us" (68), it is entirely consistent that an element of life be retained in that gruesome image of otherwise unrelenting horror and gloom.

Throughout the novel there is a certain inevitability and finality to events, of which Strelnikov's death represents but one instance. In historical terms, upon which the novel of necessity draws, the prediction made by the deaf-mute early in the book (V:16) of far more disastrous upheavals to be endured before it all finally ends, of course, comes to pass. In terms of the novel's own individual dynamics, the same sense of the inevitable prevails. Thus Tonya knows from the very first mention of Lara that she represents a formidable rival with whom she "could not possibly compete" (132). Destined to lose her husband to an unknown, unfathomed feminine force beyond her ken, her response is immediate and uncontrolled. Similarly, at Zhivago's first meeting with his son, the three-year-old strikes his father, who will eventually desert them forever, and then bursts into tears (VI:3). Also, Yury himself intimates that Komarovsky will show up one last time to reclaim Lara and take her away forever from him (XIII:12). In each case the respective character's fearful "prophecy" is self-fulfilling. What is predicted out of insecurity and uncertainty occurs—through the artifice of art—as though it were all a matter of course. Such preliminary, anticipatory sketches are thus later to find their fuller, more expanded development as self-fulfilling prophecies, by which the novel proceeds to tell its story and by which what is prefigured is eventually realized. Further, instances of heightened perception and immediate insight represent still other occasions when a character experiences (what Dostoevsky terms) a "higher reality," exhibiting an ineffable sense of being, of human being.

In an early passage taking place at the front, there is a poignant scene in which a Cossack baits an old Jew (IV:11). In the next section Russia's last czar is portrayed reviewing his troops with considerable hesitation and awkwardness. The two scenes are seemingly unrelated. But together they give rise to a discussion of the concept of a people's supposed historical mission as opposed to the idea of the sanctity of the individual espoused by Christianity. Within the context of the book's ideology, both the humiliated Jew and inept czar are uninspiring figures meant to represent anachronistic aspects of human society, whereby mass allegiance is offered some abstract religious or political concept. Explicitly identified in the novel as a world view that conceives of man as primarily a member of a people, Judaism is to be superseded by Christianity, which regards man as an individual. The problem is discussed throughout the novel from a number of perspectives, including those of Uncle Nikolai, Zhivago, Lara, and Sima, the woman in Yuryatin. In the given passage the concept of a new order, inaugurated by the inception of the Christian era, is succinctly formulated by Zhivago's friend Gordon, who asserts: "In that new way of living and new form of society, which is born of the heart, and which is called the Kingdom of Heaven, there are no nations, there are only individuals" (122). His observation culminates in the recognition of "the mystery of the individual" as being the concept most revered by Christianity. The idea is borrowed from Zhivago's Uncle Nikolai; Gordon's own expression of it, however, is evoked by an abject member of an ancient race and by that of an ineffectual czar uncertain of what role to play before "his people." The two figures and their attendant images are thus linked as a common source in rendering a particular view.

Later in the novel, when Zhivago is captured by Strelnikov's guard, he sees through the train window a schoolboy who has also been taken prisoner. He is wounded, and his head has been bandaged. Blood trickles from under the gauze, and the boy aggravates the problem by repeatedly trying to set straight his school cap over the bandage. Zhivago wonders in horror why the boy keeps adjusting the cap when it ought to be removed from his bandaged head altogether. For him the sight is symbolic of people everywhere in wartorn Russia behaving contrary to common sense. "He longed to shout to him . . . that salvation lay not in loyalty to forms but in throwing them off" (248). Zhivago's contained cry of indignation represents, in essence, an extension of his earlier discussion with Gordon. Once again, as in the case of the tormented old man (and with each individual member of the czar's troops as well), the sanctity of the individual had been violated—ironically, in the present instance, not only by the boy's captors but also by the unwitting victim himself.

In solely structural terms an image briefly introduced into the context of events produces a certain recognition on the part of a particular character momentarily made a spectator. Zhivago's strong condemnation of the excesses of the Revolution thus becomes focused on the schoolboy and is further crystallized. As a telling image, Strelnikov, too, is affected by the sight of the boy and finds it "disgraceful" (253). But how to eradicate or even alleviate the disgrace, of which the boy is only symbolic and which exists on a grand scale, is ultimately beyond his ken. And this lack accounts for his own later, personal tragedy. Ultimately a victim himself, Strelnikov will also figure at a later moment as a visual stimulus (or evocative image) by which Lara suddenly perceives what had transpired in him. Upon catching sight of the man who had been her husband, now surrounded by his guards, Lara observes: "It was as if something abstract had crept into his face and made it colorless. As if a living human face had become an embodiment of a principle, the image of an idea" (401). The sight of Strelnikov thus evokes the impression of a particular resoluteness and single-mindedness incarnate, which both Lara and Zhivago reject, and which rejection in part brings them together.

As part of the novel's basic design, Pasha is depicted as moving in the opposite direction from Zhivago, toward fixed ideas and irrevocable forms. By gravitating toward the idea of control over human life and the world, he in effect rejects fundamental life-affirming principles based on fluidity and dynamic flux, the mainsprings of which are not subject to the "laws" of any ideology nor to the (collective) will of its adherents. Yet Pasha, too, experiences a "revelation"—but of a negative kind, when Lara reveals to him on their wedding night the sordid details of her past: "His suspicious guesses alternated with Lara's confessions. He questioned her, and with each of her answers his spirit sank as though he were hurtling down a void. His wounded imagination could not keep up with her revelations." The author observes further: "In all Pasha's life there had not been a change in him so decisive and abrupt as in the course of this night. He got up a different man, almost astonished that he was still called Pasha Antipov" (97).

In essence, that very authorial observation underscores a guiding vision of the entire work: certain knowledge is attained by a given character unexpectedly, immediately, in a moment that leaves him different from before. Within the closed world of the text, *Doctor Zhivago* seeks

to convey information in condensed, highly charged form, which is perceived by the character uncritically in a flash of insight. In order to attain
a like understanding, the reader is obliged to achieve essentially the
same experience in a commensurate, coordinate manner.

The novel intends to inspire the reader with insights—into art, love,
life, and their inevitable intertwining—in the same way that the novel's
protagonist, in particular, acquires understanding. This is accomplished
through repeated striking revelations devoid of any attendant explanation. Thus all of Nikolai's observations are presented in encapsulated,
virtually aphoristic form rather than as the closely reasoned arguments
of the disciplined logician. Indeed, conventional logic finds no place
whatever in the scheme of the novel. Life is not perceived to follow logical patterns, but is subject only to unexpected events ordained by
Fate. The single exception in the work in which an idea is elaborated in
some detail occurs when Sima engages in a lengthy monologue,
expounding, essentially, the views of Nikolai. Yet, as one critic observes,
the woman herself "is on fire with the spirit of revelation" (Payne 175),
a view that might well be extended to embrace the entire work, itself
aglow with the same spirit.

The aim of the novel, then, is to transmit certain experience of a spiritual stamp from the fictional domain to the realm of the reader. In
effect, the novel itself serves as an elaborate model by which this end
is achieved.[8] Thus, within the text the pattern is always the same: the
image depicted affords a given character immediate insight, which
becomes crystallized in the mind as a result of what is perceived
momentarily in the world. Analogously, the whole array of images of
which *Doctor Zhivago* is composed are intended to offer a like experience to the reader.

Like any work of literature, *Doctor Zhivago* is oriented to the
reader—but in the particular sense that there are moments of epiphany
or of potential recognition that go beyond what any one character can
experience or know, making the reader not only the most informed
"participant" in the work (which would again apply generally to the literary text) but the one most likely to be *consistently* illuminated by
those flares that at times light the path of Zhivago in his quest for understanding. How and in what complex manner, for instance, the fates of
the two characters passing by in the sleigh become irrevocably intertwined with those of the two characters making marriage plans behind
the frost-covered window, where "a candle burned on the table, a candle
burned" (81), remains most completely revealed to the reader alone.

Likewise, beyond any single character, the reader is made cognizant of the fact that so many individuals whose lives are linked are momentarily united early in the novel at the front (IV:10); that Lara will be present at Zhivago's last hour in a room long familiar to them both; that Zhivago's poetry will serve as a source of inspiration both to friends and strangers alike, and will make for the final comment on him; that from their love a child was born to Zhivago and Lara. Many more instances might be enumerated, frequently of a strikingly coincidental nature, yet they all add up to a single tenet or statement of faith made repeatedly throughout the work: that we are all bound to one another and that our lives are marvelously and at times miraculously interconnected in the great mystery of Life, which reveals its secrets only at brief selected moments.

On another level concerned less with prosaic considerations, a more profound kind of recognition connected with the making of poetry is achieved in analogous fashion. Thus, in the mind of the novel's poet-hero, the image of a wood evokes thoughts of Lara. And, in "naming" her, he defines what she is for him.

> Ever since his childhood Yury Andreyevich had been fond of woods seen at evening against the setting sun. At such moments he felt as if he too were being pierced by shafts of light. It was as though the gift of the living spirit were streaming into his breast, piercing his being and coming out at his shoulders like a pair of wings. The archetype that is formed in every child for life and seems for ever after to be his inward face, his personality, awoke in him in its full primordial strength, and compelled nature, the forest, the after-glow, and everything else visible to be transfigured into a similarly primordial and all-embracing likeness of a girl. Closing his eyes, "Lara," he whispered and thought, addressing the whole of his life, all God's earth, all the sunlit space spread out before him. (343)

Here the essential poetic device is laid bare: the image of the forest is consciously and methodically transformed into the image of a girl, according to a pattern of transformations and interweaving of images that informs the book's overall design.

On a similar occasion Zhivago recalls his first encounter with Lara, when she was still a schoolgirl in uniform. "Often since then I have tried to define and give name to the enchantment that you communicated to me that night," he says. Inspired by his recollection of her schoolgirl image, he declares that she was "charged, as with electricity, with all the femininity in the world" (427). In developing the metaphor, the poet perceives her as possessing a force awesome in its ability to inspire love. In an instant the girl in his mind becomes transformed into the woman before him, who is for but a short time to share his life. The moment of description is one among many during which Zhivago defines for himself in poetic terms Lara's place in his life. In each instance she represents both the catalyst and the source that enables him to articulate his own perceptions and understanding of life and the world. Thus, at another moment of recognition, it is noted with regard to Lara: "You could not communicate with life and existence, but she was their representative, their expression, in her the inarticulate principle of existence became sensitive and capable of speech" (391) as a source of poetic utterance.

Although Lara is not always the inspiration for Zhivago's moments of revelation, she is inextricably bound to them. During his period of detainment by the Forest Brotherhood, Zhivago encounters an old sorceress chanting a song. The reader is informed that an old Russian folk song, "by every possible means, by repetitions and similes . . . slows down the gradual unfolding of its theme. Then at some point it suddenly reveals itself and astounds us" (362) in the manner of epiphany. The song itself speaks of

> the far end of the street, the last house,
> The last house in the street, the last window, the room
> Where she has shut herself in,
> My beloved, my longed-for love. (363)

To Zhivago's mind and ear the house in the song may well relate in symbolic fashion to the house opposite the house of sculptures, where Lara lives; and the woman, to Lara herself.[9]

The old woman concludes her mutterings and incantations on a peculiar note resembling a distorted version of an account borrowed, as the novelist observes, from the ancient chronicles and incorporated over the centuries into the oral tradition by such healers and practitioners as the old woman herself. "And the knight opened the shoulder of the woman, as if it were a casket, and with his sword took out of her shoulder blade a measure of corn or a squirrel or a honeycomb." Here the strange image is immediately given new meaning and new life in the mind of Zhivago. For, by simple association and substitution, the image of the unknown woman suffering the ministrations of her knight is transformed into another woman entirely: "Lara's left shoulder had been cut open. Like a key turning in the lock of a secret safe, the sword unlocked her shoulder and the secrets she had kept safe in the depths of her soul came to light." This thought in turn leads to a new definition, or "naming" of her, as she appears to the poet in "divine form . . . handed over, like a child tightly wrapped in a sheet after its bath, into the keeping of his soul" (367). One poetic image uttered by the sorceress is thus adapted and transformed into another conceived by Yury Andreyevich. In the mind of the latter the woman of the song appears in beloved form, and is then again abstracted into a child of divine proportion, while the "measure of corn . . . or honeycomb" is transformed into the hidden secrets of a treasured soul.

Ultimately, such transformations of imagery reflect the overall design of the novel, itself a vast mosaic composed of interrelated images. Moreover, the novel's implicitly stated *ars poetica* is both mirrored in these passages and realized in the composition of the book itself. What the novel has to say about the making of art, in other words, is reflected and illustrated in how that same novel is made. Life and art are intrinsically interconnected, Pasternak's novel asserts; a moment of revelation in the one leads, in essence, to the creation of the other. By carefully delineating its hero's thoughts and mental processes in the act of creation, the book makes its point.[10]

During Zhivago's second and last stay in Varykino with Lara and Katya, he writes at night, while mother and daughter sleep. Their peaceful rest elicits a sense of tranquillity and harmony in the mind of the poet: "The purity of their features . . . surged through his heart in a single wave of meaning, moving him to a joyful sense of the triumphant purity of being." That "single wave" affords hours of creativity extending into early morning, when Zhivago is disturbed by the mournful howling of wolves. Sighting them at the edge of the clearing, his train of thought, as well as the creative process, is interrupted. The serene image of "the two sleeping heads on their snow-white pillows" had inspired him to compose "words so simple as to be almost childish . . . suggesting the directness of a lullaby" (437, 440). But the tender image of the mother and child had been supplanted and undermined by that of "four long shadows, no thicker than pencil strokes, at the edge of the clearing" (438). Through a subtle transformation, however, which the book makes explicit, the wolves too become both symbolic and a source of further imagery, in accord with the principle that "everything was being altered and transformed."

> The wolves he had been remembering all day long were no longer wolves on the snowy plain under the moon, they had become a theme, they had come to symbolize a hostile force bent upon destroying him and Lara and on driving them from Varykino. The

> thought of this hostility developed in him and by evening it looked
> like a prehistoric beast or some fabulous monster, a dragon whose
> tracks had been discovered in the ravine and who thirsted for his
> blood and lusted after Lara. (440)

Concrete and real enough for the doctor and the woman he loves, the
wolves become abstract symbols in the making of poetry. These in turn
become further transformed into fantastic images reflecting both the
immediate threat and general hostility permeating the greater environ-
ment from which the fugitives had fled.

The danger of remaining any longer in town under the watchful
eyes of the Bolsheviks had prompted Zhivago and Lara to flee. But the
dangers that stalk them take on new form in the country as the wolves
move in closer and in greater numbers from one night to the next. The
night, however, is also a time reserved for the making of poetry, and in
this reclusive realm the specter of ravenous wolves inspires the poet to
compose "the legend of St. George and the dragon in . . . lyrical manner"
(441). For, in terms of the book's life-affirming dialectic, fearful experience is transformed into lyrical poetry. Or, conversely, as the novelist
expresses it in depicting his hero's feverish creative activity: "Every
work of art, including tragedy, expresses the joy of existence" (454).

During the course of events certain dangers fade, while new ones
emerge to take their place. Doctor Zhivago is threatened successively
by war and its aftermath, starvation, imprisonment, execution, and the
capitulation of his own weak constitution. In time the cataclysmic times
take their toll. The poet dies—but his poetry remains. Miraculously, the
woman who played such a decisive role in Zhivago's life and in the creative process suddenly reappears at his death. The coincidence may
strain credibility, but it is a powerful representative instance illustrating the novel's projected vision of life and our human interrelations.[11]
Without Lara's sudden, stunning appearance at the end, preceding her
final disappearance, Zhivago's death would appear simply an unre-
markable, ordinary event. A man who had suffered moral and physical
deterioration during hard times eventually dies of a heart attack. Her
presence, however, and her farewell make of the death scene an event
of the spirit and a celebration of life.

For the woman newly arrived from Siberia, the man at rest in the
coffin represents far more than another life that has run its course. She
sees him, in a moment of inspiration, in entirely transmuted, still vital
form: "Farewell, my great one, my own, farewell, my pride, farewell, my

swift, deep, dear river, how I loved your day-long splashing, how I loved to plunge into your cold waves" (502). Thus one last time a moment of spiritual revelation effects a wholly life-affirming transformation. The man in the coffin retains his vitality in the mind of the woman who, on this final occasion, assumes the role of the poet, and gives name to the experience of taking leave by giving it new life in the form of a new image. In such manner the individual instances of epiphany are achieved throughout this novel with the power and grace that make the work a masterpiece.

Early in the novel Zhivago exclaims: "There will be no death. . . . There will be no death because the past is over. . . . There will be no death because it is already done with, it's old and we are bored with it. What we need is something new, and that new thing is life eternal" (68). The message conveyed is that the only thing worth our allegiance is "life itself, the phenomenon of life, the gift of life" (297), which must be viewed, in a broader sense than the term is here, as an "epiphany." All aspects and functions of life are seen, in this broader perspective, as sacraments, so that life rather than death is given its due. It is the measure of *Doctor Zhivago* that the novel celebrates life in this manner, embracing all of its facets, its joys and sorrows.

3

MEMORY AS DURATION:
LOVE IN THE TIME OF CHOLERA
(GARCÍA MÁRQUEZ)

■ □ ■

Two features are essential to narrative: change and memory. Both are associated with time. Narrative by its very nature does not chronicle static situations, which are in any case inimical to the telling of story, the relating of plot. Narrative exists, on the contrary, to chronicle change. Likewise, events must be ostensibly recollected in order to be related. All of narrative is in effect ostensible recollection.

Gabriel García Márquez' *Love in the Time of Cholera* provides a stunning example of this literary preoccupation with a past that never was. In effect, the novel affords an unwitting elaboration of the workings of memory in essentially those terms that the French thinker Henri Bergson attributes to his concept of *duration*. There is, in other words, a near perfect correlation between García Márquez' novelistic treatment of memory and of the effect the past has on the present and Bergson's philosophical investigation of the same idea. Bergson proposes the concept of duration as a way of explicitly acknowledging memory as a dynamic, life-shaping force. García Márquez reveals implicitly—through the rarefied complexities of plot—how that very concept is directly related to the shaping of narrative.

Memory conveys something of the past into the present. In doing so, it allows for that something to endure. In *Creative Evolution* Bergson states that life "progresses and *endures* in time" (58). Lest the point be obscured, his emphasis falls on the idea of enduring (rather than progressing), which is at the core of his interest in duration. That basic term, in other words, contains within it the central idea of enduring. For life itself in this understanding is conceived as "a reality which *endures* [again underscored] inwardly, which is duration itself" (395). Hence enduring is equated with, or at least situated within, duration—which concept, it will be argued here, finds its corresponding place within the generic domain of the novel. As our quintessential instance, *Love in the Time of Cholera* is concerned with nothing if not the half-century-long enduring love that the hero, Florentino Ariza, feels for Fernanda Daza, the young beauty who, for several years in the absence of any personal contact, first reciprocates his expressed affection in the form of an essentially abstract, disembodied epistolary courtship, and then in the course of a single, utterly brief meeting rejects him instantly, without explanation.

For Bergson "the very basis of our conscious existence is memory, that is to say, the prolongation of the past into the present, or, in a word, *duration*, acting and irreversible" (20). He defines his key notion as the "preservation of the past in the present" (27) and as the "persistence of the past in the present" (23). In its more aggressive formulation, the latter expression is particularly appropriate to García Márquez' novel, since a seemingly "irreversible" persistence characterizes the relentless, single-minded effort of Florentino Ariza to keep the past alive.[1] Bergson defines duration as "the very life of things, the fundamental reality" (344)—which, for Florentino Ariza, is the love he has felt for Fermina Daza all his life. The French thinker declares that "duration is the continuous progress of the past which *gnaws* into the future and which swells as it advances. . . . Real duration is that duration which *gnaws* on things, and leaves on them the mark of its tooth" (7, 52; emphasis added). Not only does Bergson's understanding of duration closely coincide with García Márquez' novelistic vision, but even his repeated use of that one verb describes precisely the "gnawing" pain, desire, nostalgia, and enduring love—with the mark of *its* tooth—that Florentino Ariza feels and will not let go of for more than half a century.

In *Love in the Time of the Cholera* the passage of time is tracked in large chunks; that a half-century had passed is related numerous times (García Márquez 50, 55, 60, 68, 73, *et passim*). But the novel also evinces a certain Rabelaisian predilection for precision. Thus, on several occasions it is noted that exactly fifty-one years, nine months, and four days had passed since the hero had been rejected in love (53, 103, 288), had persevered all that time, and was now reaffirming his "vow of eternal fidelity and everlasting love" (50, 103). In the final lines of the novel precision is again evoked in the fifty-three years, seven months, eleven days and nights that Florentino Ariza had waited for precisely that present moment that concludes the novel. But this exactitude is in turn immediately countered by a decided lack of precision, enunciated in the final word of the book: "Forever"—which may well signify that just as everything in the past had been endured seemingly forever, so might everything in the future be lived in just those same infinite terms.

The novel begins with death and with the central characters already well advanced in age. All that follows right up to the concluding chapter represents an excursion back in time in order to relate all of the events that lead up to the startling, climactic moment at the close of the first chapter, when Florentino Ariza declares his undying love for Fermina Daza on the very day when her husband departs the world by leaning too far over on an already precarious ladder in an ill-conceived effort to recapture a wayward parrot. Only at the opening of the final chapter does the novel come full circle to this very point, at which things were left at the close of the first chapter. Thus the book follows a clearly evident circular construction. Although graced by numerous other chronological intricacies, the ostensibly recollected past is in effect framed by an evolving present that only at the close of the novel moves forthrightly into the future.

In like figurative terms it may also be supposed that the narrative forms a kind of loop whereby the linear temporal flow is interrupted at a point that allows for the expansive past-oriented account to unravel over most of the course of the novel prior to that moment when the book picks up at precisely that *present* moment when it had earlier been interrupted. Within that loop, however, we find a variety of chronological inversions or embedded temporal fluctuations at virtually every turn. Thus time is represented as both circular and repetitious: "Twenty-five years later, Lorenzo Daza did not realize that his intransigence in his daughter's love affair was a vicious repetition of his own past, and he complained of his misfortune to the same in-laws who had opposed him, as they had complained in their day to their own kin" (86). "The rest of the day was like a hallucination: she was in the same house where she had been until yesterday, receiving the same visitors who had said goodbye to her, talking about the same things, bewildered by the impression that she was reliving a piece of life she had already lived" (96). There is also the sense of time repeating itself in cyclical fashion. "He confirmed this with the compassion of sons whom life had turned, little by little, into the fathers of their fathers, and for the first time he regretted not having stood with his father in the solitude of his errors" (112). To greater or lesser degree these several passages illustrate Bergson's observation that "evolution is not only a movement forward; in many cases we observe a marking-time, and still more often a deviation or turning back" (*Creative* 115). Likely, that "deviation" amounts to regression when all along we had looked for and expected progression (if not exactly progress).

Oddly, time may appear exclusive in affecting certain domains while seemingly ignoring others. Thus one character testifies: "In my opinion . . . the nineteenth century is passing for everyone except us" (225). While another declares: "I am almost one hundred years old, and I have seen everything change, even the position of the stars in the universe, but I have not seen anything change yet in this country. . . . Here they make new constitutions, new laws, new wars every three months, but we are still in colonial times" (266). Time may likewise appear reversed: "In her final years she would still recall the trip that, with the perverse lucidity of nostalgia, became more and more recent in her memory" (87). And time may also seem to stop—both in the world of fantasy and in that of memory.

> He said that there were several caravelles with their sails still intact, and that the sunken ships were visible even on the bottom, for it seemed as if they had sunk along with their own space and time, so that they were still illumined by the same eleven o'clock sun that was shining on Saturday, June 9, when they went down. (92-3)

> One winter afternoon she went to close the balcony because a heavy storm was threatening, and she saw Florentino Ariza on his bench under the almond trees in the little park . . . but this time she did not see him as she had seen him by accident on various occasions, but at the age at which he had remained in her memory. (212)

> Fermina Daza was so depressed by what she had seen and heard since she left her house that . . . she avoided passing through the villages of her nostalgia. . . . When she had no other recourse and had to pass through a village, she covered her face with her mantilla so that she could remember it as it once had been. (253)

Within the convincing framework of novelistic "chrono-logical" invention, these passages allow us to concur readily with Bergson that "*time is invention or it is nothing at all*" (*Creative* 371).[2]

Yet Bergson also writes (and again underscores his point) that "*Wherever anything lives, there is, open somewhere, a register in which time is being inscribed*" (20). In *Love in the Time of Cholera* that "register" is situated in the heart of Florentino Ariza, who at one point suffers from self-inflicted shock at the realization of the passage of time: "'Damn it,' he said, appalled, 'that all happened thirty years ago!'" (219). On another occasion the reader is informed that, again shocked by the recognition of the inexorable passage of time, Florentino Ariza was "shaken by a thunderbolt of panic that death, the son of a bitch, would win an irreparable victory in his fierce war of love" (261). Time in the novel, therefore, does not exist in the abstract; it always "belongs" to, or is perceived and accounted for, by some lone figure for whom it bears meaning, at times excruciatingly so.

Perhaps most important here, then, is the recognition that time is not only cultural but also personal—for both character and reader. The latter inevitably retains certain memories of the text and its constituent events more vividly than other episodes for reasons that may well be more personal than textual. Thus, in life "we pluck out of duration those moments that interest us, and that we have gathered along its course" (Bergson, *Creative* 297). A character will likewise mark time or regard its passage in ways that might also be deemed "personal" within the fictional context. Thus, for Florentino Ariza "his only point of reference in his own past was the ephemeral love affair with Fermina Daza, and only what concerned her had anything to do with reckoning his life" (219). We get a clearer sense of such "points of reference" when it is observed that "they marked the passage of his life, for he experienced the cruelty of time not so much in his own flesh as in the imperceptible changes he discerned in Fermina Daza each time he saw her" (228). To underscore further the personal aspect of the passage of time in narrative (mirroring an equally compelling view in life), the following playful distinction makes the point.

> For women there were only two ages: the age for marrying, which did not go past twenty-two, and the age for being eternal spinsters: the ones left behind. The others, the married women, the mothers, the widows, the grandmothers, were a race apart who tallied their age not in relation to the number of years they had lived but in relation to the time left to them before they died. (260)

Affording a like understanding, but a perhaps more poignant sense of the passage of time (because it is provided from an individual rather than a generalized perspective), an aged Florentino Ariza pleads: "Don't do this to me, Doctor. . . . Two Months for me are like ten years for you" (313).

The discrepancy, of course, underscores that feature of time that renders it very personal and not at all abstract.[3]

Interestingly, the conception of time belonging to those "others" ("the married women, the mothers, the widows, the grandmothers") blatantly disregards the past, with all the experience that might be garnered therefrom, and focuses soberly and exclusively on the present, as it glides forward into the future.[4] So to that "race apart" is implicitly attributed a certain wisdom that Florentino Ariza does not have, since he "insisted on believing," as we are told, that "the memory of the past did not redeem the future" (317). Yet in compensation for that lack of redemption he is granted a life-sustaining, all-embracing memory that makes the passing years easier to bear (and wonderfully entertaining for the reader to share). "The memory of them all was with him: those who slept in the cemeteries, thinking of him through the roses he planted over them, as well as those who still laid their heads on the pillow where their husbands slept, their horns golden in the moonlight" (269). But memory need not be solely a palliative; in its unrelenting truthfulness it may also be definitive. "It was the first time in half a century that they had been so close and had enough time to look at each other with some serenity, and they had seen each other for what they were: two old people, ambushed by death, who had nothing in common except the memory of an ephemeral past that was no longer theirs but belonged to two young people who had vanished and who could have been their grandchildren" (305-6). Thus, through a common twist of an unkind fate, memory serves not only to palliate but also to relegate the past to where it belongs.

From the dual perspective of characters in a novel and of people in life, the notion that the "past is irretrievable" (Heidegger 17) argues that the past is the past and cannot be relived. But from the viewpoint of *duration*, the past is also very much a determinant feature of the present. As Bergson reiterates:

> It is into pure duration that we then plunge back, a duration in which the past, always moving on, is swelling unceasingly with a present that is absolutely new. (Creative 219)

> Real duration is that in which each form flows out of previous forms, while adding to them something new, and is explained by them as much as it explains them. (393)

But, as the French philosopher would have it, this understanding, as a form of "wisdom," relates to life itself, characterized by "that concrete duration in which a radical recasting of the whole is always going on" (394)—which, as we have just seen, takes place through the incorporation of vital aspects of the past into the present. It is our contention here that the same kind of "recasting" of present events, in light of those that preceded, informs—or, better, governs—the novel as well. For it is precisely this concept of duration, conceived in terms of and applied to the peculiar strategies and constraints of narrative, that serves as a primary conceptual element or structuring principle in the novel's creation and in the evolution of its constituent episodes that ultimately take it from beginning to end.

In abstract terms Bergson observes: "if there be memory, that is, the survival of past images, these images must constantly mingle with our perception of the present and may even take its place" (*Matter* 66). In García Márquez' novel such "mingling" is precisely what occurs in the mind of Florentino Ariza. The French thinker goes on to say that "if it still deserves the name of memory, it is not because it conserves bygone images, but because it prolongs their useful effect into the present moment" (82). What that useful effect amounts to for Florentino Ariza is that it allows him not only to recall but also to *act*—at whatever convenient moment presents itself to him as potentially available for effecting the only change in his life that has ever mattered to him: the chance to incorporate Fermina Daza into that life. Hence the French philosopher's conception of memory, as well as the Colombian novelist's, entails a notion that not only "imports the past into the present" (Bergson, *Matter* 73) but is also inspirational in effecting a dynamic present.

Further, as an artistically rendered reflection of a human figure facing a succession of threatening aspects in the fictional rather than the actual world, the literary character may (like its human counterpart) resort to sustaining temporal constructs of the imagination in order to thwart, among other threats, the passage of time. Thus, "he was still too young to know that the heart's memory eliminates the bad and magnifies the good, and that thanks to this artifice we manage to endure the burden of the past" (106). Conversely, that burden may naturally make itself felt in the personal terms noted here. "He would remember it always, as he remembered everything that happened during that period, through the rarefied lenses of his misfortune" (137). Yet such dismal preoccupations do not preclude a certain perhaps primal temporal (and spatial) survival instinct from appearing triumphant. "She navigated the disorder of the street in her own time and space, not colliding with anyone, like a bat in the darkness" (99).

But emerging supreme, as we all know, is time and the ravages it brings with it. "They were people whose lives were slow, who did not see themselves growing old, or falling sick, or dying, but who disappeared little by little in their own time, turning into memories, mists from other days, until they were absorbed into oblivion" (113). In this sad reflection people appear transformed into mist and memory. Yet memory itself, or the sense of the passage of time, may also appear transformed. "The act was an exorcism of relief for Florentino Ariza, for when he . . . walked down the dead streets without looking back, he no longer felt that he was leaving the next morning but that he had gone away many years before with the irrevocable determination never to return" (138). Here the future is transformed through a necessary survival mechanism into a past that paradoxically has not yet occurred. Yet, equally disturbing, the past may also be transformed into something that will never occur. "Her misfortune . . . was that she could never remember [the village] afterward as it was in reality, but only as she imagined it before she had been there" (254). In broader terms it becomes evident that change and memory, as paired requisites for narrative—perhaps on a par with time itself—are thus not only associated with time (as stated at the start here) but are themselves inextricably interconnected, since memory permits change, perhaps even foments it; moreover, memory is itself subject to change, as in the transformation just noted.

Not only is memory subject to transformation, however; it is also constantly in peril of its consummate eradication, as in the following joint effort at both transformation and obliteration: "With no tears, she wiped away the memory of Florentino Ariza, she erased him completely, and in the space that he had occupied in her memory she allowed a field of poppies to bloom" (206). Such an act, moreover, is quite different from simply forgetting, which would appear only to create a void or an absence devoid of either change or any attendant metaphor: "And then he wiped him from his memory, because among other things, his [medical] profession had accustomed him to the ethical management of forgetfulness" (189). That colorless act thus stands in contrast to the creative effort of the imagination by which not only memory but the self engaged in recollection may also be transformed into something other than that true self. "And so the most difficult hours passed for him, at times in the person of a timid prince or a paladin of love, at other times in his own scalded hide of a lover in the middle of forgetting, until the first breezes began to blow" (142).

Further, memory appears to be eradicated in what we may take to be a concrete form—"the reason for her weeping had disappeared that afternoon, had been pulled out by the roots, forever, even from his memory" (249)—or its eradication can appear figurative in nature: "But that night after the film he had the feeling that his memory had been erased from the drawing room" (257-58). On the other hand, there are memories that are resistant to all efforts at obliteration, and seem to retain a ghostlike (omni)presence and omnipotence all their own. "Florentino Ariza took a breath. The only thing he could do to stay alive was not to allow himself the anguish of that memory. He erased it from his mind, although from time to time in the years that were left to him he would feel it revive, with no warning and for no reason, like the sudden pang of an old scar" (336).

Affording a poetics of memory, among its riches, the novel allows that memory can be nostalgic (193), can betray (209), or can eliminate "even a spark of nostalgia" (330). Yet nostalgia, which may afford its own "perverse clarity" (223) and which may appear as only another, more sentient way of referring to memory, also operates according to its own laws of sustaining the past in the face of opposition to that preoccupation. "However, when she thought he was completely erased from her memory, he reappeared where she least expected him, a phantom of her nostalgia" (223). Yet such phantoms of nostalgic memory may also lie in wait for the other, so that the one who haunts is in turn also haunted. "Then he felt alone in the world, and the memory of Fermina Daza, lying in ambush in recent days, dealt him a mortal blow" (145). Thus, as has been shown, if memory is subject to various forces, and if at times it exerts an ameliorating effect on a seemingly overpowering reality, it also bears a certain debilitating power of its own. At times affording the sweet recollection of times past, most often in this novel memory serves mainly as a painful reminder of what was and will never be again. Except in the phenomenally determined mind of Florentino Ariza for whom a past that never happened is, paradoxically, nonetheless due to be resurrected in due time.

❋ ❋ ❋

In *Love in the Time of Cholera* the passage of time stands in direct opposition to the hero's timeless love. Although the work remains open-ended, with the main characters literally at sea and with no mooring either desired or in sight, from this opposition is derived a novel of resolution in which the hero eventually gets the girl. Yet by the time he does so, and the problem of the novel is thereby resolved, more than a half-century has gone by, and the two protagonists are by then well into their seventies. Thus, despite the fact that Florentino Ariza had engaged in "six hundred twenty-two . . . long-term liaisons, apart from the countless fleeting adventures that did not even deserve a charitable note" (152), his resolve to be united with Fermina Daza, the love of his long life, is finally achieved. The tensions of the novel depend on the hero's determination in the matter of love, on the one hand, and on the irrevocable passage of time, on the other. Time is thus dynamic in its passage, while love remains static in its steadfastness; everything changes, in other words, except Florentino Ariza's love for Fermina Daza.

In part that love is chronicled by a series of relentless metonymic associations that take the narrative from start to finish. The opening line of the book reads: "It was inevitable: the scent of bitter almonds always reminded him of the fate of unrequited love." Metonymy, especially repeated metonymies, serve precisely as "reminders"—whether of unrequited love, which is emblematic of most of the book, or of its opposite, which takes over in a remarkable reversal only at the very end. Metonymy, in any case, serves memory. Whether characterized as "the torments of memory" (3), "the maggot broth of memory" (16), "an illusion of memory" (17), or "the trash heap of memory" (219), it is still ostensible memory that the novelist must draw upon in the act of creating the narrative and actual memory that the reader must rely on in recreating the text, as an act of completion performed in multitudinous individual ways in response to the literary work.

In a hallmark statement attributed to Fermina Daza, we read that "she would always remember Paris as the most beautiful city in the world, not because of what it was or was not in reality, but because it was linked to the memory of her happiest years" (212). It is precisely such linkage that the reader encounters throughout the narrative in a series of metonymic associations that document in poetic form what the narrative relates as prosaic event. For Florentino Ariza telegrams are connected with death (55), his violin is identified with his misfortune (139), Carnival is forever poisoned for him because the "crazy woman from the insane asylum," who enchants him with "her witticism" (181), turns out to be exactly what she claims to be, and a murderess besides.

On the other hand, Fernanda Daza, "the maiden idealized by the alchemy of poetry," is associated with "heartrending twilights" (64), with "the pensive scent of white gardenias" (85), "the nocturnal perfume of withered gardenias" (278), and with "the scent of almonds that came wafting back to him from his innermost being" (255). Even if other realities become less intense and are eventually extinguished, the metonymic association remains alive in both the character's and reader's mind. Thus, "little by little the fragrance of Fermina Daza became less frequent and less intense, and at last it remained only in white gardenias" (148), the most prominent symbol of the exchange of love letters "half a century ago" that fomented the love that had convinced Florentino Ariza "in the solitude of his soul that he had loved in silence for a much longer time than anyone else in this world ever had" (48). Thus his mother claims, "the only disease my son ever had was cholera." But, as the author declares, in a deft explanation of the workings of metonymy: "She had confused cholera with love, of course, long before her memory had failed" (218). Because such metonymic associations support memory rather than diffuse it.

In perhaps equally unwitting support of our more complete understanding of how narrative is conceived and created, Bergson writes: "Inner duration is the continuous life of a memory which prolongs the past into the present . . . containing within it . . . the ceaselessly growing image of the past. . . . Without this survival of the past into the present there would be no duration, but only instantaneity" (*Metaphysics* 40). Otherwise put, and in terms of the preceding chapter, without memory there would be no lasting meaning to epiphany. For it to attain sense and value, the moment of revelation, of "instantaneity," requires that it be retained and transformed over time into the kind of knowledge that endures, into wisdom. Without memory as duration there may as well not take place the moment of revelation, what Bergson refers to as "the essentially active . . . almost violent character of metaphysical intuition" (45). For without an analogous underlying premise to Bergson's, situated *as it is*, and as I have tried to show, in verbal art, there would be no conceptual basis for the novel in general nor for *Love in the Time of Cholera* in particular.

Part II

Spatial Relations

All narrative incorporates elements of time and space. Events inevitably occur within a certain span of time and are situated in a particular place. Yet the interconnected aspects of time and space play an especially dynamic role in Nathaniel Hawthorne's "Wakefield" and Andrei Platonov's "Light of Life." Both stories essentially *derive* their respective plots from spatial and temporal concerns. Time and space are not simply integrated elements within the two stories but serve to generate the plot of each. In the nineteenth-century American tale an unprepossessing figure named Wakefield gets a notion to leave his wife. Although he disappears for some twenty years, his travels only take him around the block. In contrast, Akim, the central figure of the twentieth-century Russian story, leaves home at the age of ten, does not return for fifty-five years, and during his absence, it appears, makes virtually the entire expanse of Mother Russia his exploratory domain. Both stories, then, incorporate elements of travel—one within a very limited sphere, the other across a seemingly endless range; at least in part both depend for their interest on the length of time the respective characters are gone and on what, if anything, had been accomplished in the interim.

In the case of Wakefield, Hawthorne leaves it up to the reader to determine what might have been the motivation for this strange, unprepossessing figure to leave his comfortable hearth and home. Seemingly wanting for nothing, he goes no real distance and seeks to achieve no particular goal. He is just there—in the same town, in nearly the same place, a kind of vegetable that might have sprouted from Gogol's freakish garden. But the fact that it is "nearly" but not actually the same place is crucial. That single detail generates a dual mystery: that of Wakefield's original sudden departure, followed, many years later, by his subsequent seemingly unmotivated decision to return, both of which problems Hawthorne leaves unresolved. In the case of Akim the motivation for the child's departure is simple: the need for victuals. The family is large, and there is barely enough food to go around. So the boy takes off, as a kind of prank, never assuming that an entire lifetime will run its course prior to his return. In the interim a whole series of adventures take place, some only alluded to, others slightly detailed in brief sequential accounts. On the one hand we know that Akim heads off to make his fortune in the mines; that he serves time in the military as well as in prison; and that he marries and has a family. Yet all of these details are secondary in the sense that they only lead up to the fact that he eventually returns home. The same may be said for Hawthorne's account. But Wakefield returns to find things pretty much as he had left them; Akim returns to a very different world.

Hawthorne sums up in his opening paragraph the ostensible newspaper account, "told as truth," from which his story is derived. He considers the account "perhaps the strangest, instance on record, of marital deliquency; and, moreover, as remarkable a freak as may be found in the whole list of human oddities." The entire account is thus summed up in a single paragraph, from which "kernel" the story emerges. In temporal terms the tale undergoes a vast expansion or divergence, given the fact that upon his departure Wakefield initially "almost resolved to perplex his good lady by a whole week's absence," which ultimately balloons into "upwards of twenty years." In spatial terms the opposite is the case: "He has informed Mrs. Wakefield that he is to take the night coach into the country," but he winds up "after several superfluous turns and doublings. . . . in the next street to his own" (45-47). Time thus expands from an intended lark of a week into eccentric behavior that lasts some two decades. Yet his stated intent to go out from London and into the country affords a contrary sense of contracted space, since, "under pretence of going a journey" (45), he has barely moved away from "the little sphere of creatures and circumstances" (48), where he has spent his life.

Within the framework of this inverse relationship between time and space the story unfolds at a considered, inquiring pace: Why had he gone? Why does he return? Hawthorne does not provide answers but acknowledges that "the magic of a single night" had been pivotal. A certain "transformation" has been "wrought": in that brief period "a great moral change has been effected. . . . It is accomplished. Wakefield is another man." It now becomes as hard to return home as before it might have been originally to depart. "A retrograde movement to the old would be almost as difficult as the step that placed him in his unparalleled position" (49). Yet that essentially psychological "position" is demarcated in terms of inherently interlocking spatial and temporal relations. Thus Hawthorne employs an obvious spatial metaphor to articulate the transformation that occurs in the course of only a single twenty-four hour period: "At that instant his fate was turning on the pivot" (48). Further, as an "instant" becomes extended into a more significant passage of time, the idea of that *passage* (also a spatial metaphor) is explained, along with the attendant psychological turmoil in which Wakefield has become mired, in terms of additional such metaphor. Thus Wakefield becomes aware that "an almost impassable gulf divides his hired apartment from his former home" (50). Yet the "gulf" that divides the one spatial entity (his apartment) from the other (his home) is time itself.

Conversely, when Wakefield ruminates: "It is but in the next street!" the author retorts with an apostrophe that is essentially a reprimand: "Fool! It is in another world." Here the irrevocable passage of time is itself articulated in terms of a peculiar spatial entity that only underscores the fact that Hawthorne's "time traveler" is spatially inert. For, in a thoroughly brief reference to "another world," the author remarks: "Poor man! The dead have nearly as much chance of revisiting their earthly homes as the self-banished Wakefield" (50). This near identification of Wakefield with the dead is explained thus: "He had contrived, or rather he had happened, to dissever himself from the world—to vanish—to give up his place and privileges with living men, without being admitted among the dead" (51). The difference is that time, of course, still passes relentlessly for him—first, in smaller increments, days and weeks; then in years, first ten then twenty. Yet, in a reversal from what had been the case before, in the end Hawthorne collapses time, so that it appears to contract rather than expand. "These twenty years would appear, in the retrospect, scarcely longer than the week to which Wakefield had at first limited his absence" (51), the author speculates.

Likewise, at the end there is a further constriction of space in Wakefield's return home. That return may be seen as the fording of the "gulf" that had divided his life in two; as the ascending of the staircase he had descended years before ("He ascends the steps"); or, as the step that heralds his crossing into that "other world": "Stay, Wakefield! Would you go to the sole home that is left you? Then step into your grave!" (52). In all such derivations from the story, we see that the spatial element ultimately converges: the character returns to where he had been before, essentially having gone in a greatly delimited circle that takes him nowhere, as he accomplishes nothing. Similarly, even as time initially diverges, opening out into an "expanse" of twenty years, it is seen to converge in Hawthorne's just cited speculation that it might ultimately seem scarcely longer than the originally intended week's separation. Yet, in the labyrinth of such expansions and contractions, the author holds firm to the conviction that, "by stepping aside for a moment, a man exposes himself to a fearful risk of losing his place forever" (53), which moral (if it be such) only reconfirms the inextricable linkage between time and space, between the "moment" and one's "place."

Platonov's "Light of Life" encompasses a much greater period of time than Hawthorne's tale and an incomparably vaster domain. The author's preoccupation with time is made evident in the first words of the story, which refer to "the deep places of our memory" where a sense of time resides. The ten-year-old boy Akim tells his mother in self-fulfilling prophecy that "maybe I'll come back in my old age, when you are all dead," to which his overburdened mother replies: "You just go wherever you want; who cares if we don't see you for a lifetime!" (311) The boy circles his house several times, and then departs on his tortuous way, which may be conceived as being itself composed of ever-widening concentric circles that ultimately make of his lifelong trip a widening gyre, or vortex, a cyclical journey that takes him to the farthest point of the widest circle before contracting once again and bringing him, finally, back to his starting point, back to the village that he no longer recognizes—fifty-five years later.

On his first day's journey he only gets a mile and a half from home, but already there are certain figures who will later come to mind and appear as (once) living reminders of the earliest stages of his travels, this widening gyre. There are the people dancing whom he meets near his home, an old watchman whose job it is to oversee a "now" long demolished and forgotten bridge, and an old lame woman who shelters and feeds the boy for a time, just as he looks after her. The initial appearance of these figures anticipates concerns that will occupy a much older Akim upon his return. "A lifetime later, where is he now, that graybearded watchman of the wooden village bridge? . . . The people [dancing] . . . are any of them alive now?" (314) Naturally, the boy is not concerned with such problems at the outset of his journey. Rather, he expresses essentially the same rationale that supports his adventurous, ever-expanding sojourn as would apply equally well to Wakefield's piteous inertia: a rationale of postponement.

"It's not time yet." (312)

"There's plenty of time for going home." (316)

"He told himself that he must endure life away from home." (317)

"No, I won't go home yet; I will go someplace far away." (317)

"I won't be coming back soon, but I'll come to you all the same." (320)

Akim in fact keeps his word, only the addressee necessarily changes. The lives of those who had been a part of his childhood wanderings "have ended long ago but they exist in the feeling and memory of old Akim, beloved and immortal" (322), Platonov intones. Akim returns to a different world in which there is no longer the same river (which had been channeled into a pipe and then buried underground) and in which his childhood village is no longer there (having been paved over). But there exists a new person to come home to all the same, a young school-teacher who invites him in.

> "Grandfather," said she, "are you staying with people you came to visit?"
> "I came to visit you," he said angrily. (323)

Feeling helpless and confused, he goes home with her, unknowingly cries in his sleep at the loss of all that was known and familiar, and is cared for by her. In the morning he explains his conception of time and its passage in simplistic, humanistic terms that give meaning to the title of the tale. "I remember them, you remember me, and you will be remembered by those who shall be born after you. . . . That way each will live in another like one light" (324-25). A child had turned into an old man: "The entire life passed, a short instant of time" (321). But in compensation an old woman had been transformed into a young one: "Before him was that same eternal human being which he had known from childhood, only this human being was younger than the old lame woman and more happy than she had been." It is left to the young woman to explain what had happened. "You had gone far away and for-gotten everybody, then you returned and did not recognize us" (325). In the labyrinth of Akim's travels, in the swirl of the widening—and then narrowing—gyre, there had thus taken place numerous transforma-tions that had been effected during the relentless passage of time and within an equally restless and changing spatial field.

In both stories we find not only the intimately related temporal and spatial features that belong to all narrative and that, in these two works, are generative as well. We also recognize that the linked principles of convergence and divergence, of expansion and contraction, of both time and space are likewise essential compositional elements. The respective plots of both stories and of literary works in general depend on just such temporal and spatial "peripeteia" for their very being. Ontology, in other words, presupposes teleology. There can be no story without the author's initial and the critic's subsequent taking account of time and space.

Further, there can be no story, or only very little story, without acknowledging the tortuous psychological and physiological path—temporal and spatial—along which the hero's travails are painstakingly charted. On the part of first writer and then reader, that taking account will include in various terms and terminologies a consideration of the diverging and converging, the expanding and contracting, of both time and space within whose parameters the story is told.

In closely related terms such convergences and divergences, contractions and expansions, may be conceived both literally and figuratively as occupying a labyrinth within which time passes, as the traveler seeks his way. Interestingly, we find the predominantly spatial image of the labyrinth treated in epistemological terms (analogous to our previous consideration of time as cyclical), for "the labyrinth, too, from the beginning suggested both negative and positive senses of searching for efficacious knowledge or salvation through threatening or apparent confusion" (Gillespie 298). Significantly, then, the labyrinth, with its "pristine demonic power," models not only space but time as well in "the search for a principle of order and continuity in an apparently discontinuous universe of arbitrary relations, endless repetitions and spatial-temporal disjunctions" (Senn 225 n. 14, 227). In the obvious implication of time's inevitable passage the temporal factor clearly correlates with the spatial traversal of labyrinthine passageways. Hence the labyrinth "figures both time and space, becoming and being" (Faris 38) through the "rhythms of labyrinthine movement" (Fletcher 329), which makes it a superlative model for concluding our treatment of both time and space, as the following three chapters treat these immanent, interconnected concerns in preeminently spatial terms.

4

CONVERGENCE IN *THE MASTER AND MARGARITA* (BULGAKOV)

■ □ ■

Just prior to the start of the springtime ball of the full moon, Margarita enters apartment number 50, and exclaims: "The oddest thing of all is the size of this place—how on earth can it fit into a Moscow apartment. It's simply impossible." A little later she makes the hallmark observation: "What really puzzles me is where you have found the space for all this." Somehow that question seems applicable to the book itself: How did Bulgakov manage to put "all this" in one novel? In any case the problem of space in *The Master and Margarita* does represent a "puzzle." How to explain, among other things, the sudden metamorphosis of space, its wondrous capacity to expand and contract, as Margarita here wonders. The answer Koroviev offers the new queen of the ball is hardly instructive: "Easy! . . . For anyone who knows how to handle the fifth dimension it's no problem to expand any place to whatever size you please" (Bulgakov 247).[1] His response is playful and inadequate, as both speaker and listener must know, leaving the problem of space in Bulgakov's novel unresolved. But how can we account for the transformation of interior space into exterior space, as happens at Woland's ball? According to what novel "rules" and assumptions has that feat of spatial metamorphosis been accomplished? Such questions represent only two interlocking problems, among many, elicited by this rich, problematic novel.

Time and space are inextricably interrelated in both life and art. In the novel these two critical elements serve intrinsically as the principal axis upon which the tapestry of character interaction and resultant plot are interwoven. An initial, determining concept of both literary time and space is indispensable to the execution of any narrative, no matter how simple or complex its design might be. Time in the novel (and in life) can thus be viewed in multitudinous ways. As we have seen, it may be "experienced as something discontinuous, a repetition of repeated reversal, a sequence of oscillations between polar opposites: night and day, winter and summer . . . age and youth, life and death" (Leach 126). It can be open-ended, "boundless," or closed. In *The Master and Margarita* the temporal element remains open; at the end of the novel the hero and heroine simply retire from the world, presumably to live according to the Tolstoyan tenet that proclaims the incontestable virtue of making oneself responsible for perhaps just one other living soul. Such is the resolution of plot in Bulgakov's novel. Correspondingly, there is no conclusive resolution to the rigors of (social and political) life that the master, for one, experiences—censorship and repression, resulting from the heartless depreciation of both talent and achievement. Life, like art, can thus ultimately be valorized only for itself, for its own intrinsic quality and values that resist any final judgment or resolution. As Miguel Asturias, a writer who bears a certain kinship to Bulgakov, puts it: "A good life is life and nothing more, there is no bad life because life itself is the best thing we have" (109). This viewpoint represents, in effect, the basic philosophical underpinnings informing *The Master and Margarita*—which, if the master loses sight of the point, Margarita does not.

The compositional source of that view derives in part from the spatial relations inherent in Bulgakov's novel. Despite E. M. Forster's essentially convincing claim that in the novel time is "far more fatal than place" (29), in this novel, as Lotman puts it, "the spatial order of the world . . . becomes an organizing element around which its non-spatial features are also constructed" (*Structure* 220). What is revealed on the text's spatial plane thus represents iconically what may be found on its cognitive or epistemological plane. *The Master and Margarita* encompasses an immediate world (replete with its housing shortage and foods of the "second freshness"), from which it extends outwardly to embrace as well "a world that bears the mark of infinity." On the one hand the reader is presented with a world that is immediately graspable; on the other we are likewise offered a world of "immediate immensity." The book's "exaltation of space," in other words, "goes beyond all frontiers" (Bachelard 183-90), affording a corresponding sense of the world's infinite potential—which Margarita, more than any other character in the novel, is given to explore. Underscored by a profound contemplation of the world and its grandeur, revealed at the end from high "On Sparrow Hills," we sense finally and conclusively that enormity of possibility afforded by life—despite its endemic constraints and periodic injustices—that pervades the novel all along.

Given the inextricable intertwining of time and space in the novel form, it can nonetheless be argued that Bulgakov affords special attention to spatial concerns in this novel. *The Master and Margarita* is virtually a seamless book. In fact, in several places it is "double stitched." As is frequently noted, the last lines of the first chapter serve not only as a coda but as the opening frame of the succeeding chapter. Moreover, those lines, interestingly, reinforce our chosen metaphor, since they are themselves implicitly concerned with stitching (or lining): "Early in the morning on the fourteenth of the spring month of Nisan the Procurator of Judea, Pontius Pilate, in a white cloak lined with blood red . . ." (20). So the first chapter ends elliptically, confirming the open-ended quality of the book right at the start, while the next chapter picks up and continues beyond the ellipsis—and beyond the time and space of the novel's opening chapter to a quite different fictive world, the Jerusalem narrative, with its own temporal and spatial axes. The same such close, repeated framing serves, of course, to merge and elide other chapters of the novel (including 2 and 3, 15 and 16, 24 with 25, and 26 with 27), allowing in each instance for a change of narrator and, consequently, of point of view in a work not only in which secondary stories are embedded within the greater story as subtexts within the text but also in which their respective frames overlap.

So what can be inferred from such "overlapping" or "double stitching"? First, the intrinsic interrelation of time and space in narrative is underscored by this preoccupation on the part of the novelist. No time (and no space either) is "lost" in the practice of this framing device that leaves neither a temporal nor a spatial gap in Bulgakov's meticulously woven narrative. In these instances the segments of narrative appear virtually inseparable, just as time and space are bound by the same axis and are therefore bound to one another, as this novel implicitly strives to illustrate. By closing the gap in time, in other words, the potential gap in space is likewise closed. Or, as Uspensky notes (citing Foucault), "a verbal description of any spatial relationship (or any reality) is necessarily translated into a temporal sequence" (*Poetics* 77). Yet that exercise in "translation" appears in the present context to be necessitated additionally by Bulgakov's preponderant concern with space in *The Master and Margarita*. The novelist must leap, in effect, from one narrative to the other—from Moscow to Jerusalem and back—across both space and time. This is accomplished in the several instances just noted through a framing technique that is essentially spatial in nature, moving from one space (or setting) to another by relying upon a necessary descriptive "temporal sequence." Hence, in each such leap the temporal aspect is determinant in closing the gap (between narratives, or subtext and text), while transporting the reader and transposing the text within the spatial domain.

A striking illustrative instance is evident in the chapter "Satan's Rout," which begins thus: "Midnight was approaching, it was time to hurry." Several pages later, after Margarita has both entered and exited the tropical forest that "borders" the ballroom ("The forest soon came to an end, and its hot, steamy air gave way to the cool of a ballroom"), Koroviev announces: "Ten seconds to midnight. . . . It will begin in a moment" (257-60). And so the ball proceeds with its seemingly endless procession of horrific guests who drain and exhaust the newly crowned queen. After this great trial, however, "to her amazement she heard a bell strike midnight" (268), which effectively ends the ball that the reader—and Margarita—assumed would initiate it. Hence the ball begins, in effect, with the first stroke of midnight and ends at the last stroke. Just as space has been expanded to allow for it all to occur in one small Moscow apartment, so has time been contracted into the chronotope of zero time or anti-time, representing on the temporal plane a corresponding (although opposite) distortion to what takes place on the clearly interrelated spatial plane.[2] Yet shortly thereafter (very shortly, with only a brief dialogic interlude on the part of Woland and his next victim in line), Margarita is "deafened by cocks crowing," as the temporal sequence now appears to model the chapter's spatial expansion, resulting in the spatial plane's immediate corresponding diminishment. "The crowd of guests faded—the tail-coated men and the women withered to dust, and before her eyes the bodies began to rot, the stench of the tomb filled the air. The columns dissolved, the lights went out, the fountains dried up and vanished with the camellias and the tulips. All that remained was what had been before" (270). Hence, in this key chapter as space expands, time contracts, while the reverse is also true, testifying once more to the novel's intrinsic acknowledgment of the inextricable interdependency of these two basic novelistic elements.[3]

The problem of space in Bulgakov's wondrous account is multidimensional. It extends from the greatly delimited spheres in Woland's eye sockets (one of which contains a green eye, the other black) to the "immensity of night" (Bachelard 189), which is also his domain and through which Margarita flies naked and free. One unnatural sequence in the novel justifies another in the mind of the reader. To the Lord of Night is attributed the gross opposition contained in two different colored eyes. Meanwhile (as Yury Olesha might put it), a woman can fly. If one such supposition is accommodated by the reader's (much needed) suspension of disbelief, why not the other? But if a striking opposition rules a part of Woland's features, a peculiar symmetry determines another, as he sports platinum crowns on the left side of his mouth and gold ones on the right. Thus spatial relations in this novel clearly share with other narratives such common structural principles as binary oppositions and basic symmetries, although at the same time what is "basic" to *The Master and Margarita* might well be outlandish at best or out of place at worst in another novel.

As part of the work's intrinsic design, the oppositions in Bulgakov's novel remain inexplicably and intentionally odd. Woland's peculiar physiognomy is thus explained (away) in much the same way as Margarita's wonderment at the expansion of interior space into the realm of exteriority is dismissed by Koroviev's (earlier cited) peculiar remark. "In short—a foreigner" (12), we are told by way of accounting for Woland's strange look. Likewise, Koroviev explains things in terms of "the fifth dimension," a presumably vast domain that nonetheless he deftly leaves unexplained. Clearly deficient, such reckonings reveal only that this is a novel designed to provide more in the way of spatial distortions than logical solutions. Logic, the novel implicitly argues, belongs to the domain of philosophical disputation, while temporal and spatial transformations are the stuff of which novels (Bulgakov's in particular) are made.[4]

The kind of spatial "distortion" that *The Master and Margarita* seeks to project is the image of a world that is unbounded and forever expanding (into a hypothetical fifth dimension), with the endless potential to offer new possibility; the effort put toward realizing such potential, it might reasonably be argued, is precisely what makes the novel, in generic terms, novel. In effect, the governing creative law of Bulgakov's fictive world is that there be no natural law. Whatever happens can thus either be attributed to Woland and his retinue or to pure happenstance. But life (even fictive life) is more than just a throw of the dice. Hence, just as Bakhtin (as literary theoretician) privileges the novel as that form that remains open and unfinished rather than philosophically closed and shut down, so does Bulgakov (as literary practitioner) create a correspondent fictional universe, whose practical confines are defined and delimited only by whatever might be the limits of the human imagination.

The Master and Margarita is a magical realist text that embraces *as one* two interlocked planes: the ordinary and the extraordinary, the actual and the fantastic, the natural and the supernatural, the "real" and the "magically real." Let us posit that the first term of each such paired opposition (the ordinary, the actual, the natural, the real) has its analogue on the novel's spatial plane, understood as that space where the novel's action takes place, while the corresponding latter term (the extraordinary, the fantastic, the supernatural, the magically real) is to be associated with what may be termed "metaphysical space" where learning is achieved and knowledge acquired. Just as the latter term in each pair cannot bear meaning without some notion of the former, so is the concept of metaphysical space semantically dependent upon its immediate correlate. For every deed that is performed there must be a place for it to occur; the same applies for each individual perception or recognition. Thus, correlated with the novel's determinant epistemological plane, the concept of metaphysical space manifests its own but intimately related sphere, since none of our linked but juxtaposed notions, including the opposition between (ordinary) space and metaphysical space, can convey meaning without its immanent philosophical counterpart—what Lotman (following Toporov) refers to as its "mythological aspect," realized and made meaningful through the "merging of the contemporary and the mythological" ("On Space" 112).

On a comic level Bulgakov's novel is about how various lessons are taught to a variety of miscreants; but, more important, it also treats how knowledge is attained by other characters (Bezdomny ["Homeless"], the master, Margarita) who acquire—paradoxically, with Woland's aid—wisdom and the strength to live. As Margarita notes in a remark indicative of the carpe diem theme (incarnate in her) that pervades the book: "One should know how to seize such moments" (216). Woland helps her "to know" by giving her the opportunity to put such theory into practice. Consequently, her corresponding activities—as witch, as queen of the ball, as savior of the master, herself, and others—take place on the same epistemological plane of acquired knowledge and experience. (Woland's own activities, by contrast, do not, since he has nothing to learn.) So when Margarita says, "I may be about to let myself in for some dubious adventure" (223), we can say that all her "dubious" adventures, with their attendant learning experiences, occur within the sphere of metaphysical space.[5]

Space in *The Master and Margarita* may thus be understood in several contexts: first, synonymous with setting, it is simply that sphere in which the action of the novel takes place; second, it may refer to outer space, since Woland and his retinue, as well as the master and Margarita, all travel through the cosmos in the course of the novel; last, *space* may be understood to entail a special dimension of metaphysical space contained within, or proliferated upon, a certain epistemological plane. Thus when Margarita, newly turned witch, decides to slow down her dancing, flying broom, in order not to miss "a unique chance to see the world from a new viewpoint and savor the thrill of flight" (239), she is traveling through a particular kind of space—metaphysical space—learning, seeing, and growing, as she progresses (literally and figuratively) along her way.

Just as one may commonly speak of an individual progressing toward some goal, so is the novel teleological in its moving toward a resolution. Such progression within the novel is achieved, first, according to a poetics belonging broadly to the genre, from which is derived, second, a particular poetics or set of governing principles appropriate to a single specific work. As Uspensky puts it: "Each work presents a unique microworld, organized according to its own laws and characterized by its own spatial and temporal structure" (*Poetics* 167). Thus all novels utilize spatial concepts (verticality, horizontality; near, far; open, closed; the points of the compass) in the shared effort to model the world in verbal art. Beyond such common novelistic endeavor, however, the peculiar spatial model specific to *The Master and Margarita* allows in its own special practice for the potential contraction and expansion of space, the transformation of interior into exterior, and for a singular role to be played by the cosmos as part of that novel's setting. In addition, a primary organizational feature of the work may be revealed in still another opposition derived from the novel's spatial model: the principle of divergence as opposed to that of convergence, where the former operates to move the novel away from its intended end, while the latter seeks to resolve the novel's disparate narrative elements in the direction of a formal conclusion (if not a final resolution). This basic opposition works on several significant planes: on the level of text, by merging the Moscow and Jerusalem narratives in a final conjoining; on the level of plot and character, by affording a reunion between the master and Margarita, which entails as well a resolution of the semiotic conceptions of "home" that likewise pervade the work.

Hence the concept of divergence works against the merging of the novel's principal narratives and against its main protagonists' finding a home and each other (much as Shklovsky's notion of "retardation" might work). To effect a positive correlative on the other hand takes time, novelistic time—during which the counter-notion of convergence manages to take precedence while also taking the novel to its end. The two concepts, as will be shown, serve as counterpoints in a work that consistently seeks to achieve its own precarious balance between its plot concerns on the one hand and its philosophical ideals on the other. To effect a dramatic conclusion represents one goal, to articulate a philosophical position another. Yet the two must be ultimately reconciled in a single, sustained resolution.

The principle of convergence is exemplified in Margarita's dream, in which she imagines the master awaiting her in a dismal log cabin by a swollen stream. As she interprets it, the dream anticipates her reunion with him, since it "can only mean that he is reminding me of himself. He wants to tell me that we shall meet again . . . yes, we shall meet again— soon" (216). The same motif is repeated shortly thereafter when Margarita is seated on a bench under the Kremlin wall. There she recalls her dream and also the fact that "exactly a year ago to the hour she had sat on this same bench beside him" (218). Thus the linked motifs of the dream and the bench converge in a single theme—reunion with her lost love. Eliciting in the reader a like sense of "expectancy," we are told: "Suddenly the same wave of urgent expectancy that she had felt that morning came over her. 'Yes, something's going to happen!'" (219). According to what might be termed the "semiotics of sameness," derived from the novel's singular poetics, the quality of sameness takes on a generative role: the recurrence of an "old" event generates a new one; the repetition of an odd incident yields one that is even stranger. Hence the same bench upon which they had sat together "exactly a year ago to the hour" (can Margarita's memory be so precise?) and "the same wave of urgent expectancy" lead to a single conclusion: that "something's going to happen!"

And, of course, something does happen; Azazello appears out of thin air (one of the principal characters' principal channels of travel), seats himself beside her, and makes her an invitation on the part of a "very distinguished foreign gentleman" (221). Thus Margarita proceeds—in one of the great magical realist passages of the book—to fulfill her role as the newly crowned queen of the springtime ball. Or (again), as she puts it: "I may be about to let myself in for some dubious adventure" (223)—a great understatement from a speaker whose grand sense of adventure is tantamount in the novel to having a grand taste for life.[6]

※ ※ ※

Margarita accommodates herself to space—making it her domain with an immediacy born of a correspondingly infinite tedium: "Oh, how you bore me. . . . You all bore me inexpressibly. . . . Farewell forever. . . . I'm flying away!" (230). But freedom and space are not Margarita's chosen domain. What, then, entices her to go? Clearly, it is the imminent possibility to eliminate the tedium from her life, to see and to learn. (Even if it indulges in frequent flights of fantasy, the novel remains rooted in epistemology.) First of all, Margarita is motivated to learn the fate of the master; her method for achieving that immediate goal is to grasp the blessed opportunity—proffered by the devil—to free herself from all previous constraint. So she does not hesitate, although her guiding, enduring motivation is not to roam but to share a home. Margarita's immediate fate may be to range about in space ("The Flight"), but her cherished goal is served by the ideal of intimacy rather than immensity. In terms of the novel's governing spatial model, when the linked principles of contraction and convergence triumph over their respective counterparts of expansion and divergence, the novel's basic compositional aim will have been served: as the heroine of immensity, openness, outer space, will have achieved her goal in the found, shared intimacy of inner space.

If, indeed, "space is nothing but a 'horrible outside-inside'" (Bachelard 218), in *The Master and Margarita* the psychological motivation of the two protagonists, the vector of their tortuous journey (albeit not a concerted effort), is marked precisely by the *need* for a peaceful mooring, to end the drifting of the spirit, to get from the outside in. Bulgakov's novel begins with a fatal meeting on a bench, representing the outside world, and proceeds over the course of the novel to a more felicitous meeting between the two lovers, with the attendant promise of a spiritually comforting inside world. The repeated motif of the bench is therefore a semiotic marker suggestive of the distance still to be covered before the novel's protagonists are able to move from an outer to an inner sphere, from some place or other in the world to a place they can call "home" (also a semiotic marker, signifying an interior domain, which inherently nurtures, comforts, and protects—and is, in this novel, where one's books are kept). In this *compositional* sense, which deals with the fate of the characters, the novel is governed by a principle that dictates contraction over expansion as the primary goal. The master and Margarita are thus destined to find their way out of the realm of chaos and into a domain of harmony—according to this principle, neatly summed up by Woland's assertion that "one who loves must share the fate of his loved one" (369).

In terms (derived from spatial metaphor) both abstract and poetic, the relation between the master and Margarita, as well as their relation to the world, may be expressed thus: "It would seem . . . that it is through their 'immensity' that . . . two kinds of space—the space of intimacy and world space—blend. When human solitude deepens, then the two immensities touch and become identical" (Bachelard 203). The deepening human solitude, of which the French phenomenologist speaks, refers most poignantly in Bulgakov's novel to the master, whose will to live (reflected in his lack of will to write) has been profoundly diminished by a debilitating sense of isolation and desperation.[7] But where "the two immensities touch and become identical" is most evident in the image of Margarita, who—according to Bulgakov's novelistic plan—conspires to introduce within an ultimately inhospitable "world space" a far more accommodating intimate place.

As Lotman points out with regard to Bulgakov's artistic plan: "He makes the 'home' the center of spiritual values, which are expressed in the riches of private life, creativity and love. . . . In Bulgakov the home is an internal, closed space, the source of security, harmony and creativity. Beyond its walls lie chaos, destruction and death" (*Universe* 189-91). In this view the novel is informed by a movement away from an outer domain, marked by such chaotic, destructive forces, toward an inner sphere, "the place which is one's own, a place of safety, culture and divine protection" (185). As Bachelard observes in words that encapsulate the master's desperate point of view: "Come what may the house helps us to say: I will be an inhabitant of the world in spite of the world. The problem is not only one of being, but it is also a problem of energy" (46-47). These "problems" define precisely the master's own: his having lost the will "to be" as well as his creative energy. Thus he needs the intimacy of "the house" to break free from his imprisonment in the asylum or "anti-house" (Lotman), to escape as well the overwhelming sense of being lost in "world space" (Bachelard). The master's unexpressed ideal is, therefore, to retreat into a world that represents contraction and convergence, to return to a reduced space that offers the potential to revive an equally reduced spirit.

On the *philosophical* (rather than compositional) plane, however, the diametrically opposed linked principles of expansion and divergence likewise represent an ideal. For *The Master and Margarita* is designed as well to establish a more intimate relationship between the master's reality and "magical" reality (with its vast array of potentiality), between small and large, between *thinking* small and large. Previously, during his period of creativity the master thought and wrote boldly; now he is diminished, and his writing has ceased. It is therefore left to Margarita to behave courageously and "expansively," to fly off into the unknown in the hope of realizing her dream of a home. In this way, and on this plane, *The Master and Margarita* mediates between the limited world of man and an infinite universe that offers the chance for exploration and learning, for either failure or fulfillment. Such mediation is effected through the challenge of confrontation, as Margarita (again, more so than any other character in the novel) is obliged to confront herself and her life of petty constraint, which she can exchange for one that promises the chance for revenge, reunion, and absolute freedom.

Through her efforts the master is finally rewarded with a home, as the novel's protagonists move from "beyond" to "within" that safe domain. The immediate agent of the master's reward and the true hero of the novel, Margarita, interestingly, acts in accord with a view held by Lotman, who distinguishes a work's "mobile" persona from one that is "immobile." In observing that the former is "permitted to act in certain ways forbidden to others," Lotman argues that the mobile persona may be identified with the idea of "hero," since "the active hero conducts himself differently from the other personae, and he alone possesses this right. The right to behave in a special manner (heroically, immorally, morally, insanely, unpredictably, strangely, but always free from circumstances that are obligatory for immobile personae) is demonstrated by a long line of literary heroes" (*Structure* 243) that might well include Margarita. For she is given "the right to behave," within the constraints of Bulgakov's novelistic design, entirely in accord with the theoretical guidelines suggested by Lotman in a rare coinciding of theory and practice. Thus Margarita conducts herself "heroically" in terms of demonstrating great reserves of courage and personal dignity in her quest to be reunited with the master; she acts both "immorally" (by flying around naked in Soviet "socialist reality," by destroying Latunsky's flat) as well as "morally" (she assists Frieda in being freed from her torturous burden); she behaves "insanely" ("I can't tell you how happy I am to be leaving you! You can all go to hell!" [230]), "unpredictably" (she fearlessly agrees to be Woland's consort), and "strangely" (she asks nothing for herself in reward, even when coerced to do so).

From another, less cumbersome perspective Bulgakov's heroine may also be perceived as the novel's principal protagonist by recognizing that her persona serves as the point of resolution of what Bachelard felicitously refers to as the "infinity of intimate space" (190). In her resides the confluence of the novel's two seemingly juxtaposed principles of contraction and expansion: on the one hand she illustrates the novel's drive to seek a certain plot resolution; on the other she serves to embody its philosophical commitment to exploring courageously the infinite realm of possibility that the world can offer. In these two linked respects she is the matrix for the novel's governing compositional and philosophical principles. In her composite figure are thus reconciled these juxtaposed metaphysical sources for the creation and realization of Bulgakov's masterpiece.

"All will be as it should; that is how the world is made" (370). So proclaims Woland to Margarita at the end. So, then, how is the world made—Bulgakov's fictional universe, that is? According to what principles of governance is it ordered? In our view, as stated, it is governed largely by the related principles of contraction and expansion, of divergence and convergence. Throughout the novel Woland and his retinue have, in effect, diverged from their real appearances; only at the end does each appear in "his true aspect" (369). Koroviev sheds his clownish costume, emerging as "a knight clad in dark violet with a grim and unsmiling face" (with whom "accounts are settled" now and who "has paid his score"); Behemoth appears as "a page demon, the greatest jester that had ever been"; while Azazello is likewise transformed into "the demon of the waterless desert, the murderer demon" (368). (Only Woland's original self is left indeterminate, remaining Bulgakov's secret.) Thus does each figure eventually regain his true identity, as each returns to his true state. Likewise, Pilate is finally allowed to proceed on his course to his long-awaited meeting with Yeshua. While the master and Margarita are also granted their wish—which is also Yeshua's, as well as Woland's, in a stellar instance of the principle of convergence at work ("what I am offering you and what Yeshua has begged be given to you" [371])—to enter a realm of peace that has been their destiny all along.

In its metaphysical concerns, then, *The Master and Margarita* is devoted to the theme of homecoming—to the grand idea of entering one's real home (where love resides), of finding one's true self (where one *is* oneself), and of accepting one's assigned fate, whatever it may be. Our principle of convergence thus appears synonymous in essence with a considered triumph of truth over lie, of freedom over constraint ("You are free! Free!" [370]), of "reality" over appearance, as the principal characters (including Woland and company) retain their honesty and integrity. If in the end "all will be as it should," then truth will of course will out. But the end of the novel is also the place where night and light (Woland's darkness and the sun's brightness), as well as life and death, in their mutual reflections, finally converge as one. Hence the master's fate coincides with Pilate's: "He had been freed, just as he had set free the character he had created" (372). While, if "Dostoevsky is immortal" (342), as Behemoth boisterously proclaims, then so are Bulgakov's creations, as the master and Margarita (both subsequently revived after imbibing Azazello's lethal potion)[8] retire to that place of peace that will be theirs forever.

5

DIVERGENCE IN "THE MINISTER'S BLACK VEIL"
(HAWTHORNE)

■ □ ■

In this companion chapter to the one preceding, we again find that the spatial aspect may on occasion appear dominant as the principal organizational or structural feature of narrative. Such an occasion is evidenced in Hawthorne's enigmatic short tale "The Minister's Black Veil." If we credit the idea that "the structure of the space of a text becomes a model of the structure of the space of the universe" (Lotman, *Structure* 217), then this work would appear to offer a perspective on the world that is essentially minimalist. Nonetheless, the story is determined by an array of spatial relations that warrants consideration for what those relations might reveal concerning their meaning in the tale and, more important, for the peculiar significance surrounding the minister's veil. Hawthorne's story documents the life of a certain Reverend Mr. Hooper, who resolves to don a black veil, which he never again removes from his face. The reason for his "taking the veil" remains a matter of gloomy speculation on the part of the townsfolk of the story desirous of resolving the enigma in one way or another, whether their collective suppositions reflect positively on their "good" parson (an adjective appearing no less than nine times in the text of a dozen pages) or not. "To their imagination," the veil represents "the symbol of a fearful secret" (Hawthorne 27), although what that secret might be they cannot say.

On the day the minister dons his veil, he delivers a sermon, which "had reference to secret sin, and those sad mysteries which we hide from our nearest and dearest" (23). In addition, on that same day he presides at the funeral of "a young lady" and serves later at a wedding. Concerning the former, it is meticulously noted by one curious observer that at "the interview between the dead and the living . . . when the clergyman's features were disclosed, the corpse had slightly shuddered." Another gossipy soul later fancies that "the minister and the maiden's spirit were walking hand in hand." That evening, at the wedding of "the handsomest couple in Milford village," the bride's "deathlike paleness caused a whisper that the maiden who had been buried a few hours before was come from her grave to be married" (24-26). But married to whom? To the young bridegroom standing at the altar with another? Or to the Reverend Mr. Hooper, who, perhaps, was not so good (or not so innocent), after all? In any case, all such whispered innuendo clearly derives from the attendant stigma that the minister himself (intentionally?) incurs by his strange sartorial display.

Hawthorne terms the story "a parable," attaching to this odd designation an unlikely footnote ostensibly intended to support the veracity of the tale. The note (a kind of subtext) claims that another clergyman in New England had likewise "made himself remarkable by the same eccentricity that is here related of the Reverend Mr. Hooper." But it is also explained that this other supposedly historical personage had done so because: "Early in life he had accidentally killed a beloved friend; and from that day till the hour of his own death, he hid his face from men" (21). In marked contrast, however, Hawthorne's extended text (to which the note is but a brief appendage concerning a parallel incident) does not provide a single definitive index as to why the minister burdened himself with that apparent penance in the first place. The reader is therefore left in a quandary analogous to the one in which the story's townsfolk find themselves. Paradoxically rooted in the absence of a convincing explanation, an additional parallel is thus effected in both the reader's and characters' frustrated need to comprehend the minister's eccentric behavior. Yet the absence of a conclusive resolution ultimately discourages the reader's expectation that a unifying, convincing explanation might eventually be forthcoming.

A second significant "absence" in the tale is likewise derived from a certain tension created by another, similarly closed channel of communication. For in placing the veil over his face, the minister, in effect (paralleling the overall design of the tale, which does not reveal the rationale for his strange conduct), also deprives his fictive counterparts of a crucial level of information: namely, whatever might have been intuited from his now concealed facial expression. If we take human communication (or dialogic interaction) to be effected on two planes, the verbal and gestural, then in this story the latter is significantly reduced, affording a corresponding reduction in the potential for achieving a certain level of mutual comprehension. As the sexton innocently puts it: "I can't really feel as if good Mr. Hooper's face was behind that piece of crape" (22)—a sensed absence, of which Mr. Hooper's "plighted wife" (27) also becomes cognizant, causing her to end their betrothal and take her "farewell" in result of his refusal to "lift the veil but once, and look me in the face" (29). Thus are Hawthorne's characters, as well as his readers, left to resolve the perplexing dilemma at the center of this metaphysical mystery or purported morality tale.

While the story may well inspire more thought and critical speculation than the potential for actual resolution, a consideration of the semiotic significance of the minister's black veil nonetheless commands our attention. For it is only as a sign (rather than an object) that we can proceed to make sense of the veil (if not conclusively of the tale)—in analogous fashion to the townsfolk of the story, engaged in a like, albeit unwitting, semiotic endeavor. For the reader (if not the characters), however, the project is enhanced by the author's designating the veil on no less than four occasions a "symbol"—something, in other words (no matter how else the term might have been meant), to which meaning might legitimately be attached.[1]

Notwithstanding the fact that Hawthorne could have intuited but little, if anything, of what has been refined as current semiotic theory, and could have even less likely been cognizant of what has emerged as contemporary understanding of the symbol as a species of sign, what can be argued with reasonable certainty is that Hawthorne conceived of his term as coinciding with what we understand to be a sign. (This "coincidence" having been accomplished no less in complete, if unwitting, agreement with the philosopher and polymath, C. S. Peirce, who would later identify the symbol, bearing a relation to its object of "an imputed character," with what he termed *"general signs"* [1.558]). It has long been the case that the symbol, "one of the most overburdened terms in the field of the humanities," has been taken as a synonym for *sign*. Thus "its ubiquity suggests that *symbol* and *symbolic* are often synonyms of *sign* and *semiotic*" (Noth 115). That such is in fact the case in "The Minister's Black Veil" is clearly evident.

In that unusually appended footnote Hawthorne refers to the other clergyman's veil as being a "symbol" that "had a different import" (21). Different from what, we might well ask? And meaning what to whom? To the townsfolk of the story "that piece of crape . . . seemed . . . the symbol of a fearful secret between him and them" (27). The minister proclaims to his disenchanted intended: "Know, then, this veil is a type and a symbol" (28)—bearing, we can assume, a certain meaning. Finally, at the end, the same doomed figure exclaims: "What, but the mystery which it obscurely typifies, has made this piece of crape so awful? . . . deem me a monster, for the symbol beneath which I have lived, and die!" (33) Thus, in each instance the veil is declared, implicitly or explicitly, to bear its own semiotic "import"—if that import signify only the presence of a "fearful secret" or "mystery."

Yet beyond such vague suppositions there exists no dearth of additional *possible* referents corresponding to this intentionally indeterminate sign. First among them is the *suggestion* of "an ambiguity of sin or sorrow" (30). Intimately related is the notion of the veil signifying that each of us remains separated from all others by private thoughts, reminiscences of perhaps unworthy deeds, as well as by secret wishes and desires. It may then signify that ever receding moment, "when the friend shows his inmost heart to his friend; the lover to his best beloved" (33). But, being "a mortal veil" (29), it also signifies that which "shuts in time from eternity" (32), and is, in that sense, a sign of the imminent death that everyone must face. Or, as a kind of ornament, it may be perceived as an autotelic sign, a sign of itself, an aesthetic work (like "The Minister's Black Veil"), seeking only that we seriously regard it (not that we necessarily admire it), in what Bachelard terms "the sacred instant of contemplation" (209). So, the veil remains an ambiguous sign: it may mean any (or all) of these things; it may mean none of them.

Impossible though it is for Hawthorne to have discerned a conception of the symbol coincident with Peirce's sophisticated formulation, the philosopher's understanding of this particular sign may nonetheless serve us well in coming to grips with Hawthorne's story. For Peirce the defining characteristic of a symbol is its being habitually interpreted in the same way, as a conventional sign. "Symbols afford the means of thinking about thoughts in ways in which we could not otherwise think of them. They enable us, for example, to create Abstractions, without which we should lack a great engine of discovery" (4.531). (Does not Hawthorne exemplify Peirce's theoretical notion with a profound "Abstraction" of his own, expressed in aesthetic form?) In Peirce's thought symbols may be understood as "Signs that represent their Objects essentially because they will be so interpreted" (6.471). Yet it is precisely this dependence upon convention, habituation, the (possible) predictability of the interpretant, that Hawthorne undermines in "The Minister's Black Veil." Because, in the minister's eccentric behavior, there can be no sense of habituation for the seeker of meaning to fall back upon, no reliable interpretant to call upon. In effect, the story stymies all such efforts, reducing (in one sense) its hallmark symbol (unlike the scarlet letter) to an essentially uninterpretable sign. So, when Peirce affirms, "a *symbol* is a sign which would lose the character which renders it a sign if there were no interpretant" (2.304), Hawthorne affords an aesthetic proof of Peirce's theoretical position. Since, in the course of the tale, the "symbol" of the veil will indeed "lose the character which renders it a sign." That, in fact, is what happens as the reader (and characters) endeavors to make of the veil a sign (in accord with Hawthorne's repeated insistence that it is a sign)—but without success. So (from a certain negative perspective), the veil reverts from being a potential sign to being only an object (all that it is and all that it can be): two folds of black crape designed to conceal, rather than reveal.

In its status as object the veil is concrete, an actual physical manifestation in the world occupying a certain minimal space. As an indeterminate sign, it bears a figurative dimension, manifested in a verbal domain of metaphysical concerns. Within that realm of metaphysical abstraction, we are told that "the Earth, too, had on her Black Veil" (26), signifying not only the veil's metaphysical but also its universal aspect, from which none is exempt. Following a like principle of "nonexclusion," the minister's black veil is juxtaposed to the "veil of eternity" (32), from which no one will escape. In immediate physical terms what is concealed behind the veil is simply a single human face. In its figurative dimension, however, the metaphysical depths contained behind the mask are immense. Still, these two seemingly opposed notions may be neatly aligned in the felicitous phrase (cited earlier) of Bachelard, who explores the possibility of an "intimate immensity" (193). Within this seemingly paradoxical union is suggested the potential for communicative intimacy, on the one hand, of which Mr. Hooper's interlocutors are nonetheless deprived. On the other, also concealed behind the veil, is the untold spaciousness of the human soul, with its vast potential for secret sins and sufferings, the kind of information that Hawthorne implies but never overtly supplies.

The physical dimension converges on a single visage; the metaphysical aspect embraces the depths of the human soul. In one respect the story encompasses the minimal, virtually immeasurable space contained under the minister's veil. But it also implicitly explores a great metaphysical depth in all its mystery and immensity, as an "infinity of intimate space." The story thus poses a set of interrelated questions that seek, in effect, "a more intimate relationship between small and large" (Bachelard 190), between the physical and metaphysical, between matter and spirit. What, then, is concealed behind Mr. Hooper's veil? What secrets are contained in the deepest recesses of the minister's being? Ominous in their "subtextual" message, such queries derive equally from the (etymologically) linked physical and metaphysical domains (in the sense perhaps that "no word is metaphysical without its having first been physical" [Hutten 293]). As Bachelard observes: "Here we discover that immensity in the intimate domain is intensity, an intensity of being, the immensity of a being evolving in a vast perspective of intimate immensity" (193). What better way to describe the plight of Hawthorne's figure immersed in a drama predicated upon an intensity of opposition between a man and a world of horrified others (an "overawed . . . multitude" [27]), between the enhancing power of light and a fearful darkness, between fleeting time and eternity, ultimately between a man and himself?

In accord with the physical and metaphysical relations upon which the story is predicated, its spatial relations also allow for a series of linked, if diametrically opposed, potentials: on the one hand, there is the possibility of concealment or containment, as essentially static considerations; on the other, as previously discussed, there exists the potential for expansion versus contraction, of divergence as opposed to convergence, as related dynamic concerns. The spatial element, in other words, like the veil itself, yields its own reality—a reality that is manifested, first of all, through transformation. Thus, an old woman hobbling into the meeting house proclaims: "I don't like it. . . . He has changed himself into something awful, only by hiding his face" (22). Another remarks: "How strange . . . that a simple black veil, such as any woman might wear on her bonnet should become such a terrible thing on Mr. Hooper's face." Yet another good soul observes: "But the strangest part of the affair is [that] the black veil, though it covers only our parson's face, throws its influence over his whole person, and makes him ghostlike from head to foot" (24). What is significant here is that the veil, which would appear to contract or reduce the parson's features, is claimed instead to expand upon them (in a kind of "ghostly" transformation), effecting a change that extends over the whole of him—and, by extension, into the speakers' realm as well.

That such an encroachment—from the private sphere of the "good" Mr. Hooper into the public domain of his more or less well-intentioned flock—does indeed occur is made evident by the following authorial observation: "But that piece of crape, to their imagination, seemed to hang down before his heart, the symbol of a fearful secret between him and them" (27). According to our principle of expansion or divergence, rooted in the spatial relations that govern the tale, the veil now appears on the physical plane to extend "down before his heart." On the corresponding metaphysical plane, however, that appearance is effected according "to their imagination." Not only has the black veil, then, been expanded (in their minds), but the dread that it conveys has likewise been extended—if not to the very heart of the pastor, surely into the hearts of the townspeople. Yet they are not alone in their perceptions. For, in the bride-(not)-to-be, "in an instant, as it were, a new feeling took the place of sorrow: her eyes were fixed insensibly on the black veil, when, like a sudden twilight in the air, its terrors fell around her."

In that simile once again the principle of divergence takes precedence over convergence, as the expansion of the veil's suggestive power (as an ambiguous, indeterminate sign) instills fear and terror in those nearby. "She arose and stood trembling before him," we read, a gesture that elicits in turn the query: "'And do you feel it then, at last?' said he mournfully" (28). But what is *it* that she must feel? What is the referent here? Where is the antecedent? In Hawthorne's discarded drafts? In the townspeople's energetic collective imagination? Or is the "object" contained instead in all that has preceded? In the story itself, which has suggested all along that the veil belongs not only within the pastor's private sphere but has reached beyond into everyone's domain. So that *it* refers to the *intensity* of feeling generated (as Bachelard might conceive it), or the *horror* (as Conrad would have it), which "overwhelmed all others" (26). In any case the veil is clearly not a private matter; rather, it belongs to all and clings to all. "Thus," in accord with our governing principle of expansion and divergence, and as the author informs us, "from beneath the black veil, there rolled a cloud into the sunshine" (30)—as good a metaphor as any for the encroachment of the private sphere into the public domain.

If we consider that spatial relations establish a sense of boundaries, or operate within the context of certain already established borders, then the minister's black veil serves in the most basic fashion to create a particular boundary: between the minister and his flock, between him and his betrothed, between the man and the world outside. That is, a distinction is made at the most fundamental level between inside and outside—a basic opposition that allows for a single individual or an entire culture to set itself apart from all others. This is what the minister accomplishes, in effect, by donning the veil. He establishes a highly restrictive, closed system, whose sign is that piece of black cloth on his face, representing an ill-defined but essentially religious view. What tenets that view might entail are comprehended and adhered to exclusively by its sole proponent, although affecting in its limited sweep an entire collective.

In undertaking this role the minister has established himself, both literally and figuratively, inside a certain (religious, philosophical) sphere with respect to the rest of the world that remains outside. In result of this singular act of self-condemnation, he remains, in effect, "a man apart from men" (30). In semiotic terms, by retaining his secret motivating idea for himself alone, he is condemned to living behind a sign that will forever remain undefined.

Yet that sign might also be conceived as a discrete text, on a certain par with an artistic work, whose sense and meaning also remain ambiguous. For the minister's black veil is subject to a like critical assessment and interpretation within the literary work itself that a given work (such as "The Minister's Black Veil") might occasion outside itself. We can equate the veil with a work of art, because we can say, with Lotman, that "a work of art is in principle a reflection of the infinite in the finite. . . . It is the reflection of one reality in another" (*Structure* 210). That, after all, is essentially the point we have been making all along concerning the minister's black veil. Lotman goes on to say: "In modeling an infinite object (reality) by means of a finite text, a work of art substitutes its own space, not for a part . . . but also for the whole of that reality" (211). Our point has been that the veil, in its minimal dimensions as a concrete object, models in a maximal sense "an infinite object," namely the world, in both its physical and metaphysical reality, which, for Hawthorne's hero, are essentially one and the same.

Conceived thus as a discrete text, the minister's black veil gives rise once more to the question of what renders this text (or sign) indeterminate? Clearly, the answer resides in a certain *felt* absence—namely, of a fixed and well-defined ideology. We read that "the Earth, too, had on her Black Veil" (26). At the end the minister proclaims on his deathbed: "I look around me, and, lo! on every visage a Black Veil!" (33). Hence the metaphoric proliferation of this sign as bearing a universal quality but no clear ideology. Ambiguity, of course, is a common (positive) feature of the literary text (as opposed to manuals, handbooks, and the like, where it would be deemed negative). Beyond this surface view, however, ambiguity in this literary text—residing as well in the veil as text—represents an inherent evocative element that inspires not only an attendant sense of mystery but also a certain universality: all of us, the earth as well, are shrouded in our own unseen veils, concealing our mysteries, our secrets, our selves. The minister has thus only hypostatized (though, he does not proselytize) and made visible, as well as physical, what exists as invisible and metaphysical.

He accomplishes this by wearing a black veil that serves to frame, and therefore set apart, an essentially undefined internal universe from a far more evident outside world. As an integral sign, the veil *as frame* is also an independent text, since, in the story's terms (as well as in semiotic terms), what is most engaging is not the minister's (undoubtedly ordinary) face but the veil that covers that face. Hence the veil, not the visage, is the focus of the tale, in which the semiotic significance of the veil is that it functions in three interrelated respects: as an integral sign that unifies the text, as the frame that distinguishes a peculiar internal world from the external, and, in result of that basic function, as an independent (sub)text, deserving critical examination, within the greater text.

The veil is thus both a screen and a border, separating the seen from the unseen, the known from the unknown, the world of the living from the dead. A small piece of double folded crape that falls from above the minister's eyes to just over his mouth, the veil itself exists within a highly delimited sphere. Conceived as a discrete text or integral sign, however, the black veil is seen to *extend beyond* the minister's face. Thus, "it seemed to hang down before his heart" (27), as it "throws its influence over his whole person" (24), *extending outward*, so that "from beneath the black veil, there rolled a cloud into the sunshine, an ambiguity of sin or sorrow" (30). As an ambiguous sign and an ambiguous text, the black veil nonetheless serves unambiguously as a frame that establishes a highly delimited border (although none seem to perceive it solely as such) around the parson's face. Juxtaposed to this limited manifestation, however, is the related figurative concept of "the veil that shuts in time from eternity" (32), affording the minister's black crape an added dimension, a corresponding sense of an unfathomed metaphysical magnitude, which, paradoxically, all of its fearful beholders appear immediately, almost inevitably, to recognize.

6

THE FIGURAL LABYRINTH IN
THE GENERAL IN HIS LABYRINTH
(GARCÍA MÁRQUEZ)

■ □ ■

In Gabriel García Márquez' historical novel, recounting the last days of the great South American Liberator Simón Bolívar, the labyrinth of the title refers to a series of labyrinths that are contingent upon matters of history, geography, and biography. Each of these related considerations may be conceived in terms of spatial relations; more specifically, they appear contiguous with a set of labyrinthine pathways that consistently and conclusively result in a dead end, as "Bolívar wanders through the wintry labyrinth of his stunning decline and fall" (Martin 293). The General's role in history is ultimately choked off by endless intrigues and political machinations. His final wanderings along the Magdalena River in the northwestern region of the southern continent allow for plenty of doubling back and forth from one seemingly strategic location to another that nonetheless leads him nowhere. His life story ends in like fashion with his being literally choked on his own blood, as his hollowed-out chest collapses of its own weight, even as the man himself is reduced to less than eighty pounds, a mere shadow of his former vigorous self. Thus history, geography, and his own biography collaborate in leading the General only to his death. In this novel the labyrinth of the world does not give way to the paradise of the heart, as Comenius would have it. Rather, the labyrinth affords a kind of instantiated madness, contained, to be sure, but nonetheless born from solitudinous rumination over a past that is gone and a future that will never be, yielding a thoroughly desperate and unrelieved isolation. For this novel suggests the possibility neither of a phenomenological convergence nor divergence so much as that of an existential endless wandering in a space that accommodates one's physical presence but affords no hope of spiritual accommodation.

The image of the labyrinth draws on both iconic and symbolic properties. As a basic human symbol, the labyrinth has a pictorial history of five thousand years, which has contributed to the felt presence of an archetype or "copies of an archetype," cultural approximations that partly explain "its openness to all kinds of signification" (Senn 219, 230). Further, "the labyrinth has frequently served as a sign for the entanglements of plots and plotting," and thus bears an additional, venerable conventional aspect. We know of it culturally from ancient Greek myth and the story of the Minotaur. Modern novels likewise exploit "the labyrinth's iconic verbal properties as well as its symbolic resonances" (Faris 35, 37) in an effort to attain some level of truth in a world that has lost its spiritual moorings. In iconic terms the labyrinth—inherently a spatial construct and "a quest form, a mode of examination or exploration" (Gutierrez 90)—mirrors the wanderings and travails of the hero in the search for meaning and resolution to the vicissitudes of life.

Significant for both author and critic is the fact that "the labyrinth image . . . is characterized by a high degree of self-reflexivity on the signifier level and an equally high degree of openness and indeterminacy on the level of the signified"—that is, "the sign itself is so abstract, its features so basic and unmarked" (Senn 221, 223). The very word, then, particularly when situated in the title of a work (as in García Márquez' novel or Octavio Paz' profound meditation on Mexico, *The Labyrinth of Solitude*), appears semantically loaded right off to a degree that implies the need not only for an attendant semiotic analysis but also a phenomenological account. A "profundity," in other words, of suffering, of seeking, of striving, goes with the territory.[1]

Complementing the various figurative understandings that draw on intertwining spatial relations, an inclusive notion of a metaphysical labyrinth affords García Márquez' novel its master model, felicitously captured in the phrase "the *space of passage*" (Fletcher 329). A second, related concept derives from the image of the circle. Seemingly paradoxical in their linkage, the circle, with its attendant suggestion of endless repetition, and the ancient notion of the labyrinth, "the image of lost direction" (Frye 150), affording only an apparent contrastive series of dead ends, together represent the governing spatial relations of the novel. The two are complementary in the sense that the circle permits infinite traversals along its circumference, while the labyrinth is likewise conceived as endless, permitting an infinite series of reiterations along its circuitous path. The traveler pursuing a circular route or following a labyrinthine passage ultimately gets nowhere, as he "twists and turns between 'walls' round and round, but also back and forth" (Fletcher 334), which effectively characterizes *The General in His Labyrinth*.[2]

Thus, with no clear destination ever actually determined, the General's final journey is described repeatedly as an utterly hopeless affair, with the hapless hero "alone in the midst of the world. . . . wandering without direction through the mists of solitude" (García Márquez 153-54). All we know for sure is that "he was starting out on his return trip to the void" (85). We are told that "the officers of his entourage were sick to death of all their coming and going to nowhere" (161), while the General "continued to slog his way through this endless journey to nowhere" (163). The latter repeated expression, echoing throughout the book, amounts in effect to a kind of refrain signifying that what is depicted is indeed a "blind men's journey" (164), from which the General "no longer had a place to escape" (154). Yet all such repetition and reiteration not only sounds in thematic terms the death knell of a grand and heroic enterprise but also mirrors both structurally and verbally our two linked spatial forms, the labyrinth and the circle, with their inherent reliance upon just such repetitive behaviors. The various repeated locutions of the text thus clearly serve as verbal analogues to the spatial models that are at its core. Just as the General floats on the river, indecisively and uncertainly, so does it appear that he "would leave his work adrift" (164), a life's work that is constantly reevaluated and cruelly denigrated in light of the endless ebb and flow of historical and political change that leaves unresolved the sum total of a life that, regardless of all such reiterations, as the author states in the very last line of the book, "would never, through all eternity, be repeated again" (268).

As a related analogue, the absence of a destination in this novel is equivalent to the related issue of the absence of any origination. "The damn problem is that we stopped being Spaniards and then we went here and there and everywhere in countries that change their names and governments so much from one day to the next we don't know where the hell we come from" (184). This sense of equivalence, of relating—even equating—one situation with another (the absence of an end point with that of a beginning) is also peculiar to a book in which ontology can be debated, while teleology is thoroughly negated. Thus the General is given to say: "I've become lost in a dream, searching for something that doesn't exist" (221), according to which sad vision all goals and ideals are eradicated, while life in relation to dreams is subordinated, so that "the vast empire of his dreams" (256) takes on a reality that reality itself cannot match.

Other equivalences established in the book strike a lighter note. "It was too modest a house for so splendid a tenant, but the General reminded him that he was as accustomed to sleep on the floor of a pigsty, wrapped in his cape, as in a duchess' bed" (179). Yet all such equivalences derive from spatial imagery capacious enough to embrace the void that adheres to a life as well as to the spacious expanse of a dream, to a pig sty as well as to an elegant boudoir. In another series of equivalences that underscore the negativity, uncertainty, and lack of resolve that characterize the last days of the General, who has certainly seen better ones, the (figuratively) fallen hero observes: "Nobody wants us here, and . . . nobody obeys us. . . . It all evens out" (109). Yet that understanding, amounting to a belated philosophy of acceptance and compromise, heralds the end of a remarkably eventful life and the march, through the labyrinth, toward death.

From one perspective—that of the encoding process—the spatial imagery evoked here bears a certain literal meaning: the aim of the book, after all, is to depict the General's wandering, his seemingly endless meandering, within a recognizably lush, tropical setting rife with warring factions, whose single point of agreement is their common resentment of and resistance to the General and his dream of a united continent, variously stated but regularly reiterated.

> His ultimate hope was to extend the war into the south in order to realize the fantastic dream of creating the largest country in the world: one nation, free and unified, from Mexico to Cape Horn. (48)

> Everything I've done has been for the sole purpose of making this continent into a single, independent country. (203)

The first words on the first page attributed to the General read: "Let's go . . . as fast as we can. No one loves us here." So the lands that he and his loyalist troops traverse remain wartorn and riven with bitterly opposed factions whose (self-)destructive behaviors are presented in ways that appear as firmly entrenched as the lands they refuse to yield. By contrast, in the shift in perspective from the work's aesthetic formulation to its critical evaluation—a requisite shift from the author's to the reader's viewpoint—the book demands to be understood in terms that are figural rather than literal. Our aim is to respond to that demand.

On the second page of the novel the reader is informed that the General's "resolute gestures appeared to be those of a man less damaged by life, and he strode without stopping in a circle around nothing."

That latter phrase may well serve as epigraph both to the novel itself and to the critical endeavor at hand. His striding in a circle can be taken as both concrete and figurative, but that he goes "around nothing" clearly extends our understanding into a paradoxically richer realm of interpretation that embraces a more significant figurative dimension. Yet that greater significance belongs to the domain of the reader rather than the character. The latter sees things as hopeless. "Nobody understood anything" (10); "at times he walked around and around the room talking to himself" (71). Thus, "isolated in the midst of nothing" (199), his lifelong endeavor, he knows, will not come to fruition. The reader, in a related effort to comprehend, is granted understanding on two levels—the literal and the figural. In addition, the author provides a wealth of frequently nondialogic but always pithy utterances. Rarely indulging his figures in dialogue, he allows them lapidary speech that seeks no response. Their words remain isolated and alone. For the General in his labyrinth such absence signifies the psychology of the dead end; for the reader it signals a related phenomenology, whose labyrinthine quality it is our goal to explore.[3]

As opposed to the psychological, the physical—and at times physiological—sense of the General's labyrinth is manifested in various concrete ways. First, the body as labyrinth also figures as part of the subject of the novel. As the General's doctor observes: "Everything that enters the body adds weight, and everything that leaves it is debased" (216). But the General, ironically, becomes only more and more reduced in stature, literally and figuratively, while the story of his last days reveals only a series of debased ideals. Again, in both literal and figural terms, judging from his own image, the General is right to say: "We are the human race in miniature" (77). That observation, of course, also has meaning on a much higher but sadder level. Instancing this poignant plane, as well as the notion of the body as labyrinth coming to a literal dead end, we are told, regarding a one-armed officer whose limb had been lost in battle: "He felt the movements of his hand, the sense of touch in his fingers, the pain bad weather caused in bones he did not have" (128). Again, we see symbolically that this is a novel about nothingness, the void, an emptiness that is both physical and psychological, and that finds its representation in terms that are necessarily spatial.

The General's labyrinth is also manifested concretely in geographical as well as architectural expression. First, the world itself—"the heaving excitement of nature" (125)—can strike fear into the heart. "Night fell at two o'clock in the afternoon, the water raged, thunder and lightning shook the earth" (87). "Then the jungle began, and everything became contiguous and unchanging" (91). In terms of the kind of change imposed on the land by man, we find alteration that also amounts to a characteristic alternation. "When he abandoned the south to march north, and vice versa, the country he left behind was lost, devastated by new civil wars. It was his destiny" (113). More than that, it is his country's destiny. In spatial terms that destiny is realized as a collapsing of sorts, a folding of north into south, "and vice versa." On the one hand the geographical preoccupation of the book offers hope. "For there was the sea, and on the other side of the sea was the world" (132) and the chance for a new life. But the closer to home, the sorrier the perspective. "The nation was falling apart from one ocean to the other" (241), we are told. And it is ultimately this perspective that counts in this tale of reiterated wanderings in a labyrinth that ends in death.

Buildings and houses can also be daunting, reverberating (if not exactly reiterating) with the echoes of a bloody past. "The phantasmagorical echoes in its rooms were attributed to the spell of his soul in torment" (135); "the words, amplified and repeated by the echoes in the house, pursued the General all night" (142). But it is in spatial terms, primarily and logically, that the architectural structures of the novel have their greatest effect. "The building was immense and gloomy, and its very location caused a peculiar malaise because of its untamed vegetation and the black precipitous waters of the river that hurtled in a thundering explosion down to the banana plantations in the hotlands" (44). As with virtually every other place in the novel, the General had been there before, lending sense and credence to the notion of the world—the General's world—as being a labyrinth that allows one to traverse its circuitous paths endlessly but with no way out.

> It was the fourth time he had traveled along the Magdalena, and he could not escape the impression that he was retracing the steps of his life. (97)

> He had lived that moment in another place and another time. . . .
> It was an old dream repeated in reality. (228)

Thus each place belongs to the undepicted past as well as to the novelistic present, "idle repetitions of a drama too often seen to be believed" (17). Yet in such "repetitions" there are no apparent boundaries between the "immensity" (and gloominess) of inside and of that belonging to outside, between interior and exterior, between architecture and geography. The General's labyrinth thus admits of no evident distinction between being lost in a man-made world and wandering in the natural world. Similarly, the borders between civilized man and his primitive counterpart are erased within the General's own being, as he "tended to his insomnia by walking naked through the deserted rooms of the old hacienda mansion, which was transfigured by brilliant moonlight" (49). Within this same transfigurational space the General himself is transformed.

That transformation, as is generally so with the predominant concerns of the book, appears overwhelmingly negative. A hallmark statement of this essential negativity we find scrawled on a wall, with the General as its target: "He won't leave and he won't die" (13). Yet, in horrific transformation, he is virtually disintegrating before the eyes of his men and those of the world.

> Those who saw his scrawny ribs and rachitic legs did not understand how he stayed alive with so little body. (74)

> His white thinning hair and that look of final turmoil . . . gave her the terrifying impression she was talking to a dead man. (82)

> "Tell [him] I died! That's all, just tell him I died!" (109)

> "We'll kill ourselves! . . ."
> "No deader than we are already." (110)

> "I refuse to accept that with this journey our life is ended." (129)

> "I don't exist." (141)

> "He has the face of a dead man." (142)

> It seemed senseless to make peace with a man she already considered dead. (192)

> [He] looked like a seated corpse in the darkness of the carriage. (234)

Likewise, the General's place in history, just as his place in reality, appears destined to oblivion. Everything seems to change—for the worse. "No one would have believed he was the same man, or that this taciturn place he was leaving forever, with all the wariness of an outlaw, was the same city. Nowhere had he felt so much a stranger as in those stiff, narrow streets" (40) that he had walked so many times before and that were his domain in the past. Only now, in the dismal present, not only is the place no longer his but he himself is no longer what he was. "I am no longer myself" (44), he says, in words which can be understood both literally (he has wasted away) and figuratively (his power has also deteriorated), in both physiological and psychological terms. And it is just such paired linkages that make the book—with its temporal gradations and spatial configurations—centered on the General's travails, a set of analogous, iconic labyrinthine constructs that mirror one another seemingly endlessly.

Exemplifying this kind of pairing or linkage, affording a series of echo effects that resonate throughout the pages of the novel and that are manifested in both temporal and spatial correlations, one of the General's innumerable women from the past emerges for only a moment in his devastated present. In acknowledging a transformation that belongs not only to time but also to space—that elusive sphere that the body occupies at any given moment—the ghost of a long-ago love declares: "It's me . . . although I'm no longer the same" (76). A like (abortive) transformation is recorded on the previous page, when it is noted that "he danced for almost three hours . . . attempting perhaps to reconstitute the splendor of long ago out of the ashes of his memories." Here, too, time is transformed into space or, better, into spatial configurations manifested in a dance designed to achieve a precious alchemy that will convert ash into forgotten splendor. In addition, it is a failed transformation that also attempts to proceed from one figurative domain to another.[4]

Every feature of the book is intertwined with and reflects every other on both the sentential as well as the thematic level. Thus, in terms of geography, which derive as much from legend and history as from the lay of the land, the General's journeys, his struggles for independence, appear similarly endless. "Since the beginning of the wars for independence he had ridden eighteen thousand leagues: more than twice the distance around the world." In ostensible response to such clearly evident intermeshing of legend and geography, the immediately following sentence reads: "No one had ever disproved the legend that he slept in the saddle" (43). In a linked passage that again derives as much from (mythic) biography as from geography, the reader is told: "Less than two years before, when he was lost with his troops in the not too distant jungles of the Orinoco, he had been obliged to give orders to eat the horses for fear the soldiers would eat each other" (48).

Derived in similar manner, and infused, as is so much of the text, with a flagrant flair for poetry that inevitably enhances the sense of the intertwining of an imponderable history with an unconquerable geography, we read: "The last stage of the journey . . . was along a heart-stopping precipice through air like molten glass that only physical stamina and willpower like his could have endured after a night of agony" (66). Taking place in the here and now, which temporal and spatial loci had also shared (at one time) in a repeated sense of there and then, the entire work, in effect, amounts to a recapitulation of a single extended night of agony that García Márquez terms both figuratively and titularly "The General in His Labyrinth," a labyrinth that is here perceived as multifaceted, participating in intertwined, iconic reflections of history and geography, the linked domains of the physical and the psychological, of legend and biography.

Further, the geographic—or, better, the spatial—sphere of the book extends from interior to exterior and back, and likewise alternates between realistic depiction and fantastic assumption. Illustrating the slippage between the sense of an interior and exterior labyrinth, and between concrete and figurative description, we are told that "the bookcases in the various houses he lived in were always crammed full, and the bedrooms and hallways were turned into narrow passes between steep cliffs of books and mountains of errant documents that proliferated as he passed and pursued him without mercy in their quest for archival peace." That statement is shortly followed by the remark that "his life of fighting obliged him to leave behind a trail of books and papers stretching over four hundred leagues from Bolivia to Venezuela" (93), a spatial image suggesting immense proportions that leaves the reader in wonder. A similar conjoining of the seemingly realistic with a hint of the fantastic emerges when the river is likened to "a swamp with no beginning or end" (101), an analogy that once again suggests the sense of a (grotesquely muddy) labyrinth, affecting both body and soul, and serving as master model of this novel.

In terms of our other chosen model, the image of the circle—with its attendant morbid promise of the sojourner's remaining within a certain circumference or well-defined sphere, and never getting anywhere—suggests a like slippage from our guiding concept of spatial relations to that of psychology but with the same dead end clearly evident. Thus we find the General's longtime and long-suffering servant reiterate: "Only my master knows what my master is thinking" (14, 23, 178), a repeated remark that conveys nothing but insinuates much.

Similarly, the novelist also relegates certain problematics to a level of discourse that (like the General's labyrinth itself) leads nowhere ("no one ever knew if it was political perversity or simple distraction" [16]). Early in the novel the General himself declares his political intentions of the moment thus: "I will stay on as Generalissimo, circling the government like a bull round a herd of cows" (19). One of those cows, in turn, "reasons" as follows: "All we know is that she's well because we haven't heard anything about her" (226). That "logic" is quickly reiterated: "[She] was fine, because they had heard nothing about her" (227). Clearly, what is wrong with such circular reasoning is that it is based on nothing. Yet it conforms aptly with the governing metaphor of the novel, whose passages lead nowhere, and with the hopelessness of the book's protagonist, who "remained floating in nothingness" (112).

That protagonist likewise thinks in essentially the same terms. "My first day of peace will be my last one in power" (14), he says, still dreaming. Later the reader is informed: "From then on, that would be his fixed idea: to begin again from the beginning, knowing that the enemy was not external but inside the house" (202). Such thinking is again obviously iterative in its commitment to start over (once again), but it also presents yet another instance of the immediate linkage or slippage between the literal and the figural; for while the enemy is concrete to be sure, his being "inside the house" is once more clearly metaphoric. Still, like circular thinking contributes to the humor as well as to the overwhelming sense of hopelessness and futility that characterizes this chronicle of the great Liberator's incommensurably paltry last days.

> "There is great power in the irresistible force of love," he sighed without warning. "Who said that?"
> "Nobody," said [his servant]. . . .
> "Then I said it myself," said the General. (58)

> "Don't tell me you've conquered nostalgia," he said.
> "On the contrary: nostalgia has conquered me." (67)

> "I don't know anything anymore, General," said [the colonel].
> "I'm at the mercy of a destiny that isn't mine." (67)

Thus other figures in the novel also participate in similar forms of "logic" or related modes of varying self-defeating perceptions. In response to these and the General's own sense of an impending inglorious end, we hear various plaints and plans: "I will go where I am wanted" (15)—which appears to be nowhere. "Whatever happens, we will go to Europe" (67), a notion that is also doomed to failure. For, as the novelist tells us in an understatement that only heightens the sense of a desperate situation: "Even [Bolívar] did not seem to have a clear idea of his destination" (61), so that at the end of the book, which coincides with the end of a life, the devastated hero states in a seemingly well-documented plea that serves as the source of the novel's title and of its principal metaphor: "Damn it. . . . How will I ever get out of this labyrinth!" (267). To which exclamation, in accord with everything that precedes, there is and can be no answer and no exit.

In the midst, then, of loyalty, bravery, and an excess of high ideals, negativity—the psychology of the dead end, no exit, and no (life-affirming) answer—nonetheless prevails. Such an all-encompassing, debilitating vision finds its full summation in the following cruel observation: "The time he has left will hardly be enough for him to reach his grave" (37), a sad assessment that implicitly but convincingly underscores the inextricable union of temporal and spatial relations in characteristically stark and morbid expression. Less so but equally revealing of a psychology that has reached the end of the road, if not of the labyrinth, the following exchange suggests the irrefutable loss of an ideal.

> "Stay," said the Minister, "and make one final sacrifice to save our country."
> "No . . ." he replied. "I no longer have a country to sacrifice for."
> (37)

That sense of loss is later underscored by a remark that suggests the slippery quality of what we might otherwise consider a concrete and "solid" geography but one that is itself subordinated to the vagaries of a sickly and weakened mentality. "At this stage I even wonder if Venezuela exists" (62). Later the General will give up "wondering" and simply state directly: "[The city] doesn't exist . . . Sometimes we dream about it, but it doesn't exist" (102). Of course, it does exist. But the justification for such peculiar perceptions is not hard to find, since we are told that "America is half a world gone mad" (71), a view that characteristically finds its reiteration and like declaration in the words: "For us America is our own country, and it's all the same: hopeless" (165). Clearly, the former statement provides the rationale for the latter: it is hopeless because it is founded on madness. And on dreams that are as obsolete as the stricken dreamer himself.

Part III
Dialogic Relations

As with temporal and spatial relations, the question of human com-munication in narrative is of paramount importance. The dialogic nature of narrative becomes immediately evident in the expressed rela-tionship between author and reader, where the former presents infor-mation for the latter's consumption, resulting in a necessarily figurative dialogue that is initially unidirectional: the author "speaks," the reader "listens." Yet as soon as the reader responds, either in thought (which is bound to be virtually immediate) or in words, perhaps formulated as a critical response, the dialogue is no longer unidirectional, nor is it fig-urative in quite the same sense. If dialogue is understood in concrete terms to mean the exchange of verbal utterances between two or more speakers, then the case of author and reader (or critic) remains figura-tive. But, if we consider dialogue to occur as soon as their exists a medium by which a response is articulated (as speech) or formulated (as a written text), then any critical response may be deemed dialogic, and the relations between reader and writer (now in reversed order) are likewise seen as dialogic—in the sense that a *responsive* word in any form becomes the ultimately determining feature of dialogue.

Dialogic relations are thus commonly conceived to take place on various planes of human communication in both concrete and figurative understandings of that expression and all it entails. Do we mean by it, in other words, the verbal exchange between interlocutors exclusively, or do we prefer to extend the notion to include intertextual and cultural exchange as well? (It seems that we do.) Another such consideration encompasses the presence or absence of speech within the commu-nicative act. Can dialogue occur wordlessly, gesturally, and essentially in silence? Moreover, does dialogue need take place within the context of speakers who are cognizant of their words being received and responded to by others, or not? That is, do we consider dialogue to occur when speakers remain unaware of the impact their words have on another consciousness and, more important, when another responds to those words without the original speaker being aware of that response? These and other related questions and concerns are taken up, respectively, in chapters 7, 8, and 9. Yet, for present purposes, let us state directly that our preponderant use of the term *dialogue* throughout this book is meant to bring into clear focus that decisive moment when the word of one speaker actively engages the utterance of another and is itself engaged by that utterance.

In claiming for dialogic relations nearly unqualified universality, Bakhtin declares (in an expansive moment) that they "are a much broader phenomenon than mere rejoinders in a dialogue . . . they are an almost universal phenomenon, permeating all human speech and all relationships and manifestations of human life—in general everything that has meaning and significance" (*Poetics* 40). Broad as it is, that claim bears on this book's basic intention of inherently linking temporal, spatial, and dialogic relations as fundamental coordinates in the joint endeavors of encoding and decoding literary texts, of literary creation and literary criticism. For without time and space considerations— that is, the situating of events in a formal temporal and spatial context (accounted for by Bakhtin's chronotopic model), and without the effort at human communication—between writer and reader as well as among characters—there can be no literature.

In making his broad claim, Bakhtin comes close, on two counts, to the thinking of C. S. Peirce, who asserts that "thinking always proceeds in the form of a dialogue—a dialogue between different phases of the ego" (4.6), which refers, in effect, to different moments of the self being engaged in a lifelong struggle to understand. For Bakhtin, Peirce's for- mulation specifies the potential dialogical relationship of the speaker to his own utterances, engaged in essentially the same effort. Peirce declares even more succinctly that "all thinking is dialogic in form" (6.338), a sweeping affirmation with which Bakhtin would surely agree. Hence the equally all-encompassing premise (to which Bakhtin sub- scribes) that "any true understanding is dialogic in nature" (Vološinov 102)—a view that embraces understanding achieved (in dialogic con- frontation) within the self as well as with another individual, and that heralds the preeminent importance of dialogue as the exclusive means to attaining meaning and (mutual) understanding.

Further, just as Peirce regards the process of semiosis—the exchange of signs and their concomitant interpretation—as a poten- tially endless human activity, so does Bakhtin conceive of human com- munication in analogous terms, consistently maintaining that meaning is generated through dialogue, effected by responsive individuals in a potentially endless series of verbal encounters, whereby, ideally, "every thought and every life merges in the open-ended dialogue" (*Poetics* 293). For the Russian theorist an immanent propensity toward dialogue is *the* definitive feature of language. Language exists exclusively and unequivocally to promote dialogue, which is to say, human communication and understanding. We might add (perhaps quite unnecessarily at this point) that, from our perspective, essentially the same may be said for literature, itself a "secondary modeling system" embedded within, or superimposed upon, language, which is primary. That is, one set of relatively flexible rules, originating within a single encompassing genre that affords a work its guiding organizational principle, is embedded in another, stricter set composed of natural language, the basic material of verbal art. Not only does literature exist, then, to communicate information but also to promote on various levels (as noted) dialogic relations. Just as dialogue is immanent to language as the basis of all human communication, so is it inherent in all narrative forms.

Concerned exclusively with dialogic relations among fictive constructs (characters, that is, representing human beings), the following pages do not take up the most evident form of dialogue, understood as the concrete exchange of verbal utterances. My aim, instead, is to focus essentially on absence, which generates, in effect, a certain felt presence. Considered respectively in the chapters that follow, I treat, first, the absence of speech per se, which nonetheless allows for the emergence of a certain communicative silence, the basis for our delineation of a "poetics of silence." Second, I discuss the lack of all potential for dialogue when the (wartime) rigors of life appear most violent and rapacious, affording a consequent "nondialogic encounter." Last, I concentrate on the absence of an immediate respondent to what is initially articulated—but that will ultimately receive its conclusive response as "supradialogue." In positive terms already anticipated, we thus find dialogue present in the absence of the spoken word, and present as well across vast expanses of space and time, as one speaker's words eventually find their response or reformulation in the words of another, articulated long afterward and at great distances, in a long-awaited and finally achieved consummation of the Spirit.

7

A POETICS OF SILENCE
(DOSTOEVSKY, O'CONNOR, ENDO)

■ □ ■

In verbal art as well as in life there are only two modes of human communication: verbal and what is commonly termed "nonverbal." Yet that unfortunate negative expression would gain greatly in meaning if it were recast from a positive, more productive perspective, as "extraverbal." In such case the very nomenclature acknowledges the fact that this secondary mode contributes certain distinctive, perhaps even definitive, nuances that *add* something beyond what the spoken word is able independently to convey. In critical analyses scholarly interest has focused almost entirely on the latter to the virtual exclusion of the former—on the presence of the Word, rather than on its frequently telling absence. This may be explained in part by the fact that the ostensibly articulated word in art (as in life) is the predominant communicative mode, while the extraverbal component—that which is communicated by gesture or facial expression, particularly in the absence of speech, that is *in silence*—appears as a constituent feature of discourse that is generally perceived as supportive or reflective of the verbal message. But what if the extraverbal mode, if only temporarily or periodically, emerges as the primary means of communication? What might we learn if our focus remains concentrated on the moments in dialogue of *communicative* silence? Might we also discover instances of silence that are anything but communicative (but are nonetheless inherently informative)?

In an effort to respond to these interrelated questions, this chapter will treat three seemingly disparate artists, whose writings may initially appear almost entirely unrelated. Yet that supposition is worthy of debate and may subsequently appear quite unfounded. For there are indeed certain subtle (even clearly evident) relations shared by the great nineteenth-century Russian novelist, F. M. Dostoevsky, with two contemporary writers, Flannery O'Connor, whose inspiration derives in part from the evangelistic American South, and Shusaku Endo, whose novel, *Silence*, draws upon the Portuguese missionary experience of an insular Japan of more than three centuries ago. Yet there is also a certain incongruity in establishing literary relations that yoke the latter writer with the former two. Dostoevsky and O'Connor provide numerous instances of silence that are rich in extraverbal communication, where neither a word nor a sound is uttered but a great deal of meaning is nonetheless transmitted. By contrast, in Endo silence conceals, rather than reveals—a fact that, from our exploratory standpoint, will all the same prove telling.

Although the respective art of Dostoevsky and O'Connor treat their subject matter within very different spatial and temporal domains, there are a number of striking similarities that may be briefly noted. Both writers endow their respective heroes with a seemingly uncanny ability to comprehend another's unstated, but nevertheless communicated, point of view. Such instances of immediate and profound understanding, yielding moments of intense confrontation and resultant communication, are characteristic of each writer. When their principal characters engage one another, their discourse is always dialogic in nature; these are not souls passing the time in casual conversation but tense figures absorbed in mutual interlocution. Locked in dialogue, dueling, all facets of their encounters have meaning. Thus speech, as the primary verbal tool, is but one feature requiring interpretation among a host of extraverbal signs, including messages conveyed exclusively during periods of deliberate and sustained silence.[1]

In both Dostoevsky and O'Connor extraverbal aspects (gesture and facial expression) frequently emerge as the principal mode of communication. What is not said, in other words, is intended to be as informative as what is.[2] In the absence of speech an instance of extended silence prevails, during which some form of communication *and* corresponding comprehension is achieved. In a character's visage there is conveyed an inner vision, requiring interpretation on one level, but which is immediately grasped on another. For the character's features often simply proclaim the fact—rather than the nature—of his madness. In the dialogue of both writers there are thus two intermeshed "languages" at play. In *The Violent Bear It Away* O'Connor remarks (as a kind of hallmark statement) that "the old man insisted that his words were one thing and his actions and the look on his face another" (346). The pertinence of the observation extends beyond its immediate con-

text to encompass a conception of dialogue common to both writers—
and one that few others utilize with such intensity. Our point here, lest
it be misconstrued, is that these two writers represent stellar, but rare,
instances, O'Connor frequently and Dostoevsky extensively, when the
writer does not simply use gesture or facial description to support (or
contradict) the verbal component but employs these features in the
absence of speech, in complete silence. Dialogue for each, then, extends
beyond speech to include those extraverbal modes, which are not
merely supportive of the verbal component but exist independently
and exclusive of it, becoming, at these significant moments, the primary
communicative mode.[3]

All three writers—the Russian of a century ago, the American and
Japanese of the present—are linked by their joint concern with problems of redemption and salvation; they convey a strong sense of metaphysical homelessness, focusing upon the profound human need to
come to grips with the problem of faith. Frequently withdrawn, intro-
verted, and silent for long periods, their characters are tempered in the
twin crucibles of doubt and belief to the limits of their endurance. How
their protagonists endure their tortured god seeking is central to all
three. To reveal the high pitch of intensity at which their characters live
is the task of each. A principal theme of these apparently disparate
writers thus bears on the constant struggle to maintain one's mental
equilibrium in the face of seemingly overwhelming odds.

At the moment of initial confrontation between Dostoevsky's characters, each will try to interpret the other's expression prior to a single
word being uttered by either. Thus, at the portentous meeting between
the two women of *The Idiot*, neither speaks at first. Instead, they take
silent measure of each other, which results in a mutual understanding
that affords no possibility for reconciliation.

> The silence lasted some moments. At length an ominous look
> passed over Nastasya Filippovna's face. Her gaze grew obstinate,
> hard, and full of hatred, and it was riveted all the time upon her vis-
> itors. Aglaya was evidently confused, but not intimidated. . . .
> There was an unmistakable shade of disgust on her face, as though
> she were afraid of contamination here. . . . At last she looked res-
> olutely into Nastasya Filippovna's face and read at once all that
> was revealed in the ominous gleam in her rival's eyes. Woman
> understood woman. (549)

Such understanding amounts to the shared recognition that the two will forever remain mutually opposed, unforgiving, and unyielding.

Likewise, in O'Connor the characters "read" one another, as though the other's face up close were a text to be deciphered. "He held Tarwater's arms tightly and peered into his face as if he were beginning to see a solution, one that intrigued him with its symmetry and right-ness" (356). Yet, for these same figures, the great trick is to resist being comprehended in turn, or "known." So, they invoke a series of well-worn defensive devices to protect against a probing, threatening world—incarnate, always, in another human being.

> The boy's face darkened. His expression hardened until it was a fortress wall to keep his thoughts from being exposed. (357)

> Tarwater's face had hardened again and the steady gleam in his eye was like the glint of a metal door sealed against an intruder. (387)

Oddly, at times the skin itself seems to shift, creating not simply a new expression but a new visage, one that is both forbidding and deliberately closed to another's penetrating gaze.

> [He] watched the boy's face change, the eyes swerve suspiciously to the side and the flesh drop around the boney mouth. (351)

> The Negro sat watching his strange spent face and grew uneasy. The skin across it tightened as he watched and the eyes, lifting beyond the grave, appeared to see something coming in the distance. (446)

In all such cases the character must "read" what is conveyed by the other in the absence of speech, while not being read himself; he must see, in other words, without being seen.

Most important for both Dostoevsky and O'Connor are the eyes. One feels that for O'Connor especially they are the single most important communicative organ of the human anatomy. "It was the eyes that got me. . . . Nothing seemed alive about the boy but his eyes" (404, 416). Seemingly, all crucial information is transmitted and received through eyes that are both searching and confrontational.

> His eyes widened and an inner door in them opened in preparation for some inevitable vision. (357)

> His scorched eyes no longer looked hollow or as if they were meant only to guide him forward. They looked as if, touched with

a coal like the lips of the prophet, they would never be used for
ordinary sights again. (442)

Profound understanding is "stored" or located within "glowering eyes
still shocked by some violent memory. . . . eyes . . . blackened by the
shadow of some unspeakable outrage" (368). At the same time vital
meaning (or intention) is disseminated from such "orbits."

> His eyes as they turned and looked down at her were the color of
> the lake just before dark when the last daylight has faded and the
> moon has not risen yet, and for an instant she thought she saw
> something fleeing across the surface of them, a lost light that
> came from nowhere and vanished into nothing. For some
> moments they stared at each other without issue. Finally, con-
> vinced she had not seen it, she muttered, "Whatever devil's work
> you mean to do, don't do it here." (397)

Thus one character (somehow astutely) judges another by the eyes.
Further, one stands condemned for, and by, his eyes alone. "He had not
felt they were entirely human eyes. They were the eyes of repentance
and lacked all dignity" (364).

For Dostoevsky as well the eyes are a determining factor by which
his characters attempt either to communicate or dissimulate. In *The
Idiot* we read: "I feel as though I had seen your eyes somewhere" (100).
Those same eyes are remarked upon earlier: "There was a promise in
them of something deep. The look in those eyes seemed dark and mysterious. They seemed to be asking a riddle" (41). Each character in the
novel remains obsessed with that riddle—which, likewise, remains
impervious to resolution.[4]

Similarly, a smile in Dostoevsky will likely appear a sign of discom-
fort or pain; it either conceals the truth or reveals a strain. The same is
true for O'Connor, in whose works a smile is also enigmatic and a sign
of misery rather than joy. "An odd smile, like some strange sign of grief,
came over the boy's face" (369), a sign bearing its own distressed (hidden) meaning. "The boy was looking directly at him with an omniscient
smile, faint but decided. It was a smile that [he] had seen on his face
before. It seemed to mock him from an ever-deepening inner knowledge
that grew in indifference as it came nearer and nearer to a secret truth
about him" (415).

"Secret truths" are also approached through one character's con-
juring an image of another, so that the one sees only *his* conjured
image, his own "creation," while gazing at that other. "He gazed through

the actual insignificant boy before him to an image of him that he had fully developed in his mind" (357). They find their own self-image reflected back at them. "His black pupils, glassy and still, reflected depth on depth his own stricken image of himself" (357). Or they see themselves in one another.

> When [he] had first opened the door in the middle of the night and had seen [the other's] face—white, drawn by some unfathomable hunger and pride—he had remained for an instant frozen before what might have been a mirror thrust toward him in a nightmare. (364)

> "This is our problem together," he said, seeing himself so clearly in the face before him that he might have been beseeching his own image. (367)

What is depicted in each case amounts to a sudden awful realization on the part of a character, who confronts in the features of another an aspect of himself that he finds intolerable.[5] Such confrontation constitutes a certain final, ultimate communication conveyed in an intense and shattering manner that goes beyond speech.

Perhaps the most striking instance of "silent communication" in O'Connor occurs in *The Violent Bear It Away*, in which not a single word is exchanged between the schoolteacher and the child preacher. Their silent interaction evolves as her sermon, initially foregrounded, becomes subordinated to their gradual mutual recognition of each other, initiated by his immediate perception of her, and concluded by her subsequent denunciation of him. By filtering out here her proselytizing directed at a greater audience, there reigns only silence and that uncanny ability of O'Connor's characters to gauge and interpret one another's features.

> Simply by the sight of her he could tell that she was not a fraud, that she was only exploited. . . .

> She paused and turned her head to the side, away from th꞉ fierce light. Her dark gaze moved slowly until it rested on Rayber's head in the window. He stared back at her. Her eyes remained on his face for a moment. A deep shock went through him. He was certain that the child had looked directly into his heart and seen his pity. *He felt that some mysterious connection was established between them.* . . .

"The Holy Word is in my mouth!" she cried and turned her eyes again on his face in the window. This time there was a lowering concentration in her gaze. He had drawn her attention entirely away from the congregation. Come away with me! he silently implored, and I'll teach you the truth, I'll save you, beautiful child! . . .

She was moving in his direction, the people in front of her forgotten. Rayber's heart began to race. *He felt some miraculous communication between them.* The child alone in the world was meant to understand him. . . . She stopped a little distance from the end of the stage and stood *silent,* her whole attention directed across the small room to his face on the ledge. Her eyes were large and dark and fierce. He felt that in the space between them, their spirits had broken the bonds of age and ignorance and were mingling in some unheard of knowledge of each other. He was transfixed by the child's *silence.* Suddenly she raised her arm and pointed toward his face. "Listen you people," she shrieked, "I see a damned soul before my eye! I see a dead man Jesus hasn't raised. His head is in the window but his ear is deaf to the Holy Word!" (382-85; emphasis added)

That same accusation might be leveled at Dostoevsky's Raskolnikov (*Crime and Punishment*), who is also not yet "raised" at the moment he is confronted by his friend Razumikhin, who demands an explanation for his strange behavior. None is forthcoming, but by interpreting the look on the young student's face during a minute of strained silence, Razumikhin perceives in horror the gruesome fact that his friend is a murderer.[6]

It was dark in the corridor; they were standing near a lamp. For almost a minute they looked at one another in *silence.* Razumikhin remembered that minute all the rest of his life. With every moment Raskolnikov's intent and fiery glance pierced more powerfully into his mind and soul. Suddenly Razumikhin shuddered. *Something strange had passed between them . . . some idea,* something like a hint, something terrible and monstrous, *suddenly understood* on both sides . . . Razumikhin grew as pale as a corpse. (301; emphasis added)

In both passages the respective authorial observations are nearly identical and emblematic of the extraverbal communication that affords such dynamic confrontation. O'Connor writes: "He felt that some mysterious connection was established between them. . . . He felt some miraculous communication between them." In Dostoevsky we read:

"Something strange had passed between them . . . some idea . . . suddenly understood on both sides." These authorial observations are so close as to be nearly interchangeable.[7] Thus, not only are there thematic similarities in the two writers, but there also exists a related strong affinity for allowing extraverbal communication in its various modes to ground their characters' mutual understanding. The result is to achieve a high level of intensity within scenes of confrontation, in which both characters and reader alike seek meaning not only in what is said but also in what is not—in a speaker's gestures and expressions, in those moments of meaning-laden silence—when the reluctance or inability to speak is immediately fraught with profound significance.

Endo's *Silence* tells of the travails of a Portuguese priest's proselytizing in an intolerant seventeenth-century Japan. Unlike Dostoevsky's and O'Connor's novels, Endo's engaging work is preoccupied with *non*-communicative silence, with that silence that belongs not so much to man but that is proper to God ("the silence of God" [84]). Not Tolstoy's angry God ("Mine is the vengeance, I shall repay!" reads the epigraph to *Anna Karenina*) but Endo's missionary priest's all too silent God, especially in the face of universal pain. "Why has [God] given us this trial? We have done no wrong. . . . Why has [God] imposed this suffering upon us?" (83-84) How are we to understand that, "in the face of this terrible and merciless sacrifice offered up to him, God has remained silent" (85)? This is the problem of the book ("Lord, why are you silent? Why are you always silent?" [151]), the problem of Ivan Karamazov. Is not that Dostoevskian God wrestler's whole plaint summed up thus in pathetic paraphrase: "The silence of God was something I could not fathom. . . . surely he should speak but a word" (105-6). And further: "Why are you silent? . . . Why does this stillness continue? . . . you avert your face as though indifferent. This . . . this I cannot bear" (182-83).

That silence, which is God's, represents the principal paradox of the book.[8] But there are others, related others. "If I consented to this thought" (that God does not exist), ponders Endo's protagonist, "then my whole past to this very day was washed away in silence" (106). But if God does not exist, must not the Word, God's Word, also be "washed away in silence"? Further, if God does not speak, does not the Word become obliterated in His silence? Which notion, paradoxically, appears contrary to the world that He created—a world permeated with sound, emerging from the most amazing places. "Putting [a seashell] to his ear he listened to the faint muffled roar that issued from its deepest center" (143-44). Moreover, in this world we are enjoined to *speak*—that is, to create—to make our own (potentially) communicative sounds. But that "enjoinment" is not always fulfilled. "His eyes met those of a number of men and women staring at him with looks of pain and anguish. He was silent; they too were silent" (149). Words, verbal expression of "pain and anguish," might have been forthcoming but were not.

This absence might be explained, in part, by the fact that in Endo's novel there seems a lesser potential for dialogue than in Dostoevsky's or O'Connor's worlds. "We were silent. [They] also remained silent; their eyes seemed fixed on a speck in the empty sky" (83); "when their eyes met he would turn his face away in haste" (153). "The priest would sometimes raise his lowered eyes to scrutinize the other's face, but the expressionless countenance of the old man told him nothing" (279). The characters' faces are described as being "expressionless . . . much like puppets. . . . like masks" (52), which communicate nothing. On the other hand, when we are told that a certain communication had transpired, we remain in doubt. "Here and there the interpreter was stuck for words; yet with a face expressionless like a puppet he conveyed the meaning" (167). But how so, if (in the absence of speech) his face was "expressionless"? Conversely, at times it appears that the aim of speech may be to put an end to the talk. "As he finished speaking, he felt that his answer had been well framed. In the darkness of the hut he could clearly feel that [the other] was lost for words and reduced to silence" (137-38).

On the one hand the silence of Endo's novel is physical, almost palpable. "Yet I could sense the awful silence that enveloped the whole place. Earnestly I prayed to God. Well I knew that we should not pray for the happiness and good fortune of this world; yet I prayed and prayed that this awful noonday silence might forever be taken away from the village over which it hung so ominously" (77). Silence, then, as in both Dostoevsky and O'Connor, can be ominous. But while theirs is the ominousness that comes from either a prelude to or temporary absence of *human* communication, from the felt lack of dialogue, or even potential for dialogue, Endo's silence may be understood as being a certain property belonging to the world and as some kind of grotesque intruder upon a place designed for *sound* (human and otherwise). "What a miserable and painful business it was! The rain falls unceasingly on the sea. And the sea which killed them surges on uncannily—in silence" (92). The sea "surges" silently? How can that be? The answer is not long in coming.

"Behind the depressing silence of this sea, the silence of God . . . the feeling that while men raise their voices in anguish God remains with folded arms, silent" (93). So, beyond the physical notion of the silence of this novel lies the more important metaphysical conception of a silence that is authored by, and belongs to, God.

Better put, perhaps, between the (physical) silence of the world and the (metaphysical) silence of God there exists a certain bond *and* contention in Endo's novel. Thus, "when I set foot in the village I found myself surrounded by a fearful, eerie silence. Not a single person was there. . . . I walked the village from corner to corner in the deadly silence" (98). In this instance we are to understand that this "deadly silence" exists in the absence of people; there are no villagers to inhabit and enliven (literally) the village. Hence this silence is not metaphysical; rather, it is the silence of the world devoid, for a time, of sound. It is not the silence of God, which lasts, seemingly, and in contrast, forever. It is the silence that emanates from there being "not a sign of life" (100), which we can take to mean, conversely, that sound signifies the presence of living beings. Further, in the context of this novel—as well as in Dostoevsky, O'Connor, and numerous others—(human) sound emerges as the prerequisite sign of hope, especially, in Endo, in the absence of a response from God.[9]

Endo's novel raises another, related problem. Can the world ever be absolutely silent? Even for a moment? Is it possible for the world to be permeated with silence? We read: "The *sound* of those waves that echoes in the dark like a muffled drum; the *sound* of those waves all night long, as they broke meaninglessly, receded, and then broke again on the shore. This was the sea that relentlessly washed the dead bodies . . . the sea that swallowed them up, the sea that . . . stretched out endlessly with unchanging expressions. And like the sea God was *silent*. His silence continued" (104-5; emphasis added). The problem here is twofold: first, we are informed (both literally and figuratively), in contradictory fashion, that there *is* sound belonging to "those waves" that echo "like a muffled drum," while at the same time we learn that "like the sea God was silent." What happened, then, to the sound of the waves breaking on the shore? The preceding analogy therefore appears false; the sea is not, and has never been, silent. Only God's silence "continues" ad infinitum and ad nauseum ("even more sickening. The silence of God" [84]).

Further, we can say (with sufficient proof drawn from the novel) that the world, too, has never been silent. For the world, the physical world, exists in the presence of sound, not silence. This is made evident both literally ("The rain struck the leaves where I stood, making a noise like pebbles pattering on a roof") and figuratively ("the leaves of the tree, now dry like sand, were filled with song" [106-7]). Even when Endo appears intentionally to proclaim a realm of silence, one questions the accuracy, even veracity, of what he means to say. Thus, "When his appearance was lost from sight behind a crag, the surroundings suddenly became deadly silent *except* for the dry sound of insects fluttering in the grass" (117; emphasis added). So, this is *not* a scene, then, that had become "deadly [that is, completely] silent." Similarly, we read: "Why does this stillness continue? This noonday stillness? The sound of the flies" (182-83), which of course interrupts this imperfect "stillness." In addition, we find equally contradictory descriptions such as these: "The sea and the land were silent as death, only the dull sound of the waves lapping against the boat broke the silence of the night. . . . the darkness maintained its stubborn silence. All that could be heard was the monotonous dull sound of the oars again and again" (147). So, again and again, we see (hear) silence contradicted by sound; sound manifesting itself over and beyond silence—in a world in which only God's silence, seemingly, persists.

Thus the problems and paradoxes of this novel are not to be resolved—not quickly, in any case. But there are considerations that will take us closer to a certain resolution, one belonging to Endo. On the one hand we note that the silence of God is consistently equated with the "silence" of the sea (which is not so silent). "The sea was silent as if exhausted; and God, too, continued to be silent" (198); "all this time, over the sea, God simply maintained his unrelenting silence" (210). On the other we find that the silence of Endo's world is not absolute. Even the writer himself (inadvertently) acknowledges this, when he observes: "The tremendous stillness of the night surrounded the priest. It was not that the stillness of the night was without sound" (245). Analogously, then, perhaps we will find that God's silence, though continually bemoaned—

> Yet you never break the silence. . . . You should not be silent forever. (160)

> You are silent. Even in this moment you are silent. (204)

> Lord, hear our prayer. . . . Lord, hear our prayer! (205)

> Lord, you are still silent. You still maintain your deep silence in a life like this. (221)

is also not absolute. But to reach that resolution (Endo's), we must return to our earlier preoccupation with the human face (in the face of silence) and a pair of communicative eyes, which are, perhaps, *the* principal organ of communication, at least in our extended present context (which includes all three writers).

In this novel, too, the priestly protagonist is himself preoccupied with a face—the face of God, whose image he conceives repeatedly and hopefully, seeking an end to the silence.

> It is a face filled with vigor and strength. I feel great love for that face. (35)

> From childhood I have clasped that face to my breast. . . . if ever I had a sleepless night, his beautiful face would rise up in my heart. (67)

> his face—the most pure, the most beautiful that has claimed the prayers of man (103)

> From childhood the face of Christ had been for him the fulfillment of his every dream and ideal. (158)

So, why might not that idealized face be realized in speech?

> He felt the face of Christ looking intently at him. . . . "Lord you will not cast us away any longer," he whispered, his eyes fixed upon that face. And then the answer seemed to come to his ears: "I will not abandon you." (162)

> Now in the darkness, that face seemed close beside him. At first it was silent, but pierced him with a glance that was filled with sorrow. And then it seemed to speak to him: "When you suffer, I suffer with you. To the end I am close to you." (244)

In both instances, however, the priest *seemed* to hear what he wanted to hear. Had that visage uttered a word, or had he only heard? The question is never resolved, yet at the moment of his greatest anguish and greatest trial, it "seems" to him that the adored face does respond to his desperate entreaty. "Lord, it is now that you should break the silence. You must not remain silent. Prove that you are justice, that you are goodness, that you are love" (254). In response, long awaited (and perhaps imagined), it is "proved" by the priest's being "told" to trample on that beloved visage, the sacred image "ingrained in my soul [of] the most beautiful, the most precious thing in the world" (258), as a sign of his demonstrated apostasy before the heathen powers that be and as a means of saving the faithful, who are at the same time being tortured, while he remains safe, if not free. "And then the Christ in bronze speaks to the priest: 'Trample! Trample! . . . Trample! It was to be trampled on by men that I was born into this world. It was to share men's pain that I carried my cross'" (259).

And how is that message conveyed? How does He "speak"? As the priest recalls painfully: "the eyes spoke appealingly: 'Trample! Trample! It is to be trampled on by you that I am here'" (264). "'Trample!' said those compassionate eyes" (285), exemplifying an instance in which "God's word impinges on the human person as a two-edged sword" (Ong 12). And so the book concludes, in response to—and in the face of—everything that precedes: "But our Lord was not silent" (286), a (perceived) fact that, were it not the case, might all the same be explained (away).[10] As Ong affirms, and as Endo would agree, silence "is for man even more communicative than words. . . . sound and silence define each other. . . . For sound itself is defective in accomplishing its own aims. Silence makes up for what sound lacks" (187). Further, as Endo's priest declares: "Even if [God] had been silent, my life until this day would have spoken of him" (286)—in deeds primarily and in words secondarily—a notion that embraces novelistically and thematically what it has been my aim to express abstractly and theoretically.

In all three writers communication triumphs over its opposite within the medium of literature, itself designed as a form of communication between writer and reader. That "triumph" is accomplished through the transfer of information within two virtually indistinguishable stages, proceeding from the nonverbal plane, which exists by definition in the absence of words, to the employment of extraverbal modes that go beyond speech. The one and the other concepts, "without" and "beyond" words, allow, then, for a certain transcendence over word-lessness—the absence of speech, noncommunication, gross negativity—in favor of a certain "extracommunicative" means, by which the message is both sent and received, communicated and comprehended. Regardless of how the various respective plots are resolved (or left open) in the works just discussed, this is no mean accomplishment, as all (three) writers know, since reception and understanding of a given message is, again, a triumph in itself, modeling on a small scale the much grander linked enterprises of writing and reading a work of literature, whose processes alone—at both the encoding and decoding stages—are, respectively, their own reward.

8

THE NONDIALOGIC ENCOUNTER: *RED CAVALRY* (BABEL)

■ □ ■

There is a certain danger in defining or designating things in negative terms. A negative designation, first of all, may be understood as being subordinate in some hierarchy of values to what might constitute a possible positive correlative. Second, that potentially positive quality may require a definition of its own. The expression *nonverbal communication*, as previously noted, suggests a kind of interaction essentially lacking a verbal component. Yet this is most often not the case; nonverbal modes (gesture or facial expression) support verbal expression or momentarily take the place of words as the primary mode of human communication. In either case (again) *extraverbal* appears the more suitable expression, since it affords a positive (rather than negative) sense, suggesting *additional* supportive modes of communication. In Isaac Babel's *Red Cavalry* tales, by contrast, there is little to support what little human communication exists.

In attempting to come to grips with this determining feature of the tales, upon which much of their horror and power is grounded, I use the expression *nondialogic* in the case of Babel in lieu of a term such as *antidialogic*, which might have appeared more suitable had that expression even marginal currency. Further, dialogic relations, understood as a responsive attitude exhibited on the part of various potential speakers, would likewise have been conceived as correspondingly positive *were they to exist* in the world of Babel's startling antinomies. But is such responsiveness present at all in his antithetic universe, built from centuries-old barriers that separate, most notably, as representative extremes, Cossack and Jew? Does a potential "positive correlative" appear, then, in this starkly drawn fictive world, seemingly devoid of any basic human need to communicate? In a word the physical and brutal "Red Cavalry" rider, who tears at life, is simply not seeking understanding.[1]

That endeavor is pursued exclusively by the author's alter ego, Liutov, who, in the process of endless seeking, affords a sense of unity to the otherwise seemingly isolated tales composing the cycle.

Part of the power and the horror of Babel's civil war epic can be derived from the dispassionate juxtaposition of terrible detail coupled with lyrical evocations of both life and death.[2] "Pan Apolek" begins with the celebratory expression: "The wise and beautiful life of Pan Apolek went to my head like an old wine" (Babel 55). "The Cemetery at Kozin" concludes with the lament: "O death, O covetous one, O greedy thief, why couldst thou not have spared us, just for once?" (107). The stories are framed by both celebration and lamentation. In its epic sweep the cycle embraces the horror of violent death as well as the occasional sense of gratitude for being alive. Commentators have long noted the startling juxtapositions and striking metaphor that permeate the work as a whole. Our interest in this chapter is focused on the lyrical passages that most often frame the stories, serving either to initiate or to conclude the account on a note that contrasts with what follows or precedes. In either case, in terms of their regularly disparate and contrastive tone they may be treated as separate texts, deserving attention for their prominent place within the respective stories and for their essentially nondialogic character, which is of particular importance here.[3]

In "Sandy the Christ," for instance, the simple youth of the title speaks briefly with his stepfather, in order to get free of him and "go be a herdsman." They reach a certain practical understanding: Sandy (in a twist of irony, since he is supposed to be saintly) agrees not to tell his mother that her husband is also "tainted" with an "evil disease" in exchange for his own freedom.[4] Understanding that might be spiritual (or in any sense other than simply practical) remains muted in this tale and throughout the cycle. Thus, at the end of the account we read:

> It was only recently that I got to know Sandy the Christ, and shifted my little trunk over to his cart. Since then we have often met the dawn and seen the sun set together. And whenever the capricious chance of war has brought us together, we have sat down of an evening on the bench outside a hut, or made tea in the woods in a sooty kettle, or slept side by side in the new-mown fields, the hungry horses tied to his foot or mine. (99)

Whatever understanding arrived at here appears nonverbal (rather than extraverbal) in the fundamental sense that no words are expended; no dialogue ensues that might help to explain, here or elsewhere. Whatever truth there might be exists in the nonverbal bond between man and man and between man and horse.

A parallel depiction frames the conclusion to "The Story of a Horse," in which a fine steed is commandeered, an act that causes its owner's resignation from the Communist Party ("You've gone and lost me, commissar" [113]) and retirement from the Red Cavalry.

> And that was how we lost Khlebnikov. . . . He was the only man in the squadron to possess a samovar. The days when there was a lull in the fighting we used to drink scalding tea together. We were both shaken by the same passions. Both of us looked on the world as a meadow in May—a meadow traversed by women and horses. (114)

The reader need not ask what those same passions are. Here, too, we are *told*—just as we know that the sharing of the dawn, the setting sun, and a sooty old kettle establish lasting bonds. But the reader is not privileged to hear these lone figures engage in dialogue, to register their thoughts and responses. And this is not simply a matter of privileging diegetic over mimetic concerns, which would not go very far in explaining the governing dynamics of the stories in any case. Rather, it is a firm commitment to a nondialogic approach to the world and everything in it.[5]

While acknowledging the abiding quality of the preceding images of shared life, there remains a certain inappropriateness, even irrelevance, itself a forbidding proposition, in seeking a positive correlative to the nondialogic quality in Babel's collection of tales. This aspect will be explored here in part by concentrating on the end frames of several of the stories in the cycle. Frequently, they conclude on a note that not only does not seek a response but makes one all but impossible. What is one to answer, for example, the young woman who is made to witness her father's brutal murder in "Crossing into Poland," the first story of the cycle? Does she really expect an answer? Can one, no matter how well intentioned, articulate a response that takes account of her grief? Her question ("I should wish to know where in the whole world you could find another father like my father?" [43]) does not seek an understanding of what remains for her forever a terrible enigma—man's incomprehensible, unending inhumanity to man. And her question, in its self-contained, unseeking, nondialogic wholeness, sets the pattern for the entire cycle that follows.[6]

In a series of related instances, in other words, the final word *is* final and complete, in the sense that it seeks no further response. But, as part of the ironic horror that defines Babel's universe, such seeming wholeness is at the same time maimed and beyond hope of redemption. Nothing, no response, can ever make right what, for that young woman, is wrong for all time. This is a world in which dialogic response, were it offered, would yet prove to be of no avail. In this story a Jew cannot respond to the grief of another Jew. In succeeding stories Jew and Cossack will prove even less likely to surmount the barriers imposed by history and culture. This is not a question of communication countered by dissimulation. Rather, as far more intractable and terrifying, the stories represent instances where communication as a potential source of resolution is precluded by a reality that will not so much as suffer that possibility or potentiality.[7]

On rare occasions the message may bear a positive intention, as in the story "Berestechko," depicting a small town, occupied mostly by Jews, that "reeks on, awaiting a new era" (120). Its inhabitants are informed by the voice of the Commissar in words that close (and frame) the story: "You are in power. Everything here is yours. No more Pans. I now proceed to the election of the Revolutionary Committee" (121). His words represent only the second instance of direct speech in the tale. The preceding such utterance is made by a Cossack, who has just slaughtered an old man so adeptly as not to splash himself with Jewish blood, and who then says: "Anyone who cares may come and fetch him. . . . You're free to do so" (119). To anyone within earshot, however, the later call to freedom simply parallels this earlier call, which also claims that now "you're free." The Commissar's "good news" and the Cossack's earlier cry of hate amount to variants on the same theme: a death knell that varies only in its perhaps veiled or directly open manner. In either case any form of "resolution" remains in the hands of another, whose monologic posture does not tolerate the utterance of a further responsive, suffering word.[8]

In "Italian Sunshine" the hero, who is least adept at riding a horse or killing one's fellow man, happens upon a fragment of a letter and then comments: "Sidorov, that anguished killer of men, tore into shreds the pink wadding of my imagination" (65). One tears and kills; the other imagines—that he can attain some understanding of his fellow man: in effect, what motivates him to tear and kill. The centerpiece of the story is the Cossack's tortured writing. The same is the case in "The Letter," in which a young peasant dictates a missive home describing in simple, straightforward language devoid of all sentiment how his father had seen to his older brother's execution and how another brother had done the same for the father. In both these stories not only is the letter at the center but its respective author's voice is likewise central. In contrast, the voice of Liutov represents at best a frame to the other "speaker," a frame that is highly contrastive but not dialogic. Serving as commentator whose words in turn serve as frame, the narrator of the stories is not engaged in dialogue with those characters who accept killing as simply a part of life. In fact, the very composition of these stories precludes the potential for dialogue. Although the concept of frame is employed here figuratively, the words of the chronicler of these two tales, which "frame" their respective letters, are indeed set outside (and beyond) the words of the other. Between the two, typically, there is no structure designed to afford even the possibility of dialogic exchange.[9]

As an even further extreme of the nondialogic principle that structures and organizes these stories, affording them a profound sense of verisimilitude in the process, the story "Salt" forgoes entirely the frame supplied in "Italian Sunshine" and "A Letter" by a contrastive, dispassionate voice that comments on physical detail exclusively. As a result, by the stark omission of the psychological aspect, the stilted and artificial voice of death affords a lasting impression or is simply the only one heard. ("So I took my faithful rifle off the wall and washed away that stain from the face of the workers' land and the republic" [126].) By contrast, in "Gedali," seventh in the cycle of thirty-five stories but the first to offer even a semblance of dialogue, that semblance is articulated again in stilted terms that afford no resolution or understanding. Gedali wants a handy yardstick by which he can distinguish between Revolution and Counterrevolution. He already knows what makes for good people in hard times: his idea is to create an International composed of those who do not shoot. In ironic reversal, however, his fellow Jew undertakes to explain things by mimicking (or ventriloquizing) the voice of the Cossack, which is the voice of death: "She cannot do without shooting, Gedali . . . because she is the Revolution." As for the International, he is told: "It is eaten with gunpowder . . . and spiced with best-quality blood" (71, 72). Indulging in a kind of self-parody (of someone fascinated by death), such a forbidding "exegesis," articulated by a voice that also parodies the Commissar, who calls for Revolution, and the Cossack, who carries out that call, explains nothing and resolves nothing.[10] The enigma of death seeming to triumph everywhere over life remains.

✻ ✻ ✻

"Truth tickles everyone's nostrils. . . . The question is, how's it to be pulled from the heap." That line, like all other citations, has itself been pulled from the heap. Citing further that same speech, uttered by an unlettered Cossack ("My First Goose"), we read: "But he goes and strikes at it straight off like a hen pecking at a grain!" (77). That note of approbation is directed at Lenin, bearer of the "Truth." In the next story ("The Rabbi") truth is spiritual rather than secular—and far less abstract than revolutionary thought: thus Babel's anomalous Jew is told he must "rejoice that he is alive and not dead" (79). The scenes are contrastive; in the one story crude Cossacks are billeted on an old woman: "We slept, all six of us, beneath a wooden roof that let in the stars, warming one another, our legs intermingled" (77). In the other the Rabbi is "surrounded by the liars and the possessed" (78). One unsavory lot appears akin to another; camaraderie is once again shared: "We all of us seated ourselves side by side—possessed, liars, and idlers" (79). Only the lonely figure of the Jew moves uncomfortably between the two.

He is the link, but what do they share? In what sense are the two groups akin? The one sees truth in the words of Lenin, read aloud by the only literate one in the bunch; the other seeks wisdom at the feet of "the last of the Chernobyl dynasty" (78). But the times are such that truth is not only peripheral and ephemeral to harsh reality but also beyond the shared, common word of man. No one engages in dialogue; Lenin articulates political and economic truth ("there's a shortage of everything" [76]); the Rabbi spouts the wisdom of the ages ("The jackal whines when he is hungry, every fool has folly enough for despondency, and only the wise man can tear the veil of being with his laughter" [78]). It is tempting to set Lenin and the Rabbi in dialogue on the topic of shortages and hunger, but that would ring false, for they are not thus engaged, and neither is anyone else. The six sleep, as one dreams the nightmares of the chosen race; the others sit, amid shooting and death, awaiting the Messiah.

Or, better, one group waits, while the other creates—its own Messiah, whose frightening visage, as Gedali well knows and as Babel's fellow traveler superfluously explains, *is* the Revolution. In the absence of voices engaged in dialogic exchange, Babel delivers a series of images—a collective image of the Revolution, both in its horrific beauty, as warrior-hero ("Up to the very steps galloped Dyakov on his fiery Anglo-Arabian" [53]), and in its horrible mangled form, as victim (whose "throat had been torn out and his face cleft in two" [43]). Babel does not depict human figures engaged in dialogue; instead, he portrays the

Revolution in its carnivorous, inhuman image, devouring all that get in its way. In composite form the hallmark of that design concludes "A Letter," in which we are told: "He handed me a broken photograph. It depicted Timofey Kurdyukov, a broad-shouldered rural policeman sporting a uniform cap and a beard parted in the middle—an inert figure with prominent cheekbones and the bright stare of vacant and colorless eyes. . . . Against the wall . . . stiff as on the parade ground towered two lads, the two monstrously tall, dull, broadfaced, goggle-eyed Kurdyukov brothers, Theodore and Simon" (52). Why all the careful attention to detail in this sorry assemblage? Because that image, we are to understand, is not simply of this sad, brutal, and tragic family but extends beyond.

Nonetheless, we do find occasional verbal declarations that subsume the Revolution in their single-minded, ignorant devotion that, once again, blatantly declares from a number of linked perspectives that it will brook no interference or opposed point of view. Thus, in "Salt" the outraged letter writer declares that "we will deal mercilessly with all the traitors that are dragging us to the dogs and want to turn everything upside down and cover Russia with nothing but corpses and dead grass" (127). Similarly, in the following story, "Evening," the voice of the Revolution again declares pointedly: "you're a driveler, and we're fated to have to put up with you drivelers. We're busy shelling and getting at the kernel for you. Not long will pass and then you'll see those cleaned kernels and take your fingers out of your nose and sing of the new life in no ordinary prose" (129). Such verbal aggression documents the nondialogic quality of the times that is meticulously reflected in Babel's own "unordinary" prose.

In contemplating the virtual lack of a dialogical component in these stories, which does not constitute a failing so much as a decided virtue in documenting the horror of depicted events, we note that "The Road to Brody" is essentially composed of a legend (about Christ on the Cross and bees that will not attack: "Can't. He's a carpenter like us") and a song (about a subaltern "who drank himself tipsy with vodka the day his head was chopped off" [81]). Similarly, in the succeeding sketch, "Discourse on the Tachanka," there is not a single scrap of dialogue. (Nor is there in other pieces, including "The Cemetery at Kozin," "Prishchepa's Vengeance," "Berestechko," and "In St. Valentine's Church.") As promised by the title of the story, there follows a brief account—chock full of interesting, historical detail but devoid of a single human word—focused on a "sort of little cart . . . [that] grew to be a mobile and formidable instrument of warfare" (83). When we do hear a human voice, it is frequently at high pitch, a yell—the call to arms, the repeated call to confront death ("Come along and die for a pin and the World Revolution!" [115])[11]—uttered by some barely identified soul, such as "Korochayev, the disgraced Commander of the IV Division who fought singlehanded, seeking death." The reader is supplied with engaging descriptive fragments ("His cloak floating about him, he gal-loped away—black from head to foot, his pupils like live coals" [86]), which correlate with the equally striking speech fragments that pepper the tales, but which, in and of themselves, do not constitute the alter-nating, responsive utterances that make for dialogue.

Time is of the essence in this bloody world, where a wasted moment could tally up to a wasted life, where the disemboweled Dolgushov plaintively notes: "You'll have to waste a cartridge on me." In this world there can be no court of appeal, neither with the enemy, who "will turn up and play their dirty tricks" (89), nor with one's own best friend, who, unable to countenance another's inability to kill, had "cocked his rifle." As one isolated voice, characterized only as belonging to "a sort of lively humpback," puts it: "Nowadays everybody judges everybody else. . . . And condemns to death—it's as simple as that" (157). Here, where the line between life and death is traversed in a flash ("Afonka hid [the papers] away in his boot and shot Dolgushov in the mouth"), there is no time for dialogue ("They spoke briefly; no words reached me" [90]); there is no respite, during which to explain, to reach some semblance of understanding. Truth lies in the event depicted, rather than at the interstices of the word struggling for meaning. Here the word is secondary; action is primary. In the beginning was the deed, and it was bloody. The story of Cain and Abel becomes a tale of civil war, Babel's own chosen tale.

In this rendering the story of brother against brother is also trans-formed into that of master and man. "The Life and Adventures of Matthew Pavlichenko" follows the story of "Sandy the Christ." As the tenuous link between the two, the point of departure in each proceeds from the respective hero's earlier life as a herdsman. But there the con-nection ends: for one tells of peace attained in the interim of war, at night, under the stars; by contrast, the other relates a cruel vengeance, achieved slowly, in broad daylight. In "Sandy" the first-person perspective is provided by Babel's wandering Jew in search of a lost humanity; in "Matthew" the teller is the former herdsman turned Red General. In lyrical, rapturous tones the reader is provided with yet another image of the Revolution: "Five lost years I was like a lost soul, till at last the year Eighteen came along to visit me, lost soul that I was. It came along on lively stallions, on its Kabardin horses, bringing along a big train of wagons and all sorts of songs" (103). But that image, with its stallions and songs, is also the face of death: "because in my looks one cheek has been burning for five years—burning in the trenches, burning on the march, burning with a woman, will go on burning till the Last Judgment" (104). Here, too, there is no appeal and no reprieve, as Matthew Pavlichenko asks his former master, "and what am I going to do about my cheek?" (106), before he tramples his master's face to get back his own. Dialogue—what there is of it—again reduces to practical matters. And these are further reduced to a single, final resolution as a death warrant, articulated by the illiterate Matthew Pavlichenko, who reads aloud from a blank page Lenin's nonexistent letter authorizing murder. "In the name of the nation . . . and for the foundation of a nobler life in the future, I order Pavlichenko, Matthew son of Rodion, to deprive certain people of life, according to his discretion" (105). The lord of the manor, the jewels, and the parlor, in which he will die, recognizes, finally, his own death sentence and cries out, "Shoot me then, damned son of a bitch!" (106), acknowledging too late that, once again, there is no time left for talk, understanding, or possible reprieve.

As the briefest counterpoint, affording only a semblance of dialogue, elsewhere a quick agreement is reached on meeting certain death in joint partnership. When a fellow rider is asked by the dying hero of the story ("Squadron Commander Trunov") if he is up to facing the challenge posed by overwhelming odds, the reply appears, curiously, almost nonverbal—but typically visceral—in its oblique response: "Christ! . . . Mother of our Lord Jesus Christ!" (151). Seemingly, that fearful but determined evocation acknowledges a compelling mandate to cede one's life to the cause. (By contrast, in "Two Ivans" the shirker feigning deafness refuses, in effect, to shed "my own little drop of blood," for the sake, as he puts it, of the "power of the Soviets of mine" [158].) Again, by virtue of its understatement a profound understanding of courage is also afforded by the Rabbi's son, "the Red Army man Bratslavsky," when asked how he could leave home and face the specter of death that eventually claims him: "When there's a revolution on," he says, "a mother's an episode" (193). Although characteristically cryptic and telegrammatic, both responses represent an occasional instance in this world of "fierce and wordless brigandage" (136) when a word of immediate understanding, revealing heroic motivation, *is* exchanged.

But such exchange is quite occasional, almost accidental. As one lonesome soul expresses it, getting no response in return for his trouble: "These nights on the line are long. There's no end to them. And a man sort of gets a longing to have a talk with someone else, but where's one to get someone else, I'd like to know?" (170). The answer is, surely not on Babel's long cavalry ride. But the question remains, why not? While these snippets of life and war do not afford the luxury of time for sustained response to anything beyond immediate practical concerns, there remains another, vastly more interesting consideration: namely, that the lyrical *I* of these stories, which shifts at times from the troubled searching perspective of Liutov to another viewpoint, does not accommodate another potential voice at any given moment.[12] In a series of narratives in which the narrator constantly changes and in which the appearance and departure of its dramatis personae also seem arbitrary and dependent upon slender plot alone, the only consistent feature is the persistent absence of the other.

Babel's lyrical voice may be characterized in one prominent respect as that which, at any given moment, evokes a chilling awareness among startling and contradictory evocations of war. It is the *I* that confesses, after urinating in the dark on the face of a dead enemy soldier: "I wiped the skull of my unknown brother" (156). It is the one who proclaims: "I, who can scarce contain the tempests of my imagination within this age-old body of mine, I was there beside my brother when he breathed his last" (193). That *I*, which perceives all mankind as its brother, is readily identifiable as Babel's principal accountant, attempting to take stock of what proves ultimately unaccountable. At times the writer's unifying lyrical voice appears in barely accessible rhetorical guise that proclaims in apostrophe what could not be rendered in simple prose: "O regulations of the Russian Communist Party! You have laid down headlong rails through the sour pastry of our Russian tales" (127). In terms of more intimate address "The Rabbi's Son" begins: "Do you remember Zhitomir, Vasily? Do you remember the River Teterev, Vasily, and that night when the Sabbath, the young Sabbath crept along the sunset, crushing the stars beneath her little red heel? . . . Do you remember that night, Vasily?" (191). Here there is no shift in narrational strategy; the original lyrical voice remains present throughout to tell its pathetic tale of death. Its presence is countered, however, by the erstwhile Vasily's pronounced absence. Except for the intrusion of this proper name, there is no sign whatever of the living soul to whom it presumably belongs. "Vasily" thus appears as only a kind of prop for the telling of the tale, serving as the ready ear to whom it is told. His absence, though, is emblematic of a sustained absence throughout this gripping cycle of sad tales.

Intermittently, there are stories that are related by a voice that does not belong to Liutov, Babel's principal chosen teller. Thus, for the most part, or entirely, the following *skaz* tales are told from a different perspective from that of the majority: "A Letter," "Italian Sunshine," "The Life and Adventures of Matthew Pavlichenko," "Konkin's Prisoner," "Salt," "Evening," "The Story of a Horse, Continued," and "Treason." The remaining tales are immediately recognized by a unifying perspective that proclaims itself in tones that are both lyrical and rhetorical. Thus the opening frame of "Pan Apolek" begins in celebration: "The wise and beautiful life of Pan Apolek went to my head like an old wine" (55); while "The Road to Brody" concludes in sadness: "O Brody! The mummies of your crushed passions breathed upon me their irremediable poison. I could already sense the deathly chill of orbits suffused with tears grown cold" (82). These repeated variations of complex lyrical notes sound alternating tones of celebration and lamentation that are both life affirming and death obsessed. They identify Babel's solitary seeker, whose voice gives a sense of unity and cohesion to a collection of stories that ironically draws upon numerous disengaged voices, none of which shares in dialogic interaction with any other.

Frequently, these voices are directed at absent receivers. Thus, "A Letter" is addressed to a mother, for whom her son's dispassionate account of multiple murder and death in the family can only be devastating; "Italian Sunshine" centers on a letter addressed to a certain Victoria, whose existence may be derived solely from a flight of fancy on the part of a sick and lively imagination; "Salt" is directed to a certain "Comrade Editor," who is similarly implored to harken to the demons that haunt a distraught soldier of the Revolution on the brink of breakdown; while "Treason" likewise seeks justice from a certain "Comrade Investigator." In each instance the central narrative is addressed outwardly to some distant (nonexistent?) figure, from whom there is—and can be—no response. All these instances, therefore, model collectively the (non)dialogic structure of the work as a whole, characterized by a logical and philosophical void that is only rarely and ephemerally overcome. One cannot reach one's potential interlocutor through the mails or across the hurdles and gauntlets interposed by history and culture.

As a rare exception, such contact is marginally accomplished in "Story of a Horse, Continued," structured as an exchange of two letters. The first constitutes a message of forgiveness, directed to the commander who had forcibly requisitioned the writer's favorite mount. In response the latter is told, in effect, that it is unlikely that they will meet again other than in Hell. So the matter, it may be understood, is effectively closed. Such is the extent of whatever resolution may be sought in these tales. Elsewhere in the cycle the end result of an always marginal exchange is comparable, differing only in degree but not in kind. The stories, and the reality they depict, countenance little that passes for dialogue and even less that might be heralded as shared understanding. Yet this appears to contradict the clear presence of a pronounced lyrical voice.

That voice, after all, whatever else may be said for it, is conceived to be *human* in its possible affectation and attention. It is emitted by a clearly defined *I* and is directed toward what is presumably most felt by the speaker. In a certain sense, then, it is self-enclosed as well as self-reflective. Both characteristics, however, conform with what has here been remarked concerning Babel. His lone rider ("I was alone among these men whose friendship I had not succeeded in gaining" [199]), in fact, seeks understanding in solitary (self-)questioning. To attempt otherwise constitutes a hopeless endeavor: the Cossack already knows all that he needs to know ("I see you . . . I see the whole of you. You're trying to live without enemies" [200]); while one's compatriot Jew—immersed in the same cultural quandary that holds that human life is sacred—can, in this respect, offer no help.[13]

As the opening and closing lines of a text, the frame, as Bakhtin among others has acknowledged, occupies a special place within the given work.[14] It is situated either to afford an initial brief commentary in anticipation of what is to follow or to provide a final summative note on what has already transpired. As opening or closing frame, the lyrical passage in *Red Cavalry* is itself granted a particular strategic prominence.[15] A new and separate voice makes its brief appearance, sounding a chord of its own. But the question of *whose* own represents a problem of considerable complexity, since the new "obtrusive" voice may appear to belong to the authorial context, closely associated in this case with Babel himself, or may be attributable to a character endowed with a certain (lyrical) voice of his own.[16]

In "The Life and Adventures of Matthew Pavlichenko" the hero generally fulfills the role of narrator. The first-person perspective belongs to the former herdsman turned Red Army general. A separate introductory note, however, is sounded at the start, with an aggressive summons that increasingly evokes a sense of intimate relations between an unknown speaker and an undefined audience: "Comrades, countrymen, my own dear brethren. In the name of all mankind learn the story of the Red General, Matthew Pavlichenko." Calling immediate attention to the story's definitive feature, the choruslike clarion call serves as invitation to hear and bear witness to what emerges as a startlingly dispassionate first-person account of murder. Rhetorical in nature, those words set the tone for a tale whose subsequent speech orientation is consistently oral in the spirit of the ancient folk tradition. Structured largely from chunks of reported speech, punctuated by colloquial expressions throughout, the oral quality of the tale is unmistakable. But what the story has to recount extends beyond any established, recognizable literary tradition into the spectral realm of collectively shared years-long nightmare. Yet, first, in rambling, burlesque fashion the reader is informed by an unidentified lyrical voice of a herdsman's past that included "looking after the master's pigs."[17] It is only in the second paragraph that the lyrical voice belonging to Matthew Pavlichenko, as opposed to the one resembling a chorus in the first, makes itself heard: "And so I look after my horned cattle, with cows all around me, soaked in milk and stinking of it like a sliced udder" (100). That remark initiates "the story of the Red General, Matthew Pavlichenko," as told by himself. Hence the entire first paragraph maintains its own singularly lyrical and rhetorical tone until the principal teller of the story picks up the thread in his own distinctive voice, which contrasts starkly with the grisly tale that he has to tell.

But who is it that the "chorus" has gathered to listen and bear witness? The answer is supplied by a second lyrical apostrophe, occurring halfway through the story: "And what d'you think, you Stavropol boys, comrades, fellow-countrymen, my own dear brethren?" asks the Red General (103). Those who have gathered are clearly the down-home folk, who share the same cultural background, speech patterns, and political point of view—which expounds, simply, the idea that others (in the typically Russian paradigm of "we" and "they") are the masters, the "cold-blooded local powers" (104). In a word the collective addressees are those who *understand*, as Pavlichenko does, that "with shooting you only get rid of a chap. Shooting's letting him off, and too damn easy for yourself. With shooting you'll never get at the soul, to where it is in a fellow and how it shows itself" (106). So the story is addressed to a local bunch of "Stavropol boys," who speak the same and understand the same. Further, the lyrical voice of the story that sings of murder and slow death, ostensibly belonging to Pavlichenko, is also collectively theirs. In this engaging case addresser and addressee appear to merge in a thoughtless abandon that consistently results in mutilation and death.

In another respect, however, the illiterate Matthew's story is very much *his*. For it establishes his particular rhetorical skill in telling his tale with humor, with vaunted good will that is false, and with a certain disinterest that thoroughly belies the determined will to vengeance that is also eminently his but not his to the exclusion of others with similar ambitions. Here, again, the individual case slides into that strange overriding universal set that Babel explores in all its gravity and horror. Within the cycle, after all, vengeance—seemingly for its own sake and for a whole spate of personal and "political" reasons—figures as a prominent theme. As a case in point, "Prishchepa's Vengeance," told in a single page, takes on epic proportion in a work that exemplifies Babel's mastery of the small form. Nowhere is his skill in rendering encapsulated horror, brutality, and the sense of life as both powerful and awful more tellingly revealed than in this miniscule masterpiece. Not a word of dialogue is uttered, nor is there a single utterance that might in isolation be termed lyrical. Yet the entire piece rings, paradoxically, with that very quality—in response to the closing lines of the preceding piece (shortest in the collection), "The Cemetery at Kozin,"[18] which follows "Pavlichenko." Those lines that implore, "O death . . . why couldst thou not have spared us, just for once?" receive their fullest response in "Prishchepa": No, not once, not ever—because I, Prishchepa, who am wordless (in contrast to the garrulous Pavlichenko) am also death incarnate. And no one shall be spared. Not even myself. In the words of Pavlichenko, who says it all for all the "boys" and their ilk: "I don't spare myself, and I've more than once trampled an enemy for over an hour. You see, I want to get to know what life really is, what life's like down our way" (106). Prishchepa also goes back "down our way" to get his own, to tear at life, to wreak death—with no one spared, not even once. The answer to the plea closing the preceding sketch is thus contained in the account that follows.

Prishchepa accomplishes his bloody deed alone; Matthew Pavlichenko does the same ("I went over alone, without the detachment" [104]). By contrast, in "A Letter," in which vengeance is also accomplished, this time against a hated father, the deed is performed collectively: "We got on our horses and did two hundred versts—I, brother Simon, and the fellows from our settlement who wanted to come along too." The "fellows" equate with Pavlichenko's boys: those who think the same and act the same; or, better, those who act without thinking at all. Here they are needed. Otherwise, how would Simon have "lined up all the fighting men in the yard according to army custom," in order to "finish off Dad?" (50). That choice unfeeling language belongs to the idiot youngest brother Kurdyukov, who dictates the letter. While the account seemingly reaches a nadir for lack of all human emotion, it does not represent an isolated instance. Other such voices, belonging for the most part to other distraught letter writers and disillusioned petitioners, are also heard as needed counterpoint to the lyrical tones that are sounded throughout.

Lyricism in the tales may be evoked by an unidentified voice functioning as chorus, as individual teller of a given tale, or, in an extended sense, it may be manifested throughout an entire piece by virtue of a certain corresponding extended lyrical note. This is the case in "Prishchepa," whose subject is not simply the loss of parents sucked into the vicious whirlpool of death and vengeance repeatedly wreaked, as the principal reward of civil war. Its subject, rather, is the return to childhood, a typically lyrical theme rendered here in thoroughly atypical fashion. What the hero manages to accomplish in the midst of murder and pillage on the grand scale is to reconstruct his forever lost childhood world ("Prishchepa went back to his despoiled home and arranged the furniture he had taken back in the places he remembered from childhood"). In this cardinal sense this brief horrific piece constitutes a simple inversion of a universal lyrical theme. When, at the end of "two whole days and nights" of violent, hysterical mourning, "Prishchepa untied his horse, leaped into the saddle, threw a lock of hair into the flames, and vanished" (109), he had taken farewell of his childhood and returned for good to the terrible world of civil war adulthood. Related in a thoroughly dispassionate manner, its universality is concealed by a screen of seemingly inhuman brutality, its lyricism veiled by content too terrible and alien to contemplate. Yet Babel's point, repeatedly made from behind the screen and veil of the poetry of inverted lyricism, is that these things, too, are human. In this world of civil war, where brother kills brother, father murders his own flesh and is in turned killed by the same, Prishchepa is your brother. In total accord with this strange, strained poetics he is the representation of the human face likewise inverted.

❉ ❉ ❉

An instance of a chorus appearing as the lyrical voice in an opening apostrophe occurs only in "Matthew Pavlichenko." The tale is unique to the cycle in that respect. The voice of Liutov, Babel's fellow traveler and alter ego, also initiates most notably in lyrical form "Pan Apolek," extolling the apostate's "wise and beautiful life." But his anguished voice (not unlike his brother Prishchepa's, had the latter been afforded the power of speech) bemoans the loss of a childhood steeped in learning: "O the rotted Talmuds of my childhood! O the dense melancholy of memories!" (69). (Prishchepa, too, suffers from memories of a lost world.) Those tortured words are contained in the first lines of "Gedali." The old man whose name serves as title to that story is afforded his own lyrical voice in the lines that introduce "The Rabbi."

> All is mortal. Only the mother is destined to immortality. And when the mother is no longer among the living, she leaves a memory which none has yet dared to sully. The memory of the mother nourishes in us a compassion that is like the ocean, and the measureless ocean feeds the rivers that dissect the universe. (77)

This speech is distinctly attributed to Gedali. In a poetics of lyrical inversion, however, we are not surprised to recognize that not a single mother appears in these stories, except as the intended recipient of a message bearing awful tidings ("A Letter") and as the destined receiver of similar bad news ("The Rabbi's Son," in which the young hero referred to in the title of the tale explains that, in the face of revolution, "a mother's an episode," as he lies naked and dying in a railroad car).[19]

Cossack mother and Jewish mother, in the universality of their predicament, are thus fated to share the same monumental grief. Nevertheless, the image of the mother exists in the tales only in recollection and memory, which is where Gedali appropriately places her in his lyrical flight devoted to Her. He is, however, not the only one to recall her; Liutov also evokes her healing image in successive metaphors: "Evening wrapped about me the quickening moisture of its twilight sheets; evening laid a mother's hand upon my burning forehead" (76). Elsewhere she is evoked thus: "Night comforted us in our miseries, a light wind fanned us like a mother's skirt, and the grass below sparkled with freshness and moisture" (129). Although cloaked in wondrous metaphor, she is nonetheless not there. And without her, no matter the stunning lyrical note briefly sustained, there will be no one to "nourish in us a compassion that is like the ocean." Hence the poetics of inversion is likewise sustained: Matthew Pavlichenko shows no compassion for his former master, while Prishchepa shows none for his former neighbors and villagers.

Nor does the principal first-person speaker of the tales, whose voice (lyrical and otherwise) links the stories within a single framework. True to his name, Liutov (meaning "fierce"—ironic in the context) is portrayed acting in brutal manner in a number of instances. In "After the Battle" he strikes a cripple: "I pushed the epileptic away and struck him in the face. [He] fell sideways to the ground and began to bleed from his fall" (186). In "Zamoste," demanding food, he threatens the old woman upon whom he is billeted: "I'll burn you . . . I'll burn you and your stolen calf" (171). Likewise, in "My First Goose," in which the need to feed an empty belly is matched by a need for acceptance, he is again violent ("'Christ!' I muttered and pushed the old woman in the chest with my fist" [75]). By his trampling the goose, both needs are momentarily satisfied. Yet this comes at a cost—the Cossacks sleep well, he does not. The story is positioned in the cycle between "Gedali" and "The Rabbi," both of whose main represented voices counsel compassion and restraint. Nonetheless, in the absence of Mother and in the midst of war the anomalous Jewish companion to these fiercesome horse riders bares his own inverted human face. In doing so, however, "my heart stained with bloodshed, grated and brimmed over" (77). In effect, that closing lyrical note resolves the paradox of this and similar instances of incongruous cruelty: in felicitous ironic turnabout the human face that the hero tries (unsuccessfully) to reject nonetheless emerges from a soul that "brims over" all of its own.[20] Only at the end is a balance achieved; the Cossacks no longer scorn him, while he suffers no corresponding loss of self. Although the campaign is lost, a modicum of success crowns the private battle.

As in "My First Goose," a strategic final lyrical note frames a number of the tales in the cycle, affording a temporary respite (but not the final word) from a struggle that rages not only on the battlefield but internally as well. Thus, "After the Battle" concludes on a similar note of despair at not having "achieved" an inhuman visage in the face of overwhelming odds that one do so.

> The village was swimming and swelling, and blood-red clay was
> oozing from its dismal wounds. The first star glimmered above me,

and fell into the clouds. Rain lashed the willows and spent itself. Evening flew up to the sky like a flock of birds, and darkness crowned me with its watery wreath. I felt my strength all ebbing away. Bent beneath the funereal garland, I continued on my way, imploring fate to grant me the simplest of proficiencies—the ability to kill my fellow-men. (187)

While that oft-quoted concluding line represents in itself a much celebrated paradox, it is further supported and enhanced in this remarkable passage by the stated sense of deteriorating strength on the part of Babel's lyrical persona. For it is just that paradoxical "ebbing" of the desire and ambition to shoot that is life affirming. Exhausted by the need to load up and kill, he remains human and himself. This means as well, in this anomalous case, that he remain true to the spirit of the old Gedali. In his own lyrical manner the latter declares: "Yes, I cry to the Revolution. Yes, I cry to it, but it hides its face from Gedali and sends out on front nought but shooting" (70). Hence the sorry figure, who implores "fate" the ability to shoot, happily represents the sole exception to Gedali's blinded vision.

The intrusion of a frequently contrastive lyrical passage in the cycle figures more prominently as the closing frame than as one that opens a piece. A comparable note is rarely struck at the start, and then to far less effect. Retained for the end, the lyrical note achieves its goal by virtue of what it is. Stark and unrepentant lyricism serves almost by definition as a reminder that the persona of a given tale is nonetheless human and that what is perpetrated in the name of whatever warring cause is effected as well by a humanity that has been fragmented and has consequently lost the spiritual sense of itself that Gedali manages to retain.

But the old man is not alone in this respect. While tales related by the "alien" voice of the one who tears at life ("A Letter," "Italian Sunshine," "Salt," "Treason") do not end positively or hopefully, this type is nonetheless granted a lyrical voice of its own. Matthew Pavlichenko delights in the year of Revolution, making it the chief object of his affection: "Eh you, little dear Eighteen, my sweetheart! Can it be that we shan't be walking out with you any more, my own little drop of blood, my year Eighteen?" (103). Similar self-contained lyrical notes appear tellingly on the lips of other speakers as well. Resigning from the war, Khlebnikov writes "with tears that are not fitting to a soldier but that will go on flowing all the same, slashing my heart, slashing my heart till it bleeds" (113). Confronted by certain death, another fighter (as noted) mutters, "Christ! . . . Mother of our Lord Jesus Christ!" (151), in which a lyrical note and a curse converge; while one, unwilling to shed that "little drop," cries "wildly, throwing sand over his face" (158) in frenzied reaction to the idea of relinquishing his life for some abstraction embodied in the "year Eighteen." Pavlichenko is thus not the only Cossack lyricist here. Others also strike poetic, lyrical notes of their own. And they are not alone. "Dusty, endless, the brigade stretched out like a line of peasant carts on the way to a fair" (93). Hovering over that brigade is a spirit that sounds its own decisive note. For in response to the nondialogic quality in Babel that appears so negative, there is manifested a positive, human aspect as its lyrical correlative.

9

SUPRADIALOGUE: *DOCTOR ZHIVAGO*
(PASTERNAK)

■ □ ■

The structure of *Doctor Zhivago*, as stated earlier, is in many respects unique. Its concluding chapter is a collection of poems ostensibly composed by the novel's central figure. The preceding sixteen prose chapters are themselves further divided into numerous individual scenes, focused on a predominant image, which may be likened to separate cinematic shots. In this respect the novel lends itself to discussion of the relations between narrative and cinematic technique. It also seeks a certain reconciliation between specific incidents documented in prose and then later reformulated as poetry, affording a sense of "dialogue" between the two classic modes of expression. Our intent here, in returning to Pasternak's novel, is to consider dialogue primarily in its concrete sense, rather than range across an entire figurative spectrum, to which the term or its derivatives seem, in recent usage, naturally to gravitate. Metaphoric interpretation, nevertheless, will also find its place here in response to the poetic qualities of the work itself. In broad outline my aim is to concentrate upon a specific complex aspect of the novel, its dialogic structures in complex interrelation, and to demonstrate that, within this singular work, they are worthy of attention as principal features accounting for its singularity.

Upon initial consideration *Zhivago* may appear an odd choice for dialogic analysis, since, in a work strongly disposed toward metaphoric formulation and figurative description, the diegetic aspect strongly predominates over the mimetic. Far more is told, in other words, than is shown. In a striking number of instances the reader is simply informed of an event's occurrence, rather than presented with the causal detail by which it took place. As cited in the first chapter, Zhivago's most profound liaison is thus communicated in these spare terms: "Two months had now elapsed since the day when, instead of going home from Yuriatin, he spent the night at Larisa Feodorovna's" (Pasternak 302). In conformity with this terse narrative mode the characters' speech, in particular, is presented in utterly sparing, laconic fashion. The frequency between the author's recapitulation of events by presenting his characters' exchanges in the form of either indirect or quasi-direct speech appears to outweigh greatly the presentation of their direct speech.[1] Hence the reader is made privy firsthand to the characters' dialogical engagements only relatively rarely—and with the added inescapable sense of their truncation. One must therefore rely principally on the author's summative accounts, within which are incorporated at times only isolated fragments of his characters' speech. Rather than fault *Zhivago* in these respects, I will take the work on its own terms. This entails acknowledging the novel's striking paucity of dialogue within a study whose aim is to concentrate precisely on the various contrastive modes depicting such communication.

The presentation of the characters' own speech, generally a prominent feature of narrative, is indeed lean, appearing as a possible debit rather than credit. Yet, paradoxically, the concept of dialogue in the abstract is enhanced and broadened by virtue of its particularized, special use in *Zhivago*. Whereas dialogue, characterized by a virtually requisite employment of direct speech, would appear to be an unmarked feature of narrative in general because of its proliferated use, in Pasternak's novel, by contrast, it is a distinctly marked element—and worthy of further attention in this respect alone. Specific to the work at hand, in other words, the stated fact of there having been a talk (with few specifics and even less of the characters' own words provided) appears unmarked; while dialogue, presented in some dimension and detail as such, rather than simply cited as an event having taken place, remains for this novel marked. Thus, at the meeting early in the book between Zhivago and Misha Gordon the reader is informed: "In the past few days they had talked of everything in the world." But only a few nonspecific details follow to illustrate the point: "Gordon had learned his friend's ideas about the war and its effect on people's thinking" (116), we read. Previously, it is stated: "They were talking, as they had done all these nights and days" (115). Yet not a word of all that talk ("of everything in the world") is communicated to the reader.

During her period of convalescence (after shooting Komarovsky) Lara is offered financial assistance, moral support, and a place to live by Kologrivov, the father of her childhood friend. "And in spite of her protests, her tears, and her struggles" (95), he obliges her finally to acquiesce in his magnanimity. Not a word of hers is reported. At this same time, when Lara attempts to convince Pasha to renounce her ("I am a bad woman. You don't know me, someday I'll tell you. . . . But enough, forget me, I'm not worthy of you"), his response, likewise, can only be surmised. The reader is informed instead that "there followed heart-rending scenes, each more unbearable than the last" (95). Similarly, during Pasha and Lara's wedding night the reader is told that "they talked till morning." But not a single word of their discussion is reported. What we learn instead is that "in all Pasha's life there had not been a change in him so decisive and abrupt as in the course of this night" (97). Later, at the couple's farewell party, a single brief and inconsequential exchange between the two concludes on the note: "But there's a lot to talk about" (98). Nothing further is ever communicated.

As a final striking case in point, during the only meeting between Zhivago (as an adult) and his uncle Nikolai, a former priest and independent-minded philosopher, the reader is informed that "for Yury Andreyevich the encounter was a tremendous, unforgettable event"; that "theirs was a meeting of two artists"; and that "their talk was full of exclamations, they paced excitedly up and down the room, marvelling at each other's perspicacity." But the reader is not made privy to a single word of their discussion. Rather, we learn that "they informed each other of all that had happened during their separation" and that "they began to speak of the things that really matter to creative minds" (178)—tantalizing information at best. In fact, there is not a single instance in the entire novel of direct speech conveyed between Zhivago and his uncle. Nor is a single word directly communicated between Zhivago and his half-brother Yevgraf. From these related characteristic features it may well be claimed that *Doctor Zhivago* is an implicit work, in which much is left untold, while even more remains unsaid.

Nonetheless, such assessments, couched in seemingly negative formulation, afford an already noted positive dimension as well. This apparent contradiction defines, in large part, the purpose here. Having acknowledged, on the one hand, the truncated nature of dialogic interaction in *Doctor Zhivago*, our principal aim is to concentrate upon those features of the novel that enhance and extend the idea of communicative exchange, determined by a highly distinctive dialogic poetics. In short, *Zhivago* varies markedly from general novelistic technique and, in such variance, allows for a greater dimension to the concept of dialogue in narrative than appears to have been accounted for by certain theoretical treatments. In discussing the problem, let us consider briefly the approaches taken by the Prague School theorist Jan Mukařovský and by Bakhtin, whose lifelong preoccupation with the question of dialogue is presented succinctly, for present purposes, in his late published writings.

In "Dialogue and Monologue," an essay that stood virtually alone in addressing the issue (aside from the as yet unknown monumental work by Bakhtin), Mukařovský calls for a resolution to the problem of the relationship between monologue and dialogue.[2] There he defines monologue as "an utterance with a single active participant regardless of the presence or absence of other passive participants" ("Dialogue" 81). All that is needed for monologue to take place, in other words, is a single speaker, who may be the only one present to hear his own words. In apparent agreement Bakhtin abbreviates a similar formulation in his later unfinished writings: "Monologue as speech that is addressed to no one and does not presuppose a response" (*Speech* 117). Further, in conformity with Prague School thinking, Mukařovský posits the alternation of speech between two speakers as being fundamental to dialogue.[3] That is, the dialogic mode requires that the speakers undertake roles that are alternately active and passive. This feature represents the principal opposition at play in the distinction between monologue and dialogue, as elaborated by Mukařovský.

For Bakhtin, however, neither speaker is ever passive, even when silent. Rather, each is constantly engaged in an effort to rebutt, convince, or even mock the other while strategically modifying his position with respect to what has so far been articulated and in anticipation of what might yet be said. Such emphasis not only upon the role of the speakers but also upon that of their respective word serves to focus more sharply upon the complexity of dialogic interaction. For it goes beyond the simplistic recognition of heralding alternating speech as the fundamental dialogical principle by acknowledging the internal dynamics at play, at each respective pivotal moment, when one speaker's utterance serves to evoke a new considered dialogic response from the other. Neat in theory, dialogic engagement in *Doctor Zhivago*, as we shall see, is motivated at times quite differently.

Notwithstanding Bakhtin's elaborate typologies of inherent complexities and respondent strategies, it has been argued that "to be read as dialogue, a literary text or segment of a text must be divided into alternating speeches attributed to different speakers" (Veltruský 599). Interestingly, in conformity with such basic, minimal definition Bakhtin also has occasion to speak of dialogue in essentially the same terms.

> The boundaries of each concrete utterance as a unit of speech
> communication are determined by a change of speaking subjects,
> that is, a change of speakers. . . . One observes this change of
> speaking subjects most simply and clearly in actual dialogue
> where the utterances of the interlocutors or partners in dialogue
> . . . alternate. (*Speech* 71-72)

The Russian theorist thus acknowledges in telegraphic manner these
same basic suppositions but hints, significantly, at their entirely elementary character:

> The narrow understanding of dialogue as one of the composi-
> tional forms of speech (dialogic and monologic speech). One can
> say that each rejoinder in and of itself is monologic (the absolutely
> minimal monologue) and each monologue is a *rejoinder from a
> larger dialogue.* (117; emphasis added)

Dialogue is thus conceived on a fundamental level as being composed of
interlarded monologic speech elements. But to suggest that "the division
into speeches delivered by alternating interlocutors [is] the ultimate cri-
terion of what is a dialogue and what is not" (Veltruský 599) goes but a
short distance in providing an understanding of what intricacies are at
work in eliciting and maintaining dialogical interaction. On the other
hand, the notion of making rejoinder—during a seeming "monologic"
moment—to a certain "larger dialogue" accords greatly, as conceived
here, with the overall manifestation of dialogue found in *Doctor Zhivago.*
    While thus implicitly crediting the Prague School's fundamental
description of dialogue, Bakhtin further declares the importance of
interlarded monologic speech as *framed structures*, constituting individual texts of varying scope and dimension. The opening and closing
statements of an utterance represent the boundaries of speech that not
only initiate and conclude a given argument but also serve as points of
tangency, as it were, between the utterances of one speaker and
another. Within the monologic structures constituting dialogue, opening and closing statements are thus especially significant. "For they
are, so to speak, sentences of the 'front line' that stand right at the
boundary of the change of speech subjects" (Bakhtin, *Speech* 89 n. i).
Therefore, the question of what strategies go into the "framing" of an
utterance—that is, how the utterance is initiated and concluded—is
deemed crucial to an understanding of dialogic speech.
    This same concern is particularly appropriate when attempting to dis-
tinguish between the various modes of reported speech, especially

when the category of quasi-direct speech comes into play. A heightened awareness of the making and breaking of frames applies as well to the problem of isolating and distinguishing between various narrative voices and between shorter narratives or subtexts incorporated within the greater narrative. Thus it is observed that "the analyst must determine what shall count as the elementary units of narrative and investigate the ways in which they combine" (Culler, *Structuralist* 205). Such proposal is tantamount to arguing for a poetics of framing—of establishing the borders of a given text's subtexts or elementary units. To analyze the framing of the text and its constituent narrative components is crucial to the critical enterprise. As Bakhtin puts it: "In order to understand, it is first of all necessary to establish the principal and clear-cut boundaries of the utterance" (*Speech* 112). Yet, as *Doctor Zhivago* readily illustrates, discerning the borders of an utterance constituting a given monologue or dialogue (also a challenging distinction in this novel) may not be an easy task.

In considering the problem of monologue and dialogue as fundamental modes of verbal interaction within narrative, and as central to the elaboration of a general poetics of the novel, *this* novel will serve to illustrate both the broad applicability as well as inadequacy of the foregoing theoretical perspectives. In *Zhivago*, in other words, the preceding theory bears at times a striking relation to Pasternak's unusual novelistic technique—but, as might be expected, it applies at best in skewed fashion.

First, Bakhtin's emphasis upon the importance of a speaker's opening and closing statements appears somehow muted in *Doctor Zhivago* or motivated by a different set of aesthetic and ideological concerns than those theoretical views just outlined. Since the "dialogue" within the novel so often is composed of essentially isolated monologic statement, the opening and closing utterances, as previously instanced, do not so much function as borders or points of relative tangency between two sets of utterances as they serve principally to frame or set off the monologic fragment, which nevertheless has its place within the larger dialogue. Thus, when Bakhtin notes "the seams of the boundaries between utterances" (*Speech* 119), the question arises whether such "seams" are relevant to *Zhivago* and, if so, whether they do indeed show? Rather, one might better acknowledge that Pasternak has both revised and extended the concept of dialogue, so that the possibility of alternating monologic speech does not appear to account for the extended form of dialogue that informs the novel. In this work various characters carry on the work "toward the conquest of death," as Nikolai puts it, without necessarily being aware that such is their "work" or that others are engaged in that same effort. Nor are they likely to be aware that they are engaged with others in an ongoing dialogue concerned precisely with elaborating the nature of this endeavor as the making of art or the articulating of a life-affirming philosophy.

Second, let us return to Bakhtin's previously cited view that "each monologue is a rejoinder from a larger dialogue." Such theoretical standpoint represents a prominent compositional principle of Pasternak's novel, within which the larger dialogue is implicit but frequently obscured. As a result, there is also a strong sense of fragmentation in the work—of dialogue being abruptly resolved into a single monologic component expounded by a single speaker (most often the novel's protagonist) upon a variety of topics, including the nature of Marxism, the Revolution, the making of art, a general theory of history and theology. As a case in point, early in the novel Zhivago is asked to comfort his ailing future mother-in-law. The reader is informed: "And there and then he delivered a whole impromptu lecture" (67). That declaration may well serve as a hallmark statement to the novel in its entirety, containing numerous such instances, when either Zhivago, his shadowy uncle Nikolai, or the even less defined figure of Sima (in Varykino) all deliver "impromptu lectures" or, simply, extended monologues that are clearly fragments of a larger dialogue, to which these characters' various speeches contribute over the entire work.

Thus, Lara observes to Zhivago, regarding Sima: "You and she are extraordinarily alike in your views" (410), to which Zhivago later provides the (internal) dialogical response: "Of course, she's taken it all from Uncle Nikolai" (415), implicitly acknowledging the greater interwoven dialogue of the novel that, paradoxically, so frequently appears as monologue. Although Nikolai remains the original source of these views, when Sima remarks that "something in the world had changed. . . . Leaders and nations were relegated to the past" (413), she is, in effect, also echoing the views expressed by both Zhivago and Gordon during their earlier talk (IV:12). Such echo effects are achieved in the novel when the voices of its principal speakers (including Nikolai, Zhivago, Lara, and, to a lesser degree, Sima) ventriloquize a specific series of related ideas, with one voice predominating at times over the others, each of whose speech contributes an extended monologic piece within the novel's mosaic-like dialogic configurations. In accord with this supradialogic model, Zhivago observes upon overhearing the

women's talk that "they were having a conversation that was more like
a lecture Sima was delivering to her hostess" (410). Yet all such apparent monologues in the novel represent a composite supradialogue
(embracing "suprapersonal values" [de Mallac 319-25]), within which
the book's major themes—death and resurrection, art and immortality,
history and theology, revolution and dissolution—are expressed.

Nikolai initiates one such theme when he observes that "man does
not die in a ditch like a dog—but at home in history, while the work
toward the conquest of death is in full swing; he dies sharing in this
work" (10). At the same time in this early monologic speech he contributes to an incipient "dialogue" carried on by the protagonist and others—again, for the most part, as isolated speeches. Zhivago's extended
monologue at the ailing woman's bedside (III:3) is thus heralded by the
opening thematic one-word utterance, "resurrection," which serves as
epigraph to the speaker's theme at hand but might also fulfill a similar
function with regard to this fully developed theme in the novel, as initiated by Nikolai and further expressed in various related contexts by
Zhivago. He concludes by saying: "There will be no death because the
past is over; that's almost like saying there will be no death because it
is already done with, it's old and we are bored with it. What we need is
something new, and that new thing is life eternal" (67-68).[4] Zhivago
thus expresses, in poetic paraphrase, his uncle's philosophical thought.

When Nikolai reports in his notebook, "and then, into this tasteless
heap of gold and marble, He came . . . and at that moment gods and
nations ceased to be and man came into being" (43), he is here, too, ini-
tiating not only an important theme of the novel but also a related
extensive dialogue among its characters. Illustrating the point, a discussion between Zhivago and Gordon (treated in chapter 1 from a different perspective) begins with the bare stated fact: "Once again . . . it
was night, and they were talking" (119). Zhivago launches into an
account of how he had witnessed the unimpressive figure of the czar
reviewing his troops at the front: "I suppose that there were such things
as 'peoples' under the Caesars—Gauls or Scythians or Illyrians and so
on. But ever since, they have been mere fiction." (It is this viewpoint that
Sima will reiterate later in the novel.) He goes on to deny their viability
in the face of the New Age of individual man and concludes by decry-
ing that "facts don't exist until man puts into them something of his own,
a bit of free human genius—of myth." At this point, as another kind of
hallmark statement, and as a prelude to his own views, Gordon inter-
jects the remark: "And now I'll tell you what I think about the incident

we saw yesterday" (121). Similarly derived from Nikolai's teachings, his uninterrupted speech of two pages—typical of the novel's supradialogue—concludes the passage and the discussion.

Although of paramount importance (by virtue of their profound influence on Zhivago, among others), Nikolai's words are conveyed as direct speech only rarely. In fact, we hear from him for the last time relatively early in the novel (given his importance), when he bursts into the family's Moscow apartment, exclaiming: "They're fighting in the street. . . . You've got to see it. This is history. This happens once in a lifetime" (190). That the utterance is sounded by Nikolai is particularly appropriate, since he is the novel's main philosopher of history. Likewise, Zhivago is its premier analyst of the Revolution. The one is concerned principally with abstract philosophical and historical theory, the other with trying, against great odds, to sort out current events. One way in which the latter emerges as the preeminent hero of the novel is that, on numerous occasions, he is the only one given to speak—frequently, at length. Thus, at one point he says to Lara: "I'll go on talking. I'll talk for a long time. Just think what's going on around us" (146). He is also the one most given to air his views, publicly. When he proposes a toast at a family gathering (VI:4), he admonishes his guests, oddly, to "stop talking in the corners and listen carefully." On this occasion Zhivago likens the Revolution to a "sea of blood" that will sweep all before it (182). Shortly thereafter, however, he heralds the Revolution as being possessed of "genius. Only real greatness can be so unconcerned with timing and opportunity" (195). That one moment of appreciation for the cataclysm, however, is short-lived. "Only once in his life had this uncompromising language and single-mindedness filled him with enthusiasm. Was it possible that he must pay for that rash enthusiasm all his life?" (381).

During a moment of spectacular coincidence at the front, when the novel's extraordinary web of intertwined destinies is explicitly remarked, Lara, preoccupied with the thought of other than providential destiny, exhorts in response to the horror of war: "O God, O God . . . don't let me doubt that you exist" (118). Later, also at the front, late at night, Zhivago hears the wind intone his own personal plaint: "Tonia, Sasha, I miss you, I want to go home, I want to go back to work" (127). At the end, after Lara's departure from his life, he declares aloud: "Farewell, farewell. . . . Farewell, my only love, my love forever lost" (450). And then, as though "almost saying to the lingering afterglow," he states reassuringly—to no one: "Thank you, thank you, I'll be all right" (451). In all these instances the utterance is directed to absent addressees: God, as it were; Zhivago's wife and child; the love of his life; and thin air. These declarations, nonetheless, model the dialogic structures of the novel. For a speaker may just as well be addressing an absent other, so frequently is there no response forthcoming. What the speaker has to say may appear to sink in the void. In numerous instances, however, the evocation of an echo effect counters this otherwise gloomy impression with the sense of the speaker's word being transmuted within a series of ever enhanced meanings.

As another illustration of this echoing technique, Lara hears in church: "Blessed are the poor in spirit. . . . Blessed are they that mourn. . . . Blessed are they which do hunger and thirst after righteousness. . . . Happy are the downtrodden" (49-50). Lara perceives that the droning message is for her; she is its rightful addressee. Later, hurrying for shelter from the strikes, uprisings, and accompanying bullets, but feeling herself in harmony with those bullets, Lara perpetuates the message she has heard in church, echoing it in a different chord, however, as she now blesses those who are firing: "Blessed are the downtrodden. Blessed are the deceived. God speed you, bullets" (53). Similarly, in response to one of the many extraordinary coincidences that make of the novel a delicate latticework of intersecting destinies, Lara implicitly returns to her thoughts of an earlier time: "The boys are shooting. . . . Good, decent boys. . . . It's because they are good that they are shooting" (51). But now the boys who had played at insurrection have grown up and are men serving and dying within a defeated army. "And now they were shooting again, but how much more frightening it was now! You couldn't say, 'The boys are shooting' this time" (128). In both the case of the message received in church and of that formulated in her own heart, in response to the historic cataclysm she cannot escape, the sense of the original formulation is necessarily transmuted.

Retaining, by contrast, the original meaning of previous formulations, Lara's farewell speech to Zhivago is dialogic in the sense that she picks up unwittingly on themes, as a kind of response, that are articulated earlier by Zhivago in another context and with another interlocutor, about which she could not have known. Hence Zhivago observes (none too gently) to his captor, Liberius, the leader of the Forest Brotherhood, that the idea of "Reshaping life!" runs counter to his own philosophy of life. "People who can say that have never understood a thing about life" (338). His passionate observation is followed more than a hundred and fifty pages later by Lara's ironically triumphant declaration at Zhivago's bier: "But the small problems of practical life—things like the reshaping of the planet—these things, no thank you, they are not for us" (502). Once again, then, in the final scenes such echoes afford the sense of the characters in the novel contributing to a dialogue—contained within the bounds of the book for sure but nonetheless appearing as somehow borderless and unframed, without beginning or end.

There are several principal modes of presentation by which the dialogic interaction in the novel is truncated. In the barest possible mode, as noted, the fact that a certain dialogue has taken place represents all the information afforded the reader. This form appears as a kind of "pure" diegesis on the order of an official report. As a second possibility, only one character is given to speak, although the presence of other potential interlocutors is made clearly evident (precluding an instance of soliloquy). Third, in the absence of an "external" interlocutor, a character may engage in internal dialogue (or "inner speech"), frequently presented as a kind of dispute (and, partly, as quasi-direct speech).[5] Finally, a character's speech may be simply abbreviated, concluding, perhaps, elliptically. In all these generic instances the concept of dialogue, in its concrete sense, is retained as a principal characteristic.

Not only is dialogue carried on between two interlocutors, where perhaps only one of those present is speaking. There are also instances of dialogue between what Peirce calls "different phases of the ego" (4.6), in which a single figure is engaged in a kind of internal debate. Early in the novel we hear Komarovsky's contriving utterances (conveyed through Lara's recollections): "Good heavens, Lara, what an idea! I just wanted to show you my apartment. We're so near" (25). Lara's hesitation and doubts are communicated in Komarovsky's words; hers are not given. The passage is framed, however, by Lara's own related thoughts: "Mother is his—what's the word . . . He's mother's. . . . Then why does he look at me like that? I'm her daughter after all" (24). Here the novelist intrudes upon his burdened young heroine to situate "the girl from a different world" more securely in time and place. But her thoughts, in turn, are also made to obtrude—and finally to regain (as at the beginning of the passage) their prominent place, as the reader learns to what extent the girl is haunted by the stalking figure of the much older man. This information is conveyed in short alternating paragraphs containing Lara's ruminations followed by the novelist's interpolations, concluding in their seeming mergence, and thus rendering an effect of dialogue embedded within dialogue: the girl's internal discourse, which, it appears, is concurrently in dialogue with the novelist's observations.[6]

> It was all this waltzing that had started it. What a crazy business it was! . . . Of course, one reason why you allowed anyone to be so familiar was just to show how grown up you were.
>
> She could never have imagined that he danced so well. . . . She could never have dreamed there could be so much effrontery in anyone's lips when they were pressed for such a long time against your own.
>
> She must stop all this nonsense. Once and for all. . . . There loomed an imperceptible, a terrifying border-line. One step and you would be hurled into an abyss. (26)

The dialogic counterpart to Lara's earlier injunctions and admonitions appears somewhat later in the same chapter. Illustrating a modern instance of the pathetic fallacy,[7] the passage begins with the sound of raindrops pattering on metal and ends with their serving as nature's harmonious accompaniment to Lara's tears. Again, Lara's ruminations are interwoven within the novelist's description of events, with her tortured thoughts given deserved prominence. "How had it happened? How could it possibly have happened? It was too late now, she should have thought of it earlier. Now she was—what was it called?—a fallen woman. She was a woman out of a French novel. . . . O, God, O God, how did it happen?" (45). Earlier she had struggled to find the appropriate word that would pertain to her mother as Komarovsky's concubine. Now she must seek the word that applies to herself. The parallelism between the two sections is further heightened by the complementary sense of an internal dialogue embedded within a narrative fabric in which the sensibility of a young girl is interwoven with that of a mature perspective.

Section 6 of "The Hour of the Inevitable" is devoted to Pasha's like internal conflict concerning his life with Lara. Here the reader is at first provided a straightforward account of the couple's new life together in Yuriatin during the past four years. (We know that approximately that much time has passed only because there is noted the existence of a three-year-old daughter.) This is followed by an account of Pasha's thoughts during a sleepless night. He had become an insomniac, the reader is told, providing the occasion for him to come to a fatal decision that irrevocably affects his life and that of his family. His internal dialogue is rendered in quasi-direct speech that derives partly from the word of the author but that concludes with Pasha's own. "So what was he to do? He must set his wife and daughter free from this counterfeit life. This was even more important than to liberate himself. Yes, but how? Divorce? Drown himself? What disgusting rubbish! He rebelled against the very thought. 'As if I'd ever do anything of the sort! So why rehearse this melodrama even in my mind?'" This latter fragment is all that is provided directly. Yet the resolution to his internal debate is made clearly evident by the mention of an army train rolling through the night and into Pasha's consciousness. "Pasha Pavlovich smiled, got up, and went to bed. He had found a way out of his dilemma" (108).

In the following passage Lara reacts to a decision that is never verbalized. That Pasha makes some kind of response (whether verbal or nonverbal) to her tortured cries is implied in her speech but is also not reported. "Pasha, Pashenka . . . don't leave us. Don't do it, don't. . . . You're ashamed to change your mind? And aren't you ashamed to sacrifice your family to some crazy notion? You a volunteer! . . . Tell me honestly, for the love of Christ, without any fine phrases, is this really what Russia needs?" (109). In these two companion scenes Pasha ruminates on his married state and comes to an irreversible decision. Although likewise isolated in its presentation, Lara's poignantly detailed reply is nevertheless dialogic, since it is distinctly responsive—to a choice, however, that remains essentially opaque for Lara *and* the reader, who is left uninformed about the substance and manner in which Pasha's decision is communicated. Thus his necessarily isolated thoughts are paralleled by her similarly isolated verbal response. Further, on a higher thematic level Pasha and Lara's lack of communication is later contrasted by Lara and Zhivago's special communion.

As a related form of internal discourse, Zhivago's diary (composed at Varykino and paralleling Nikolai's writings as a kind of incorporated subtext) similarly deserves note. Within its pages he reports on the state of his carrot and radish supplies, ruminates on the mystery of childbirth, the phenomenon of dreams, and on the nature of a "secret, unknown force, an almost symbolic figure," or "hidden benefactor," needed in everyone's life (277-87). Although it is reported that Evgraf, in fulfilling this role in Zhivago's life, spent some two weeks in Varykino, not a word of the brothers' (presumed) talks is communicated to the reader. Rather, we are informed that "he went often to Yuriatin, and then vanished suddenly as if the earth had swallowed him" (287). Curiously, much the same can be said for virtually all of the characters of the novel.

Their life stories are never so much completed as they themselves seem summarily to disappear from the scene. Thus, Zhivago "broke through the crowd . . . took a step, another, a third . . . and did not get up again" (491). While "one day Larisa Feodorovna went out and did not come back. . . . She vanished without a trace and probably died somewhere" (503). In such manner are the two main characters dispatched.

Upon Lara's disappearance from his life, Zhivago's internal debate ("What have I done? What have I done?" [449]) takes on complex form. Usurping, as it were, the author's role, he projects Lara's supposed thought as extended monologue of his own invention. This projected thought is framed by his suppositions. "She is thinking: It's wonderful that things have gone so well, they couldn't be better. . . . That's what she must be thinking" (450). His unrelenting inner turmoil is matched by a like complexity of thought, whose dynamics are explained thus: "A double monologue was going on in his mind, two different kinds of monologue, the one dry and businesslike, the other addressed to Lara, like a river in a flood." The moments of grief and havoc are conveyed, then, by a "double monologue," complemented, however, by a clear dialogic response to her absent being: "Farewell, Lara . . . farewell, my love, my inexhaustible, everlasting joy." One line of thought is directed toward practical concerns ("The first job is to survive"), the other (addressed to Lara) toward the making of art: "This is how I will portray you. . . . That was how life's storm cast you up on my shore, O my pride, that is how I'll portray you" (451-52).

Similar to internal dialogue, but greatly extended and fragmented, a character may appear to be in dialogue with himself without necessarily being aware of the fact. This is particularly so regarding the subject of art and art making. Zhivago tells his ailing mother-in-law, quoting St. John, "There will be no death" (68). Later, preoccupied with thoughts of death, he ruminates on the making of art. "More vividly than ever before he realized that art has two constant, two unending concerns: it always meditates on death and thus always creates life. All great, genuine art resembles and continues the Revelation of St. John" (89-90). These (present) thoughts are a continuation of those accorded Tonia's mother and are thus internally dialogic, transcending immediate temporal considerations. In addition, they also represent a fuller development of Nikolai's thought and are thus a continuation of the extended dialogue that Zhivago and others maintain with their mentor throughout the novel. From this important related perspective the voice of the dimly sketched Nikolai is the most resonant in the novel. Virtually all of the philosophical debate, whether it be internal, and the property of a single character, or more overtly dialogical, echoes that voice from which it all emanates.

The quality of voice per se bears a special value in the novel. At the very beginning Zhivago, as a child, hears the voice of his mother calling to him. "The ghost of his mother's voice was hallucinatingly present in the meadows. He heard it in the musical phrases of the birds and the buzzing of the bees. Now and then he imagined with a start that his mother was calling him" (11). Later, as an adult, he hears a woman's voice in a dream (283), which, later still, he recognizes as belonging to Lara (291). After Lara's departure from his life the significance of his mother's voice and Lara's merge. "As in his childhood, when after his mother's death he heard her voice in the bird calls . . . so now his hearing, accustomed to Lara's voice and expecting it as part of his life, played tricks on him and he heard her calling, 'Yurochka!' from the next room" (454-55).

At times a proliferation of unknown voices attains a certain prominence. As with the voices of the women in his life, these may bear a positive connotation, and are themselves intrinsically valuable. Their existence alone is life affirming, such as "the voices of children playing in the streets coming from varying distances as if to show that the whole expanse is alive" (391). Or they may be voices heralding uncertainty. Thus, part 1 ends with a clamor of voices: "Big news! Street fighting in Petersburg! . . . The revolution!" (128). Beyond the climactic immediacy of the moment, however, such clamor, representing the varied manifestations of isolated speech, model, in effect, the sense of incipient dialogue characteristic of the novel. Although a certain paucity of dialogue has also been registered here, the complementary recognition of its ever-present *potential* is an important related feature that dramatically illustrates Bakhtin's view that an inherent propensity toward dialogue is a distinctive property of language. That view is especially evidenced by the sense of a chorus, repeatedly projected, each of whose member voices contributes to an awareness of the reigning chaos, confusion, and vitality of the time. The feeling of such turbulence is accomplished either by a cacophony of voices all speaking, seemingly, at once or by a series of isolated voices, each enunciating only a single utterance.

In the entire chapter "The Highway," for instance, there are only a few speakers already known to the reader. The others are invented ad hoc, it seems, to articulate some fleeting sentiment or point of view. In such cases the utterance takes precedence over the character expressing it;

that is, the speech of the unknown figure is more important than the speaker, who exists within a melee of voices, in order to have a single ephemeral say. This factor is evidenced consistently at generic "grass-roots" meetings (VI:12; X:6), at which elemental, raw human emotion is conveyed in this manner. When goaded by Gints in the beginning of the novel to remember their duty, army deserters respond in threatening cacophony. "Several hundred voices rose in an uproar. . . . hate-filled, hysterical trebles predominated: 'The nerve! Just like in the old days! These officers still treat us like dirt. So we're traitors are we?'" (153). Frequently, the chorus is composed of anonymous voices, which are acknowledged as such: "'scoundrels,' yelled voices in the queue" (216). "Bewildered voices rose from the group" (226). Fragments of dialogue are thus "snatched" from speakers, as, for example, from those catering to, and those riding, the train to the Urals.

> "Hey, you! Where are you off to? Where's my money? . . . Stop!
> Stop . . . I've been robbed! Stop, thief! There he goes, that's him,
> catch him!"
> "Which one?"
> "That one, the one who's clean-shaven and grinning."
> "Is that the one with the hole in his sleeve?"
> "Yes, yes, catch him, the heathen!"
> "The one with the patched elbow?"
> "Yes, yes. Oh, I've been robbed."
> "What's going on here?"
> "Fellow over there bought some milk and pies . . . and went off
> without paying."
> "That shouldn't be allowed. Why don't they go after him?"
> "Go after him! He's got straps and cartridge belts all over him.
> "He'll go after you." (219-20)

Those who are armed and released from work details have their anonymous say as well. "Hey, Grandfather! I'm not shirking, I'm too young to work, my nanny won't let me." "Hey, Marva, don't saw off your skirt, you'll catch cold!" "Hey, young one, don't go to the wood, come and be my wife instead!" (240). Others are less secure and filled with fear.

> "Well, we're in for it. Now we'll never go."
> "Yes. It won't be soon."
> "It's an armored express—must be Strelnikov."
> "Must be him."
> "He's a wild beast when it comes to counterrevolutionaries." (235)

Most poignant, perhaps, and vital as well, are the voices of those condemned by their fellows of the Forest Brotherhood.

> "Forgive me, comrades. I'm sorry, I won't do it again, please let me off. Don't kill me. I haven't lived yet. I want to live a little longer, I want to see my mother just once more. Please let me off comrades, please forgive me."

> "Good comrades, kind comrades! Is this possible? In two wars we fought together! We stood up and fought for the same things! Let us off, comrades, have pity on us. We'll repay your kindness, we'll be grateful to you all our lives."

> "Judas! Christ-killer! If we are traitors, you are a traitor three times over, you dog, may you be strangled."

> "Don't humble yourself! . . . We die as martyrs for our ideals at the dawn of the world revolution. Long live the revolution of the spirit! Long live world anarchy!" (355)

In a novel notable for its sparseness of direct discourse, not only is the quality of isolated speech, or voice per se, an equally noteworthy feature but, paradoxically, so is dialogue itself a category bearing a strong positive value. At times this is made emphatic, even hyperbolic: Lara and Zhivago's "subdued conversations, however casual, were as full of meaning as the dialogues of Plato" (395). At others it is clearly implicit. When Strelnikov emerges from the snow-covered expanse into the realm of candlelight for the final time, the reader is informed that he and Zhivago "had been talking for hours. They talked as only Russians in Russia can talk, particularly as they talked then, desperate and frenzied as they were in those anxious, frightened days" (456). Strelnikov, we are told, "was evidently keeping to himself some important secret that burdened him, while pouring out his heart all the more effusively on every other subject" (457). Those subjects are briefly and sporadically sketched, while his "secret" suicide plan is poetically rendered shortly thereafter as "red beads that looked like rowanberries" spilled on the early morning snow (464). Their talk is effectively completed, however, and its autotelic quality made evident, when Lara is informed at the end by Yevgraf of its having taken place, to which she responds: "Well, thank God, thank God, that's better" (497).

In this work, replete with hallmark statements, Lara's remark—broadly extended—serves to affirm the value placed on dialogue in its varied modes of expression and completion. This includes dialogue as generic to exchanges among individuals well known to each other ("They had dialogues of this sort" [179]); dialogue in its most incipient stages, as isolated voices within a seeming chorus of elliptical, inconclusive speech; and internal dialogue conducted by a single soul in dispute with itself. It also includes speech that, appearing to be monologic, more accurately represents a continued supradialogue, expressed as a series of sustained echoes that responds to an original series of thoughts and ideas, whose richness bears continued refraction from new perspectives. Moreover, from the present perspective what appears monologic in the novel may well be conceived as dialogic; first, when it constitutes either an overt or "hidden" *response* to some utterance made (in speech or in thought) by a given character, transformed, in effect, into a displaced interlocutor; and, second, when it represents, as we have just seen in the case of Zhivago and Strelnikov, an essentially unwitting response (by Lara) completing *their* dialogue, whose extraneous completion is entirely consistent with the novel's overall thematic plan.

As a concluding hallmark statement drawn from the novel but highly applicable to the present endeavor, we read: "This is a transitional period, when there is still a gap between theory and practice" (260). While that surmise (in a variety of contexts) will very likely always apply, the case of *Doctor Zhivago* nevertheless goes a long way toward showing that art, in oblivious and felicitous fashion, always somehow confounds theory. And, in their related modes of development, both are likely the better for it. Yet, within a framework of potential cross-fertilization, art and theory also provide each other a source and justification for their respective existence as well. Thus, in referring to "real dialogue," conceived as "daily conversation, scientific discussion, political debate," Bakhtin, in effect, makes the point of this chapter, when he declares:

> The relations among rejoinders of such dialogues are a simpler and more externally visible kind of dialogic relations. But dialogic relations, of course, do not in any way coincide with relations among rejoinders of real dialogue—they are much broader, more diverse, and more complex. Two utterances, separated from one another both in time and in space, knowing nothing of one another, when they are compared semantically, reveal dialogic relations if there is any kind of semantic convergence between them (if only a partially shared theme, point of view, and so forth). . . . Dialogic relations are thus much broader than dialogic speech in the narrow sense of the word. And dialogic relations are always present, even among profoundly monologic speech works. (*Speech* 124-25)

Should *Doctor Zhivago* appear "profoundly monologic," it has been my intent here to demonstrate that it is in appearance only. For, in the terms just outlined, Pasternak's novel may well be understood to be governed by a dialogic poetics, articulating in a variety of ways—through echo and chorus effects, by means of temporally and spatially "displaced" dialogic response, and, paradoxically, through extended, seemingly monologic speech—the principle that human communication is effected freely by individuals participating in the human drama, on numerous planes, unbounded by time and space, as in life itself.

Literary Models: Practical Conclusions

■ ☐ ■

In the introductory pages I argue, in sum, that a model is devised to provide an interpretation. It establishes a conceptual framework that facilitates the formulation of ideally convincing hypotheses. Several questions yet remain to be answered. How does a model serve to accomplish this? Just what is it that we want to accomplish? What limitations, in other words, might we wish to put on a model for the express purpose of literary, rather than scientific, analysis? And is there some difference in aims and intentions between these two modes of approach?

Science, for one thing, takes into account mechanical models, three-dimensional constructs designed to appear isomorphic (that is, exact in detail and relations, if not in size) with respect to the subject at hand. This concept of model clearly has no place within our purview or within the study of literature. Since its object of study belongs to the mind, to metaphysical issues rather than physical realia, literary analysis naturally employs abstract models for its investigations. Such has been the case uniformly in the chapters that compose this book. Models employed in literary study are necessarily abstract, we may assume, since they are meant to correlate with works of the imagination.

To understand better this fundamental correlation, we need note that all of human communication is embraced by signs that are either verbal or visual. As Lotman observes: "Over the entire history of mankind, no matter how far back we penetrate, we find two independent and equal cultural signs: the word and the picture. Each of them has its own history. But for the development of culture it seems that the presence of both types of sign system is necessary" (*Cinema 5*). The same may be true of individual literary models and of modeling systems in general. Dependent though they are upon narrative, a mode of communication that is purely verbal, each of the models belonging to the preceding chapters can be derived either from verbal or visual forms. That is, with regard to the latter, we have (wittingly and unwittingly) utilized ideal conceptual frameworks that can be pictured and are therefore of invoking a certain psychological, visual representation—one, in other words, that can be conceived in the mind even if it has not been drawn. As Peirce felicitously puts it: "that which is displayed before the mind's gaze" (4.531), or, at least, can be displayed, as I claim here. At the same time, of course, we have also employed models that are purely abstract, which is to say, purely verbal, and which practically could not be diagrammed for the purpose of literary criticism and analysis.

In terms of the three rubrics comprising this book—temporal, spatial, and dialogic relations—it would of course be impossible to treat every conceivable manifestation of each such relation. Yet these discussions are nonetheless meant to be broadly inclusive. Hence the first chapter, as I have argued, provides a paradigm of linearity in narrative designed to encompass all instances of chronological inversion. The following chapter treats time in its immediacy as momentary and momentous, as opposed to conceiving it (in chapter 3) as endlessly extended and endured. Thus, within a theoretically infinite range of possible linear inversion stands "the moment of revelation" at one end of the spectrum and "memory as duration" at the other. Essentially the same such argument, mutatis mutandis, holds for the rest of the book.

Part 2 likewise treats two opposing spatial aspects, convergence and divergence, where the latter is conceived to open the text to further exploration and consideration, while the former seeks to bring it to a close in presenting a conclusive resolution. Both, as we have seen, incorporate the potential for a labyrinthine search for answers and for the development of the same. Beginning with two mutually exclusive considerations, part 2 closes (chapter 6) with the ancient concept of the labyrinth as a model that incorporates both these opposing considerations within an (again, theoretically) infinitely complex configuration of narrative possibility. Similarly, in the concluding triad of chapters the respective discussions range from silence as a mode of communication to what we have termed *supradialogue*, where the one may be said to "precede" responsive speech, while the other goes beyond it. Encompassing a broad spectrum of communicative possibility, part 3, then, also reveals itself as being broadly inclusive of a subject whose manifestations are manifold.

Each chosen model throughout the book introduces a key concept as the hub from which all of the spokes, as it were, of the given argument extend. That common metaphor (from among much of the figurative expression employed here) may be diagrammatically rendered in quick order. The same is true of our model of linear relations, particularly in terms of its syntagmatic frames, or subtexts, within the greater narrative text. By projecting a single plane, in other words, with references to past and future indicated as forward and backward "movement" along that plane, such linear relations might readily find their pictorial representation. This is not true, however, for our remaining treatments of time in narrative. For the two diametrically opposed concepts of epiphany and duration clearly do not lend themselves to diagrammatic representation. They remain verbal and abstract, although nonetheless useful and meaningful as core conceptual frameworks in confronting a necessarily endless series of idiosyncratic representations of novelistic time.

Parts 2 and 3 of the book are contrastive in at least one sense: all of the spatial considerations of the former may be diagramatically conceived, yet none of the concerns of the latter may be likewise visually rendered. The linked concepts of convergence and divergence may thus be depicted as the closing or opening of a cone, or as two sets of vectors superimposed upon the same conic image directed oppositely. Similarly, the labyrinth (in its various manifestations) requires no elaboration as to how it may be visually represented. In contrast, the central notions of part 3—silence, the "nondialogic encounter," and supradialogue—do not lend themselves to pictorial representation. Concentrating on dialogic relations, they remain rooted in purely verbal, abstract concerns that necessarily and exclusively correspond with the word as sign rather than with the sign as picture. Yet, corresponding with these two primordial, universal sign forms of human communication, there appears an overall correlation with models as conceptual tools for exploration and investigation. How we as human beings communicate, in other words, may correspond in terms of these two basic sign forms with the like endeavor of seeking to create analogous forms by which to explicate and elucidate. Like metaphor, the model (as analogue) may similarly be shown, then, to have its roots in the most basic modes of human communication. From this speculative intimation I will return to two final considerations: a brief assessment of my overall goals and intentions in the employment of models as conceptual tools and how they may relate generally to the aims of literary, as opposed to scientific, modes of inquiry.

Efforts to elaborate a comprehensive theory of literature found an early spokesman in the Russian Formalist Boris Eikhenbaum, who, in the 1920s, remarked with a certain optimism: "It has at last become clear that a science of literature, inasmuch as it is not merely a part of the history of culture, must be an independent and specific science with its own field of specific problems" (O'Toole and Shukman 17). Should that view eventually be realized, literary study might then take its place as an accepted discipline within the proliferating community of recognized sciences. And that at a time of renascence that has grown incrementally. Hence a contemporary critic's accurate discernment that "literary criticism has . . . become a professional activity as never before" (Brooks vii) appears a gross understatement today. What this revitalization has entailed, in part, has been a current widespread commitment to the revival of poetics as a systematic theory of literature designed to account for the special way in which meaning is produced within verbal art. Let us suppose, then, that a concern with elaborating a poetics or all-embracing theory of even a single genre therefore legitimately constitutes the literary theorist's principal concern.

As a contrastive position, however, it might be postulated that the absolute individuality of the artistic text be regarded as a diametrically opposed counterpoint to the concept of an all-encompassing theory. This view might likely proclaim the text as fundamentally irreducible to certain common elements (beyond such generalized features as plot, character, and setting as essential components). Were it to be deemed otherwise, the argument would run, the work would ultimately be divested of its definitive sui generis aspect. But, as a correlary to this opposing view, the very concept of genre would of necessity be logically reduced to only a theoretical concern largely devoid of the potential for practical application. Such a contrastive viewpoint declares the individual work unique by definition, requiring, therefore, that it be analyzed independently and exclusively. From this same hypothetical standpoint, moreover, there can be no convincing, logical basis for the elaboration of a general poetics; rather, there may evolve through independent efforts at concrete literary criticism only the "poetics" of the single individual text.

Since the endeavor to establish a viable poetics is intended to embrace an entire series of works, or specific genre among many, this view would appear logically incapable of accommodating such an effort. Yet the same position must also be assessed positively with regard to its affirmation of the primacy and autonomy of the work itself, as opposed to subordinating its originality and unique quality to the periodically proclaimed need for a consistent and uniform method of interpretation. The suggested opposition between these two hypothetical contrary positions thus reduces to the question of whether to attribute a certain primacy to the highly particularized encoding process, by which the work comes into being as a unique entity, or to privilege a presumably effective, broadly applicable decoding procedure by which it might be convincingly analyzed. Although conveniently employing a kind of shorthand here (which should not obscure the distinct difference in roles between that of writer and critic), what is at stake between these two opposing views is nevertheless adequately expressed in such spare terms.

From this seeming opposition appear two mutually opposed stands: one proclaiming the possibility at least of realizing an incipient, all-embracing poetics or theory of genre; the other insisting upon the "inviolable sanctity" of the individual literary text. Yet both views reflect independent, positive values: the former affirms a potential scientific legitimacy for literary criticism; the latter asserts the unequivocal hegemony of the text itself. Hence the literary theorist is consistently challenged to establish a synthesis between the two, whereby the single text retains its individuality and specificity, while at the same time its place as part of an established genre, following a set of conventional norms and constraints within that genre, is likewise implicitly acknowledged. This synthesis affording a balanced, generally accepted viewpoint, presupposes first of all an effective genre theory that would establish the place of the work within the basic categories of literary discourse. One need not, in other words, define ad hoc one's subject of inquiry when there already exists a common—perhaps not fully delineated—regard for what that subject entails. In yielding an analysis of a given work aimed at being systematic and, in this sense, scientific, however, it is necessary for the researcher to ground further one's efforts within a certain ordering principle or "pattern of coherence," designed to yield a more general, potentially useful methodological approach.

In elaborating a model affording that needed framework, the critic may take recourse in concrete or metaphorical terms, in purely verbal or pictorial expression, which, in all cases, would yield a descriptive model, encompassing through a certain abstract schema the principles defining and delimiting the subject at hand. Yet, in striving to provide a systematic study, it is a feature peculiar to contemporary literary criticism—but one central to the problem addressed here—that the critic is obliged at each instance of critical engagement and from within a vast multitude of distinct critical approaches to elaborate seemingly ad hoc the appropriate "theoretical framework" that would afford the particular study its conviction and credibility. But, once having elaborated that descriptive model, designed to evoke the bounds by which the subject is defined, the critic is then far better equipped to accomplish his chosen analytical task.

If at the same time, however, a detailed methodology applicable not only to the given instance is delineated, yielding a potentially instructive occasion for other critical ventures, the model employed might then be designated as not solely descriptive in function but also, on some level, prescriptive. In affording a kind of procedural sketch in perhaps sequential and hierarchical order, such a model would offer a more detailed manner of approach or concrete methodology. Since the emphasis falls upon procedure as an even more inclusive framework, the prescriptive feature—or series of strategies intended to account, ideally, for all possible instances—is then superimposed upon the descriptive. The descriptive aspect of this hypothetical, combinative model then would account for the possible interaction among the constituent features of the given subject, while the prescriptive aspect would detail a method by which other related generic considerations could be subjected to further critical analyses. The purely descriptive model attempts, then, to explain *what* it is that confronts the critic; the prescriptive suggests *how* it might be integrated within an ordered analysis. One provides a description of a single given case exclusively; the other offers a more generalized analytical strategy.

It therefore remains to consider certain implications regarding the potential for what has been termed—perhaps prematurely (for more than a half-century)—a "science" of literature. The idea of a science of literary studies is here understood to refer to the establishment and application of a systematic set of premises upon which individual efforts at literary criticism might be founded. This challenging proposition can be approached in the necessarily delimited terms of the two prior distinctions. First, by analogy with the previously posited definition of a theoretical descriptive model, such purported science is conceived in terms of its ability to provide ordered information in systematic fashion. To be defined as necessary, codified, and standardized, literary terms would be ordered according to specific interrelations or hierarchies, the latter to be determined in their turn. According to such a hypothetical program, detailed schemata (or descriptive models) would be derived from broad conceptual frameworks, allowing for individual literary works to be described and analyzed. Second, analogous to the prescriptive aspect of the previously proposed model, it might encompass a "normative" mode, intended to elucidate a concrete, broadly applicable methodology. In this generic instance such emphasis engenders the ability to specify a method by which the researcher might proceed with his specialized endeavor. Rather than be confronted solely by a set of terms and their possible interrelations, the critic is presented, in however broad fashion, a practical mode for their application.

A science of literature, conceived in terms of the first theoretical model exclusively, may thus be viewed as a form of genre theory, affording the ordered presentation of descriptive information. Or, determined in terms of the latter prescriptive mode, incorporated within the former as an additional aspect, and yielding a certain further methodological guidance, it would be constituted as a more complex, combinative, or bipartite model. But whether the latter may indeed suit the purposes of literary criticism, and, more important, the vast heterogeneous construct—the institution of literature as a whole—upon which it is founded, constitutes a final consideration. For, in response to the question, still contested, as to where the text is ultimately located, the critic may argue that the text "must be in the mind of the reader: it is the product of the interaction between the structures the author has provided and the structuring energies of our minds. So each generation, each social group, each individual reader creates his own text; in fact . . . each time we read, we create a new text" (O'Toole 225-26).

Clearly, if one conceives of the text in such terms, the likelihood of promoting or adhering to a prescriptive approach would be largely precluded, since the focus of attention—the literary work itself—is transmuted according to the conceptions and experience of its perceiver. Whether the question, then, is formulated in terms of current reader-centered notions or by attributing to the work itself a certain polysemic quality, a positively assessed ambiguity, there appears, in either case, a peculiar state of flux clearly not to be nailed down by any single prescriptive method. Instead, the work may more likely be considered from the perspective of various descriptive models, each potentially capable of revealing certain notable features through the close interaction of the artistic text and related, complementary model—one, moreover, that implicitly heralds the importance of devising models that recognize the individualized use of language as the basic material constituent of verbal art.

As Bakhtin rightly argues, "Language in the novel not only represents, but itself serves as the object of representation" (*Dialogic* 49). In the making of a model (as in the entire critical enterprise), that "object" must be given its originary, basic due. Hence the critic must strive to seek a balance between the application of language-oriented models and the individual linguistic usage of the given writer's own specialized idiom. As a result of this endeavor, literature is granted, first (and as it should be), its special status as a unique semiotic system, where one code is prominently embedded within another—the literary within the linguistic.

Further, this understanding illustrates Lotman's notion of literature as a secondary modeling system, derived from and modeled upon natural language as the primary one. While the latter "system" is represented by human language in all its multifarious manifestations, the former is conceived to embrace the full range of humanity's other communicative mechanisms, including art, first of all, in its unlimited proliferation. From this standpoint the individual work of art as a unique representative instance of a secondary modeling system would be acknowledged as such by the proposed implementation of a descriptive model that implicitly recognizes its sui generis status as an original and unrepeatable language construct. Yet that work would reflect as well an individual poetics that at once partakes of the generic norm, while generating a superimposed code that is strictly its own.

One theorist observes in judicious fashion that "semiotics can only define experimentally (which means text by text) the procedures adopted—these form part of a catalogue that must always remain open" (Segre, *Semiotics* 23). He makes a good point, particularly in the case of literary studies, which inherently acknowledges as axiomatic the individual literary text as unique. Yet, by adopting procedures that include the employment of models that are necessarily open to modification, revision, and therefore ad hoc adaptation, we are in a position to proceed beyond the ongoing contribution of single entries into that always-to-remain-open catalogue. This is not to restate, or reformulate, the structuralist call for broadly applicable global constructs but, rather, to affirm, in theory and practice, the need for literary study to acknowledge the concept of model as basic both to its overall theoretical approach and corresponding individual analyses in the study of literature in general and narrative texts in particular.

NOTES

Chapter 1

1. As Genette puts it: "To study the temporal order of a narrative is to compare the order in which events or temporal sections are arranged in the narrative discourse with the order of succession these same events or temporal segments have in the story, to the extent that story order is explicitly indicated by the narrative itself or inferable from one or another direct clue" (35). This understanding essentially defines our project here.

   Further, time in the novel may be either static or dynamic. In the former case the narrative is occupied (for some number of pages, rather than a period of novelistic time) with description. Time is employed in a "dynamic" sense during the narration of events (Mendilow 23). It is this latter dynamic aspect, in its various linear manifestations, that will serve as our present focus.

2. In critical discussions of this "constant," however, a crucial distinction often appears blurred, as when theorists define the story *(fabula)* as "the representation of the action in its chronological order and causal relations" (Fokkema 40). Or: "What characterizes the *fabula* is by definition its chronological and causal ordering of events." The two considerations may not be readily equated, however, because "causal logic does not coincide with temporal logic, even if it implies it" (Segre, *Structures* 40, 21).

   As Barthes affirms: "Indeed, there is a strong presumption that the mainspring of the narrative activity is to be traced to that very confusion between consecutiveness and consequence, what-comes-*after* being read in a narrative as what-is-*caused-by*. . . . narrative, on account of its very structure, tends to establish a confusion between consecutiveness and consequence, between time sequence and logic" (248, 251). Or, as Aristotle put it long ago: "It makes a great difference whether . . . events are the result of . . . others or merely follow them" (*Poetics* 1452a21). A succession of events may thus not be immediately inferred as being causally related by virtue of their simply being sequentially ordered.

3. While the reader first of all "faithfully follows the itinerary of the plot, a synthesis progressively added up in memory constantly tends to rearrange itself into *fabula*, in other words, to acquire and take into account each new clarification concerning the logical-temporal order of events. . . . Even before serving as a theoretical hypothesis, the *fabula* is thus an absolutely essential moment in understanding a narrative text" (Segre, *Structures* 18).

4. Mendilow implicitly equates these two basic concepts: "The story proper, or in other words, the fictive present" (104). Genette terms the same concept "the first narrative" (48). It is initiated, Sternberg contends, by "the author's finding it to be the first time section that is 'of consequence enough' to deserve full scenic treatment [and] turns it, implicitly but clearly, into a conspicuous signpost, signifying

that this is precisely the point in time that the author has decided . . . to make the reader regard as the beginning of the action proper" (20).

5. "One of the traditional resources of literary narration," *anachrony* is defined as "all forms of discordance between the two temporal orders of story and narrative"— that is, "discourse" or "plot" (Genette 36, 40). Sternberg argues for further distinctions between *fabula* and *sjuzhet*, story and plot (8-14), while Chatman makes his axis of distinction "story" and "discourse," in accord with the title of his book— all of which makes common currency a thing of the future.

6. As Genette rightly observes, "a narrative can do without anachronies" (88). But as Rimmon-Kenan points out: "Strict linear chronology . . . is a conventional 'norm' which has become so widespread as to replace the actual multilinear temporality of the story and acquire a pseudo-natural status" (17). With more than one character, in other words, each may follow his own time sequence within the various episodes comprising the plot. But while the account may indeed unfold on as many levels as there are characters, here we will essentially follow the conventional norm, which affords a "unilinear" impression within those episodes.

7. "Narrative thus appears as a succession of tightly interlocking mediate and immediate elements" (Barthes 270). Conversely, "the literary text may be conceived of as a dynamic system of gaps" (Sternberg 50).

8. As Genette points out: "The ellipsis, or leap forward without any return, is obviously not an anachrony but a simple acceleration of the narrative" (43).

9. These distinctions essentially correspond to Genette's categories of external analepsis, internal analepsis, and mixed analepsis, respectively. Following his broadest delineations, such retrospective views serve to inform the reader of various "antecedents," to "fill in, after the event, an earlier gap in the narrative," or to retrace what has already been covered by it, thereby allowing for "the narrative's allusions to its own past" (50, 52, 54).

10. Or, as Bakhtin puts it: "Language in the novel not only represents, but itself serves as the object of representation" (*Dialogic* 49).

11. For indices are "integrative units. . . . bits of *information* used to identify or pinpoint certain elements of time and space" (Barthes 246, 249).

12. As Mendilow expresses it, "the essence of drama in fiction lies in the creation of a feeling of a fictive present which moves forward" (131).

13. Yet in *Anna Karenina* "time flows differently for different characters" (Alexandrov 160), since "temporal indicators" show that certain characters (Kitty and Levin) at times lag behind others (Anna and Vronsky) by as much as nine months. To accommodate this feature our model would have to be "drawn" with a segmented primary plane to account for the several main plot lines comprising Tolstoy's novel.

14. The proleptic (anticipatory) segment may even extend into some never-to-be depicted future domain, as with the closing lines of *Crime and Punishment* and *Resurrection*, respectively.

> But that is the beginning of a new story, the story of the gradual renewal of a man, of his gradual regeneration, of his slow progress from one world to another, of how he learned to know a hither-to undreamed of reality. All that might be the subject of a new tale, but our present one is ended. (Dostoevsky 527)

> That night a new life began for Nekhludov, not because the conditions of his life were altered, but because everything that happened to him from that time

held an entirely new and different meaning for him. Only the future will show how this new chapter of his life will end. (Tolstoy 430)

15. The same might apply when the concern is less lofty or less philosophically weighty, as when Tolstoy comments in *War and Peace* on doctors and the practice of medicine: "It is the work of their life to undertake the cure of disease, because it is for that they are paid, and on that they have wasted the best years of their life" (612).

16. "By transferring the events to the mental plane, [interior monologue] can dispense with ordinary chronological sequence and forward moving continuity; for these are valid only by external standards, and have no justification (apart from the convenience of the reader) in the evocation of mental processes where associative memory follows purely private and individual laws of sequence" (Mendilow 75).

17. As Meyerhoff explains: "the inner world of experience and memory exhibits a structure which is causally determined by *significant associations* rather than by objective causal connections in the outside world. To render this peculiar structure, therefore, requires a symbolism or imagery in which the different modalities of time—past, present, and future—are not serially, progressively, and uniformly ordered, but are always inextricably and dynamically associated and mixed up with each other" (23-24).

18. Gleb Struve argues that Tolstoy "was probably the first major European writer to make a conscious and extensive use" of interior monologue ("Monologue" 1110).

19. These related theoretical concepts are applied critically to *The Brothers Karamazov* in Danow, *Dialogic* 167-98.

20. Mukařovský explains further: "Motivation is a basic requirement of plot construction. . . . On account of reciprocity, motivation has at the same time a progressive and a regressive character. When the initial member of a motivational bond appears, it evokes an expectation in the perceiver; the next then directs the perceiver's attention backwards to what has already been perceived" ("Detail" 198-99).

21. Following Tomashevsky's terminology, indexical signs that generate further text may be equated with the conception of *dynamic motifs*, which "are central to the story and which keep it moving"; indices that serve only to anticipate may be regarded as equivalent to *static motifs*, which "do not change the situation" (139).

In accord with Tomashevsky's distinctions, Barthes posits the linked concepts of "cardinal functions" or "nuclei" and the less significant "catalyses," where the latter "are no more than consecutive units," while the former "are both consecutive and consequential . . . the risk-laden moments of narrative" (248).

Chapter 2

1. Various critics acknowledge this feature of the novel. "*Doctor Zhivago* inevitably acquires something of the effect of a series of epiphanies" (Payne 172). "Pasternak's [art] is poetry of the epiphany; each self-enclosed mirror-like moment reflects the universe, and all of them build up to a great summation. . . . Indeed, the whole of *Doctor Zhivago* is an epiphany" (Muchnik 391-92). "The book presents, as it were, an invitation to share some mysterious and beautiful insight into life" (Silbajoris 19).

"No image can replace the intuition of duration," writes Bergson (*Metaphysics* 27-28), "but many diverse images, borrowed from very different orders of things, may, by the convergence of their action, direct consciousness to the precise point where there is a certain intuition to be seized." That "seizing," so to speak, corresponds to what we refer to here as an instance of epiphany.

2. A sense of fragmentation in the novel has been remarked upon in various ways. "Pasternak's novel consists of a chain of loosely connected parables" (Dyck 120). Each chapter is divided into "short vignettes" (Rowland 12). The novel "can be broken down into . . . hundreds of separate lyric notations" (Gifford, *Novel* 184). The work "is a series of intense episodes united, paradoxically, in their very separateness" (Muchnik 348).

3. In chapter 9 of this book the concept of an "expansive," broadly encompassing form of dialogue (or "supradialogue") is treated.

4. There is a fair consensus of critical opinion regarding death and resurrection as being the principal theme of the novel, as confirmed by Wilson ("Doctor" 216), Jackson (148), Obolensky (161), and Muchnik (352), who rightly observes that "the dual nature of death as both destructive and creative is a ruling idea of the novel" (357).

5. "Therefore art is also an effort of resurrection, and its immortality dwells in other men's minds as a gift that the artist has made of himself. Death is thus transformed in the miracle of art" (Silbajoris 25).

6. Although the state of mind during which poetry is conceived and written is amply detailed (XIV:8), it is the lack of psychological examination of the characters' interrelations that is noted here.

7. Earlier a similar image to that of the woman bowed over the coffin is elicited when Zhivago is taken ill. Again there is an accompanying epiphanic moment. "He had complained that Heaven had cast him off, but now the whole breadth of Heaven leaned low over his bed, holding out two strong, white, woman's arms to him. His head swimming with joy, he fell into a bottomless depth of bliss as one who drops unconscious" (Pasternak 395). Lara's care thus has its (immediate) healing effect.

 Later, at the end, Lara of course can do nothing, yet the fact that she still "talks to the deceased as to the living" (Grigorieff 341) is yet another symbolic detail suggestive of the novel's governing metaphor of resurrection.

8. Or, as Wilson suggests: "The whole book is an enormous metaphor for the author's vision of life" ("Legend" 16). And, further: "For Pasternak, the whole of life properly seen is a revelation" (Gifford, *Pasternak* 185).

9. Zhivago is thus "able to understand Lara's significance for him in terms of the imagery used by [the old woman]. When Yury escapes to her from the partisans, she has become symbolized by the rowan tree, the actual one standing outside the camp, and the other in [the] song" (Gifford, *Pasternak* 187).

10. Part of that point is that, "in an almost literal and fantastic sense," Zhivago's whole life is transformed into the poems at the end. "Zhivago becomes his poems, as if in a fairy-tale. . . . An individual's sense of the force of life ripens him for his own—and for the ultimate transformation. As Mary Magdalene says in Zhivago's poem 'Magdalene,' 'I will grow up to resurrection'" (Reeve 135).

11. "Not only are coincidences part of a deliberate structural pattern, but . . . they also have a deeper meaning and are expressive of the main thematic design of the novel. . . . Such chance encounters are for Pasternak part of a mysterious intertwining and interlocking of human destinies" (Struve, "Hippodrome" 231-33).

Chapter 3

1. Although Heidegger argues that "the past is what is past, it is irretrievable" (19), this is not so in the mind of Florentino Ariza, for whom such irrefutable logic is entirely irrelevant. For him, rather, there is only "a present which is always beginning again" (Bergson, *Matter* 139), affording a renewed, rich potential in the process.

   That potential might be defined thus: "If one possessed the present completely, one would possess a summing mechanism in full and perfect operation, and that mechanism would be total memory. For the present in theory is a summation of an infinite past" (Fletcher 340). For, as Bergson argues: "Consciousness means memory," and, conversely, "there is no consciousness without memory" (*Metaphysics* 26, 40).

2. Drawing upon Aristotle, Heidegger makes essentially the same point when he states: "Time too is nothing. It persists merely as a consequence of the events taking place in it. . . . Time is that within which events take place" (3), an argument that precludes the idea of time as being absolute.

   Likewise, again eschewing the notion of time as absolute, Bergson argues: "The essence of time is that it goes by; time already gone by is the past, and we call the present the instant in which it goes by" (*Matter* 137)—all of which suggests that time is only something (and not really some *thing* at all) we nominate.

3. In relating "spirit" to time, Heidegger recalls Augustine, whom he paraphrases thus: "In you, my spirit, I measure time; you I measure, as I measure time" (6). Heidegger's English translator and commentator notes that "a more conventional translation reads: 'Tis in thee, O my mind, that I measure my times'" (24). In either understanding (spirit or mind), clearly time is associated with what has been termed here mundanely a certain "personal" quality. Heidegger concludes that his original question, "What is time? became the question: Who is time? More closely: are we ourselves time? Or closer still: am I time?" (22)

   In the same spirit Bergson explains that "what I call 'my present' has one foot in my past and another in my future. . . . The psychical state, then, that I call 'my present,' must be both a perception of the immediate past and a determination of the immediate future" (*Matter* 138), both of which, of course, are "mine."

4. Or, conversely, as Heidegger has it, defining the "time of the present" thus: "Everything that occurs rolls out of an infinite future into an irretrievable past" (18).

Chapter 4

1. Koroviev's curious explanation may be condensed in the consistently felicitous and sagacious expression of the French philosopher and phenomenologist, Gaston Bachelard, who observes: "Poetic space, because it is expressed, assumes values of expansion" (201).

2. In a brief paraphrase Joseph Frank captures the essence of what takes place here when he notes in the abstract: "an image is defined not as a pictorial reproduction but as a unification of disparate ideas and emotions into a complex presented spatially in an instant of time" (11). Exhibiting a wealth of detail, Bulgakov's novel stunningly exemplifies, especially here, how numerous and various are the "disparate ideas and emotions" that might be artistically rendered "in an instant of time."

3. That interdependency is evident in part because "past and present are apprehended spatially, locked in a timeless unity that, while it may accentuate surface differences, eliminates any feeling of sequence by the very act of juxtaposition"

(Frank 63). This view may well be applied to Bulgakov's novel, in which a "feeling of sequence" is reduced, if not completely eliminated, "by the very act of juxtaposition," most notably of the Moscow and Jerusalem narratives.

4. As Lotman aptly and conclusively explains: "Although its appearance would not be possible outside the determinate space of the plot, each new text alters that space, with which it effects a dynamic correlation" ("Space" 112-13).

5. Moreover, that sphere helps to determine her adventures. As Toporov states (with regard to Dostoevsky), encapsulating much of the present argument: "As in the cosmological plan of myth, space and time are not simply the frames (or a passive backdrop), within which the action unfolds; they are active (and, accordingly, determine the hero's conduct), and in this sense they are largely comparable to the plot" (238).

In addition, in the context of the "brigand" *(razbojnik)* in the nineteenth-century Russian novel—a character type with which Margarita shares certain common features—Lotman makes the point: "The prevalence of plots of this type is related to the fact that they afford the possibility of depicting the entire spectrum of society from top to bottom and effectively juxtapose the so-called criminal element with the seemingly proper stratum of society. This creates a broad sphere for the development of plot with an enormous range of possibility" ("Space" 107). In terms of Bulgakov's heroine, who functions within a similar sphere, that "enormous range" might well include Margarita's outrageous antics, coupled with her equally generous behavior.

6. One is reminded of the line in *Doctor Zhivago*: "Talent in the highest and broadest sense means talent for life" (Pasternak 68).

7. As David Patterson explains: "Because the loss of place is definitively linked to the exile of the word, homelessness is bound to wordlessness" (44).

8. The "merging of the contemporary and the mythological" (noted earlier) becomes evident in this "revival" since "often in mythic texts real death is substituted for by a faked one" (Lotman, "Space" 112).

Chapter 5

1. What that meaning might be remains ambiguous. Poe's "The Masque of the Red Death" (also a kind of parable), in contrast, suggests unambiguously by its very title that the mask (an equivalent term, virtually, to Hawthorne's *veil*) worn by an intrusive figure come upon a carnivalized scene is a clear and evident sign of the Red Death that threatens all and sundry.

Adding to the ambiguity of our semiotic endeavor is the fact that Hawthorne also refers four times to the minister's black veil as being an "emblem." For our purposes we will treat it as a symbol exclusively, since, as Thomas A. Sebeok points out, an emblem is, in any case, "a subspecies of symbol" (121).

Chapter 6

1. "What is remarkable throughout is the fact that usually no attempt is made to deal concretely with the labyrinth as signifier. Such seems to be its semiotic potential that simply to name it in its metaphoric functions is enough to produce the desired effect" (Senn 225).

Nonetheless, proceeding beyond such naming, a student of the labyrinth laboriously treats it as a sign "of complex artistry," "of inextricability or impenetrability," and "of difficult process," among numerous other considerations (Doob 66-91).

2. A careful reader of literature and labyrinths expresses the intricate relations between time and memory and between the labyrinth and the circle in compelling fashion that essentially obliterates any dichotomy between the labyrinth and the circle, in effect merging the two: "García Márquez structures Bolívar's memories back through spirals of time. . . . the spirals of memory intersect the linear progress of Bolívar's trip. . . . For García Márquez, the labyrinth offers an image of forms within the turbulent circles of memory" (Davis 113, 114, 122). Nevertheless, it pays to recognize as well the general effect of wandering in the labyrinth, where "the 'faculty' that fails to work in the maze is [precisely] memory" (Fletcher 339). Equally appropriate to the novel, it is argued that the image of the labyrinth may go beyond Frye's notion of "lost direction" (cited earlier) to suggest "lost origin . . . lost plan, lost orientation, lost position" (Fletcher 340), all of which applies to the General's last days, as chronicled in this carefully researched (as García Márquez is at pains to explain in a curious afterword) fictive biography.

3. As one analyst rightly observes: "The speech of [García] Márquez' central characters typically tends to the lapidary and the aphoristic. It is not a baring of the soul, or an elaboration of a view, so much as the summary expression of an inner process which could not perhaps be made either fully conscious or fully rational. It preserves its own mystery and asks to be met by its hearer in the same spirit" (Bell 145).

4. Yet another way of regarding the novel's iconic qualities is expressed thus: "Every few pages García Márquez inserts another woman. Their very presence, since most of them are said to belong to Bolivar's glorious past, allows a labyrinthine exploration of his life before his final journey, and the ebbing of his passion in bed (or in the hammock), as in the episode of the young girl who leaves him in the morning as virginal as she was the night before . . . mirrors the ebbing of his life" (Palencia-Roth 57).

Norman O. Brown takes the argument a step further: "The woman penetrated is a labyrinth. You emerge into another world inside the woman" (48).

Chapter 7

1. From one considered perspective the relationship between sound and silence is expressed thus: silence is "of a piece with sound, for it is sound's polar opposite: sound and silence define each other. Words must be interspersed with pauses, silences, to be understood. Indeed, the deepest understanding . . . comes often in the silence that follows an utterance, as the effects of the words reverberate without sound" (Ong 187).

Another viewpoint acknowledges the presence of "silence in monologue" and "silence in dialogue" as active forces in communication (Neher 16). That same perspective ignores (or expands upon) the obvious point that words are interspersed by moments of silence, stating instead that "within the word one has to apprehend silence" (10), and further that silence "is everywhere present in the absence of the word" (18), allowing, then, for a *potentially communicative* presence, which is valorized over a correspondingly diminished notion of absence.

Finally, in accord with what has preceded, we read: "Language and silence belong together: language has knowledge of silence as silence has knowledge of language. . . . Speech is in fact the reverse of silence, just as silence is the reverse of speech. There is something silent in every word, as an abiding token of the origin of speech. And in every silence there is something of the spoken word, as an abiding token of the power of silence to create speech" (Picard 16, 24).

Such views encapsulate in abstract, even poetic, expression the present argument.

2. As Ong puts it: "Man is rooted in 'speaking silence'. . . . when we thus think of silence as communicating, we are likely to think of it as a kind of speech" (2-3). Neher, likewise, refers to the "voice of silence," arguing that "silence is only another word, a transmutation of the word . . . .it is the delicate and subtle 'pianis-simo' of the word [which] only serves to justify and strengthen the agreement of the whole" (17, 59).

3. The two writers share a number of features in common. The talks between Tarwater and each of his uncles (*The Violent Bear It Away*), for instance, are rem-iniscent of Dostoevsky's extended verbal duels. In the first part of the novel Tarwater's great-uncle attempts to argue him into faith; in the second the school-teacher tries to reason him out of it. In *The Brothers Karamazov* Ivan plays a sim-ilar role with his brother Alesha. In fact, the atheistic older brother relates "The Grand Inquisitor" precisely in order to dissuade the young novice from his chosen path. By contrast, in *The Possessed* Stavrogin, as mentor to Shatov and Kirillov, assumes both roles, infecting the former with an all-embracing faith and the latter with an opposing atheistic viewpoint that prescribes suicide as the ultimate demon-stration of man's freedom.

In O'Connor's novel the two ideas—the acceptance or rejection of faith—become oddly merged. Tarwater drowns the idiot child, first, to determine what lit-eral sense he might find in the rite of baptism and the attendant notion of being born again but also to demonstrate (to himself first of all) that he does not have faith and that he is "free of it," knowing as he does that the child will not come back to life. Yet, by virtue of the peculiar dialectic operative in the work, he comes away from it all with a sense of having felt "the call." What takes place in the world thus has no effect on the mind of the boy, which has long been fixed. Such reversal of expectation is also reminiscent of Dostoevsky. We need only recall Raskolnikov's firm resolve not to kill the old pawnbroker, just prior to his murdering her, or Stavrogin's seemingly determined resolution to take up lonely citizenship in the Swiss canton of Uri, before committing suicide. In these instances as well some-thing deeply internalized seems bound to have its way, despite the best efforts of certain "external" conscious decisions to sway.

Other parallels between the two writers may also be briefly remarked. Both Raskolnikov's and Ivan Karamazov's suffering results from wrestling with the prob-lem of faith, as is the case with Hazel Motes (*Wise Blood*), the would-be preacher of a church without God, and with Tarwater, the misguided follower of John the Baptist. Similarly, dialogue at its most serious is situated in places that are dreari-est. Ivan and Alesha discuss the existence of God in a seedy tavern (just as Raskolnikov and Svidrigailov have their talk in similar surroundings), while Tarwater and his uncle have it out, also on the problem of faith, in a dingy diner, just prior to the adolescent's ritual drowning of the idiot child, in a tragic travesty of baptismal rite. Thus, as an innocent, unwitting victim of the older boy's internal struggle and violent turmoil, the child figures in a sacrificial role similar to that of the old pawn-broker and her sister (*Crime and Punishment*), Nastasya Filippovna (*The Idiot*), and Fedor Karamazov (*The Brothers*), in which each is the victim of another's will to power and corresponding need to understand. For both Dostoevsky and O'Connor understanding is accomplished, paradoxically, by the perpetration of a crime—as much against oneself as another. In brief, the notion of victim or sacrifice (significantly, both words are the same in Russian) is central to the existential vision of both writers. Someone always has to pay for another's discord, as does the suffering character himself. In Dostoevskian terms the seemingly endless cycle of pain and suffering can only be broken by taking responsibility for oneself—and for others.

4. Prince Myshkin is captivated by Nastasya Filippovna's eyes, under whose spell he alone perceives a lurking, self-destructive madness. Rogozhin's are no less striking and strangely suggestive of much the same thing. Both the doomed woman and the man obsessed with her send their fearful messages through the same channels—mutely, poignantly, and to no avail. Neither feels compassion for the other; only Myshkin is haunted by them both: by a pair of eyes that are plaintive and hopeless and by those that express an even worse desperation. Gleaming like hot coals, the latter pair repeatedly signifies Rogozhin's hidden presence: at the railway station ("I saw two eyes that looked at me just as you did just now" [199]); in the dark corridor ("Those two eyes, *the same two eyes*, met his own. . . . Rogozhin's eyes flashed" [226-27]); and in the church ("I fancied I saw his eyes. . . . But why? What's he here for?" [568]). Finally, rather than be saved, Nastasya Filippovna will take refuge in those dark, shining, mad eyes—from the possibility of life. ("Nastasya Filippovna had caught his eyes in the crowd. She rushed at him like a mad creature" [577]). Much earlier in the novel, in attempting to learn the truth of the man, Myshkin silently confronts Rogozhin. "Not sitting down but standing motionless, he looked Rogozhin straight in the eyes for some time: at the first moment they seemed to gleam more brightly" (198). Which is to say, in a Dostoevsky novel, more threateningly.

5. In Dostoevsky prominent instances of such sad confrontations include Raskolnikov's respective meetings with Sonya and Svidrigailov (*Crime and Punishment*); Ivan's confrontation with his devil ("Ivan Fedorovich's Nightmare") and his interviews with Smerdyakov (*The Brothers Karamazov*). As an attendant feature of these confrontations and "as an integrated feature within dialogue, the moment of silence bears information . . . on some level of meaning" (Danow, *Dialogic* 17), which necessarily demands interpretation.

6. "Because the unsaid and the unsayable desire at that moment to be said" (Neher 18)—or, at least, to be understood.

7. In fact, one might meaningfully incorporate a line from the passage by Dostoevsky, just cited, within O'Connor's context (where the child preacher is substituted for Raskolnikov): "With every moment [*her*] intent and fiery glance pierced more powerfully into his mind and soul." Likewise, the same is possible in reverse, by applying a line from O'Connor to Dostoevsky: "He felt that in the space between them, their spirits had broken the bonds of . . . ignorance and were mingling in some unheard of knowledge." In each case, moreover, that "unheard of knowledge" amounts to the recognition of another's godlessness—of the killing off of what is best in oneself.

8. Personalized, that paradox emerges as "the agony of one to whom presence is denied because vocal communication is denied." On the other hand, "any manifestation of the sacred . . . suggests personal presence" (Ong 114, 163). And any such "manifestation" is, of course, precisely what the priest is seeking in only a single Word from his Lord, since "[voice] itself is the manifestation of presence" (Ong 168), including, in the context of Endo's novel, sacred presence.

Or, as Neher puts it, simply: "God is silence" (11). And, as Picard likewise affirms: "Silence points to a state where only being is valid: the state of the Divine.

The mark of the Divine in things is preserved by their connection with the world of silence" (20). But such (basic) resolutions remain opaque for Endo's tortured, searching, imploring priest, who seeks but a Word.

9. Yet the absence of such response may also be reformulated as a kind of presence that places in clear perspective the relation of God's silence to man's existential predicament: "Man does not put silence to the test; silence puts man to the test" (Picard 17), a notion that fairly encapsulates the principal theme of *Silence*.

10. Thus, Endo's Japanese Grand Inquisitor ridicules his Catholic prisoner with the words: "I have been told that you said . . . that the Christ . . . told you to trample— and that was why you did so. But isn't this just your self-deception? just a cloak of your weakness?" (280). The cruel point is supported, in effect, by Buber's claim that "in the end, man, having attained to clear knowledge, must recognize that every alleged colloquy with the divine was only a soliloquy, or rather a conversation between various strata of the self" (22). However problematic the term *soliloquy* might be, Buber is nonetheless remarking an instance of *dialogic* communication, unique unto itself, that takes place, of necessity, *in silence*, in what Peirce terms "a dialogue between different phases of the ego" (4.6) and what Lotman refers to less elegantly as "auto-communication," "internal speech," or "internal communication" ("Models" 99).

Chapter 8

1. In classic understatement, Trilling describes the Cossacks as "without mind or manners" (18). They are rightly characterized in existential terms that are equally primitive as "nomads who ride in search of nothing but the sense of their own natures" (Falen 132).

2. As one student of Babel comments, "The primary narrator sees beauty in horror and the horror of that beauty" (Sicher 69).

   Concerning the stories' origins, Terras remarks: "As far as their genesis is concerned they are closer to the lyric poem than to the epic narrative" (152). Sicher, on the other hand, having it both ways, speaks of an "epic lyricism" (69).

3. See Lotman's discussion of the frame as a potentially distinctly separate text (*Structure* 209-17).

4. Falen points out that "Even Sashka's betrayal of his mother links him with Christ, recalling as it does Jesus' refusal to recognize his own mother (Matthew 12:47-48) and his admonition that those who would follow him must forsake their families (Matthew 19:29)" (177). Yet the analogy seems infelicitous: forsaking is one thing, betraying is another. The disease, after all, is communicable, as everyone knows, including the dimwitted Sandy.

5. Dialogue is rarely mentioned in critical studies of *Red Cavalry* and then only cursorily. As an exception, too much is granted, with seemingly little reflection upon a sweeping generality that does not hold up, when it is claimed that "the stories consist of accounts by first-hand narrators and of dialogue" (Grongaard 62-63). Such a view does not take into account those stories in which there is no dialogue whatever or in which there is only a single line of direct speech ("In St. Valentine's Church").

   Much closer to the mark is this assessment: "In its integration into the cycle's stylistic system, dialog comes to function as another 'fragment' of the total verbal pattern, as a constituent element in the verbal elaboration of the stories, adding another level to their rich stylistic mosaic" (Luplow 88). Terras, likewise, rightly states that "there are but few dialogues of any length." He also speaks of "brief, racy dialogues (always 'stylized'!)" and of there being "shreds of dialogue" (150, 153). These observations correlate with Ehrenburg's remarks to the effect that Babel "attributed great significance to dialogue" in the sense that "dialogue in his stories is so distinctive and clear that at times a single phrase reveals a character's entire moral aspect" (7, 8).

6. While some commentators find hope residing in the belly of the pregnant Jewess, one also regards the young woman's question as "unanswerable" (Carden 131). That concisely expressed view may be extended to embrace the cycle as a whole, which offers an abundance of horrific description with no resolution.

7. Sicher observes that "revolution and modern warfare do not usually pause to respect nostalgia and lyricism" (38), a certain understatement. Yet the same can be said with regard to the virtual lack of an occasion for responsive talk in Babel's cycle.

8. Hence, "there is no dialogue between the two perspectives. . . . Gedali [representing one point of view in the cycle] and Vinogradov [the commissar of the story, representing another] are impoverished by this absence of dialogue, while Ljutov, who is drawn to both perspectives, is unable to unite them into a single vision; their existence within the confines of his single consciousness does nothing to reconcile their antagonism" (Klotz 164-65).

9. "In a certain sense, then, the stories . . . are static, and this quality is sometimes emphasized very clearly by the fact that the story is set within a frame" (Grongaard 30).

10. Thus, "the apparent dialogue between Ljutov and Gedali is in fact two juxtaposed monologues. Instead of a synthesis there is an unresolved tension, both in the argument and in Ljutov's consciousness" (Klotz 163).

11. Literally: "For a pickled cucumber and the World Revolution!"

12. Or, put differently: "Babel places narrative voices between himself and the reader, voices which are not *personae* for the author, but which are yet not fully distinct from him. In this way the author keeps the reader in doubt as to his position; the reader is caught in a web of ironies and ambiguities, some of which are created by the narrator and his complex character, some by the author's unclear overview, and some by a combination of both" (Luplow 24).

13. For additional discussion of this problem, see Danow, "Paradox."

14. For Bakhtin the frame is positioned as the "front line" of an utterance or text (as we will have occasion to note again later), and that position is strategic (*Speech* 89 n. i).

15. In more general terms it is explained: "For the expansiveness of narrative Babel substitutes rhapsodic rhetoric and an intense lyric concentration upon images" (Ehre 72). Further: "The Babelian short story at its best seems to realize that poetic balance between thought and image, line and color, movement and structure in a way which is characteristic of great lyric poetry" (Terras 156).

16. Concerning the problem of distinguishing between Babel and his narrator, one reader refers in facile manner to "the stories told by the sophisticated Lyutov-Babel" (Ehre 66). Another supports this implicitly encapsulated view: "But the truth of the matter is that Babel has not carefully distinguished the narrator from the author, and the stories slide back and forth across the boundary between the two functions" (Carden 124). A more convincing argument suggests that "Lyutov is not merely a *persona* for the author, but must be distinguished from the separate and

ultimately controlling authorial overview" (Luplow 10). An earlier reader appears to have it both ways in a paradoxical assessment, in which the latter, concluding phrase is surely the more compelling: "The character using the first person singular . . . is often identical with the writer himself, and yet he is not so much a person as a point of view" (Poggioli 236).

17. One commentator perceives the initial choruslike voice as belonging to Pavlichenko: "The archaic is given special emphasis in the introduction by the fact that Pavlichenko talks about himself in the third person" (Grongaard 57). But does he? Perhaps that extraordinary lyrical voice of the opening apostrophe does not belong to the untutored, illiterate shepherd turned Red Army commander.

18. This "short prose poem" is neatly summed up thus: "Almost verbless, it is an incantation, singing through the inscriptions on the gravestones of a dead world surviving only as memory" (Ehre 73).

19. As one critic suggests: "In [the young man's] dying words he attempts to refute Gedali's view that 'only the mother is eternal.'" Further, the irony is pointed up that, "if Ilya Bratslavsky has indeed escaped, it is only through the agency of death; his search for a new identity has returned him to the bosom of the eternal mother-earth" (Falen 158-59). Another point of view has it that "she is also an 'episode' for Lyutov. In the course of the book he struggles against the webs of nostalgia that tie him to the mother, and in the final story, 'Argamak,' he breaks free to join the epic march of the Cossack army" (Ehre 84).

Concerning the collective plight of the mother in wartime, Dolgushov's succinct request ("The Death of Dolgushov") is most to the point: "You'll write and tell my mother how things were" (89).

20. One reader rightly speaks of "lyrical epiphanies," of which the coda just noted represents a classic instance (Lee 249).

Chapter 9

1. Distinctions among these three forms of reported speech are discussed in valuable outline by Vološinov (141-59).

2. The essay was originally published in 1940.

3. The Prague School distinguishes (in its 1929 "Theses") between "alternately interrupted (dialogic) speech and unilaterally uninterrupted (monologic) speech" (Steiner 12).

4. Zhivago's expressed sentiment is remarkably close to Bakhtin's gripping pronouncement: "Nothing is absolutely dead: every meaning will have its homecoming festival" (*Speech* 170). In this confluence of theological thought, the poet/novelist and literary theorist express essentially the same idea, in like aesthetic fashion.

5. Quasi-direct speech, as Bakhtin explains, is "generally one of the most widespread forms for transmitting inner speech in the novel" (*Dialogic* 319). "Quasi-direct speech involves discourse that is formally authorial, but that belongs in its 'emotional structure' to a represented character, whose inner speech is transmitted and regulated by the author" (Bakhtin, *Speech* 130 n. 15).

Strelnikov's troubled ruminations concluding chapter 7 illustrate the form. "Suppose his wife and daughter were still there! Couldn't he go to them? Why not now, this very minute? Yes, but how could he? They belonged to another life. First he must see this one through, this new life, then he could go back to the one that had been interrupted. Someday he would do it. Someday. But when, when?" (253).

6. Lara's admonitions to herself coupled with the novelist's interpolations are described in abstract terms by Vološinov: "Thus relations between reported speech and authorial context . . . take a shape analogous to the relations between alternating lines in dialogue" (157).

7. As a kind of poetics in a very minor key, providing a certain justification for such "fallacy," the reader is informed at one dramatic moment: "There was something in common between the disturbances in the moral and in the physical world" (192).

WORKS CITED

Abrams, M. H. *The Mirror and the Lamp: Romantic Theory and the Critical Tradition.* Oxford: Oxford Univ. Press, 1953.

Achinstein, Peter. *Concepts of Science: A Philosophical Analysis.* Baltimore: Johns Hopkins Press, 1968.

Alexandrov, Vladimir E. Relative Time in *Anna Karenina. Russian Review,* 1982 (41:2), 159-68.

Allende, Isabel. *The House of the Spirits.* Trans. Magda Bogin. New York: Bantam, 1986.

———. *Eva Luna.* Trans. Margaret Sayers Peden. New York: Bantam, 1989.

Appelfeld, Aharon. *Badenheim 1939.* Trans. Dalya Bilu. Boston: Godine, 1980.

———. *The Healer.* Trans. Jeffrey M. Green. New York: Grove Weidenfeld, 1990.

———. *Katerina.* Trans. Jeffrey M. Green. New York: Random House, 1992.

———. *Unto the Soul.* Trans. Jeffrey M. Green. New York: Random House, 1994.

Aristotle. *Poetics.* Trans. W. Fyfe. Cambridge, Mass.: Loeb Classical Library, 1965.

Asturias, Miguel Angel. *Mulata.* Trans. Gregory Rabassa. New York: Avon, 1982.

Auerbach, Eric. *Mimesis: The Representation of Reality in Western Literature.* Trans. Willard R. Trask. Princeton: Princeton Univ. Press, 1953.

Babel, Isaac. *The Collected Stories.* Trans. Walter Morison. New York: Meridian Books, 1960.

Bachelard, Gaston. *The Poetics of Space.* Trans. Maria Jolas. New York: Orion, 1964.

Bakhtin, Mikhail (M. M.). *The Dialogic Imagination: Four Essays by M.M. Bakhtin.* Trans. Caryl Emerson and Michael Holquist. Austin: Univ. of Texas Press, 1981.

———. *Problems of Dostoevsky's Poetics.* Vol. 8 of *Theory and History of Literature.* Trans. Caryl Emerson. Minneapolis: Univ. of Minnesota Press, 1984.

———. *Speech Genres and Other Late Essays.* Trans. Vern W. McGee; eds. Caryl Emerson and Michael Holquist. Austin: Univ. of Texas Press, 1986.

Barthes, Roland. An Introduction to the Structural Analysis of Narrative. *New Literary History,* 1974 (6:2), 237-72.

Bell, Michael. *Gabriel García Márquez: Solitude and Solidarity.* New York: St. Martin's Press, 1993.

Bergson, Henri. *Creative Evolution.* Trans. Arthur Mitchell. New York: Modern Library, 1944.

———. *An Introduction to Metaphysics.* Trans. T. E. Hulme. New York: Liberal Arts Press, 1955.

———. *Matter and Memory.* Trans. Nancy Margaret Paul and W. Scott Palmer. New York: Zone Books, 1988.

Black, Max. *Models and Metaphors: Studies in Language and Philosophy.* Ithaca: Cornell Univ. Press, 1972.

Borges, Jorge Luis. *Labyrinths: Selected Stories and Other Writings.* Eds. Donald A. Yates and James E. Irby. New York: New Directions, 1964.

———. *The Book of Sand.* Trans. Norman Thomas di Giovanni. New York: Dutton, 1977.

Bridgman, P. W. *The Logic of Modern Physics.* New York: Macmillan, 1961.

Brooks, Peter. Introduction. In Tzvetan Todorov, *Introduction to Poetics.* Vol. 1 of *Theory and History of Literature.* Trans. Richard Howard, vii-xix. Minneapolis: Univ. of Minnesota Press, 1981.

Brown, Norman O. *Love's Body.* New York: Random House, 19ʳ

Buber, Martin. *Eclipse of God: Studies in the Relation* ᵗ   ᵗligion and *Philosophy.* Westport, Conn.: Greenwood Press, 19ᵗ

Bulgakov, Mikhail. *The Master and Margarita.* Trans. Michaᵗ   ᵗny. New York: Meridian, 1985.

Carden, Patricia. *The Art of Isaac Babel.* Ithaca: Cornell Univ. Press, 1972.

Carpentier, Alejo. *The Lost Steps.* Trans. Harriet de Onis. New York: Noonday, 1979.

Chatman, Seymour. *Story and Discourse.* Ithaca: Cornell Univ. Press, 1978.

Clark, Katerina and Michael Holquist. *Mikhail Bakhtin.* Cambridge, Mass.: Harvard Univ. Press, 1984.

Culler, Jonathan. *Structuralist Poetics: Structuralism, Linguistics, and the Study of Literature.* Ithaca: Cornell Univ. Press, 1975.

———. *The Pursuit of Signs.* Ithaca: Cornell Univ. Press, 1981.

Danow, David K. Lotman and Uspensky: A Perfusion of Models. *Semiotica,* 1987 (64:3-4), 343-57.

———. *The Dialogic Sign: Essays on the Major Novels of Dostoevsky.* New York and Bern: Peter Lang, 1991.

———. *The Thought of Mikhail Bakhtin: From Word to Culture.* New York: St. Martin's Press, 1991.

———. The Paradox of *Red Cavalry. Canadian Slavonic Papers,* 1994 (36:1-2), 43-54.

Davis, Mary E. Sophocles, García Márquez and the Labyrinth of Power. *Revista Hispanica Moderna,* 1991 (44:1), 108-23.

de Mallac, Guy. *Boris Pasternak: His Life and Art.* Norman: Univ. of Oklahoma Press, 1981.

Devi, Maitreyi. *It Does Not Die.* Chicago: Univ. of Chicago Press, 1992.

Dillon, George. *Constructing Texts: Elements of a Theory of Composition and Style.* Bloomington: Indiana Univ. Press, 1981.

Doob, Penelope Reed. *The Idea of the Labyrinth: From Classical Antiquity through the Middle Ages.* Ithaca: Cornell Univ. Press, 1990.

Dostoevsky, Feodor (Fyodor). *Crime and Punishment.* Norton Critical Edition. Trans. Jessie Coulson. New York: W. W. Norton, 1964.

———. *The Idiot.* Trans. Constance Garnett. New York: Bantam, 1971.

———. *The Brothers Karamazov.* Norton Critical Edition. Trans. Constance Garnett; revised by Ralph E. Matlaw. New York: W. W. Norton, 1976.

Dyck, J. W. *Boris Pasternak.* New York: Twayne Publishers, 1972.

Ehre, Milton. *Isaac Babel.* Boston: Twayne Publishers, 1986.

Ehrenburg, Ilya. Introduction. In I. Babel', *Izbrannoe* (Selected Works), 5-10. Moscow: Izdatel'stvo khudozhestvennoj literatury, 1957.

Endo, Shusaku. *Silence.* Trans. William Johnston. New York: Taplinger, 1980.

Falen, James E. *Isaac Babel: Russian Master of the Short Story.* Knoxville: Univ. of Tennessee Press, 1974.

Faris, Wendy B. The Labyrinth as Sign. In *City Images: Perspectives from Literature, Philosophy, and Film*. Ed. Mary Ann Caws, 33-41. New York: Gordon and Breach, 1991.

Fletcher, Angus. The Image of Lost Direction. In *Centre and Labyrinth: Essays in Honour of Northrop Frye*. Eds. Eleanor Cook et al, 329-46. Toronto: University of Toronto Press, 1983.

Fokkema, D. W. Continuity and Change in Russian Formalism, Czech Structuralism, and Soviet Semiotics. *PTL: A Journal for Descriptive Poetics and Theory of Literature*, 1976 (1:1), 153-96.

Forster, E. M. *Aspects of the Novel*. New York: Harcourt, Brace and World, 1927.

Frank, Joseph. *The Idea of Spatial Form*. New Brunswick: Rutgers Univ. Press, 1991.

Frye, Northrop. *Anatomy of Criticism: Four Essays*. Princeton: Princeton Univ. Press, 1973.

García Márquez, Gabriel. *One Hundred Years of Solitude*. Trans. Gregory Rabassa. New York: Avon, 1971.

———. *The Autumn of the Patriarch*. Trans. Gregory Rabassa. New York: Avon, 1977.

———. *Love in the Time of Cholera*. Trans. Edith Grossman. New York: Alfred A. Knopf, 1988.

———. *The General in His Labyrinth*. Trans. Edith Grossman. New York: Penguin, 1991.

Genette, Gérard. *Narrative Discourse: An Essay in Method*. Trans. Jane E. Lewin. Ithaca: Cornell Univ. Press, 1980.

Gifford, Henry. *The Novel in Russia: From Pushkin to Pasternak*. New York: Harper and Row, 1964.

———. *Pasternak: A Critical Study*. Cambridge: Cambridge Univ. Press, 1977.

Gillespie, Gerald. *Garden and Labyrinth of Time: Studies in Renaissance and Baroque Literature*. New York: Peter Lang, 1988.

Grigorieff, Dmitry. Pasternak and Dostoevsky. *Slavic and East European Journal*, 1959 (3:4), 335-42.

Grongaard, Ragna. *An Investigation of Composition and Theme in Isaak Babel's Literary Cycle Konarmija*. Aarhus: Arkona, 1979.

Gutierrez, Donald. The Labyrinth as Myth and Metaphor. *University of Dayton Review*, 1983, (16:3), 89-99.

Harré, Rom. 1970. *The Principles of Scientific Thinking*. Chicago: University of Chicago Press.

Hawkes, Terence. *Structuralism and Semiotics*. Berkeley: Univ. of California Press, 1977.

Hawthorne, Nathaniel. *Selected Short Stories of Nathaniel Hawthorne*. New York: Ballantine Books, 1989.

Heidegger, Martin. *The Concept of Time*. Trans. William McNeil. Oxford: Blackwell Publishers, 1992.

Hesse, Mary B. *Models and Analogies in Science*. London: Sheed and Ward, 1963.

Holquist, Michael. *Dialogism: Bakhtin and His World*. London and New York: Routledge, 1990.

Hutten, E. H. The Role of Models in Physics. *British Journal for the Philosophy of Science*, 1954 (4:16), 284-301.

Ivanov, Viach. Vs. The Category of Time. *Semiotica*, 1973 (8:1), 1-45.

Jackson, R. L. *Doctor Zhivago: Liebestod* of the Russian Intelligentsia. In *Pasternak: A Collection of Critical Essays*. Ed. Victor Erlich, 137-50. Twentieth Century Views Series. Englewood Cliffs: Prentice-Hall, 1978.

Joyce, James. *Stephen Hero*. New York: New Directions, 1944.

Klotz, Martin. Poetry of the Present: Isaak Babel's *Red Cavalry*. *Slavic and East European Journal*, 1974 (18:2), 160-69.

Leach, E. R. *Rethinking Anthropology*. London School of Economics Monographs on Social Anthropology no. 22. London: Univ. of London, Athlone Press, 1961.

Leatherdale, W. H. *The Role of Analogy, Model and Metaphor in Science*. Amsterdam: North-Holland, 1974.

Lee, Alice. Epiphany in Babel's *Red Cavalry*. *Russian Literature Triquarterly*, 1972 (2), 249-60.

Lotman, Jurij [Yuri, Ju. M.]. *Semiotics of Cinema*. Trans. Mark E. Suino. Michigan Slavic Contributions no. 5. Ann Arbor: Michigan Slavic Publications, 1976.

———. *The Structure of the Artistic Text*. Trans. Ronald Vroon. Michigan Slavic Contributions no. 7. Ann Arbor: Michigan Slavic Publications, 1977.

———. Two Models of Communication. In *Soviet Semiotics: An Anthology*, 99-101. Baltimore: Johns Hopkins Univ. Press, 1977.

———. O sjuzhetnom prostranstve russkogo romana xix stoletija (Space in the Nineteenth-century Russian Novel). In *Trudy poznakovym sistemam* (Studies in Sign Systems), 1987 (20), 102-14.

———. *Universe of the Mind: A Semiotic Theory of Culture*. Trans. Ann Shukman. Bloomington: Indiana Univ. Press, 1990.

Lubbock, Percy. *The Craft of Fiction*. New York: Viking Press, 1957.

Lukács, Georg. *The Theory of the Novel*. Trans. Anna Bostock. Cambridge, Mass.: MIT Press, 1971.

Luplow, Carol. *Isaac Babel's Red Cavalry*. Ann Arbor: Ardis, 1982.

Martin, Gerald. *Journeys through the Labyrinth: Latin American Fiction in the Twentieth Century*. New York: Verso, 1989.

Mendilow, A. A. *Time and the Novel*. New York: Humanities Press, 1952.

Meyerhoff, Hans. *Time in Literature*. Berkeley: Univ. of California Press, 1955.

Morson, Gary Saul. Who Speaks for Bakhtin? A Dialogic Introduction. *Critical Inquiry*, 1983 (10:2), 225-43.

Muchnik, Helen. *From Gorky to Pasternak:Six Writers in Soviet Russia*. New York: Random House, 1961.

Mukařovský, Jan. *Aesthetic Function, Norm and Value as Social Facts*. Trans. Mark E. Suino. Michigan Slavic Contributions no. 3. Ann Arbor: Michigan Slavic Publications, 1970.

———. Detail as the Basic Semantic Unit in Folk Art. In *The Word and Verbal Art: Selected Essays by Jan Mukařovský*. Trans. John Burbank and Peter Steiner, 180-204. New Haven: Yale Univ. Press, 1977.

———. Dialogue and Monologue. In *The Word and Verbal Art: Selected Essays by Jan Mukařovský*. Trans. John Burbank and Peter Steiner, 81-112. New Haven: Yale Univ. Press, 1977.

Neher, André. *The Exile of the Word: From the Silence of the Bible to the Silence of Auschwitz*. Philadelphia: Jewish Publication Society of America, 1981.

Noth, Winfried. *Handbook of Semiotics*. Bloomington: Indiana Univ. Press, 1990.

Obolensky, D. The Poems of *Doctor Zhivago*. In *Pasternak: A Collection of Critical Essays*. Ed. Victor Erlich, 151-65. Twentieth Century Views Series. Englewood Cliffs: Prentice-Hall, 1978.

O'Connor, Flannery. *Three by Flannery O'Connor*. New York: Signet, 1962.

Ong, Walter J. *The Presence of the Word: Some Prolegomena for Cultural and Religious History.* New York: Clarion, 1970.

O'Toole, L. Michael. *Structure, Style and Interpretation in the Russian Short Story.* New Haven: Yale University Press, 1982.

O'Toole, L. M. and Ann Shukman, eds. and trans. *Formalist Theory.* Russian Poetics in Translation no. 4. Oxford: Holdan Books, 1977.

Palencia-Roth, Michael. Gabriel García Márquez: Labyrinths of Love and History. *World Literature Today,* 1991 (65:1), 54-58.

Pasternak, Boris. *Doctor Zhivago.* Trans. Max Hayward and Manya Harari. New York: Modern Library, 1958.

Patterson, David. *The Shriek of Silence: A Phenomenology of the Holocaust Novel.* Lexington: Univ. Press of Kentucky, 1992.

Payne, Robert. *The Three Worlds of Boris Pasternak.* Bloomington: Indiana Univ. Press, 1961.

Peirce, Charles S. *Collected Papers of Charles Sanders Peirce.* Eds. Charles Hartshorne and Paul Weiss. Cambridge, Mass.: Harvard University Press, 1931-35.

Picard, Max. *The World of Silence.* Chicago: Henry Regnery, 1952.

Platonov, Andrei. *Collected Works.* Trans. Alexey A. Kiselev. Ann Arbor: Ardis, 1978.

Poggioli, Renato. *The Phoenix and the Spider.* Cambridge,Mass.: Harvard Univ. Press, 1957.

Ramras-Rauch, Gila. *Aharon Appelfeld: The Holocaust and Beyond.* Bloomington: Indiana Univ. Press, 1994.

Reeve, F. D. *Doctor Zhivago:* From Prose to Verse. *Kenyon Review,* 1960 (22:1), 123-36.

Rimmon-Kenan, Shlomith. *Narrative Fiction: Contemporary Poetics.* London and New York: Methuen, 1983.

Rowland, Mary and Paul. *Pasternak's Doctor Zhivago.* Carbondale: Southern Illinois Univ. Press, 1967.

Sebeok, Thomas A. *Contributions to the Doctrine of Signs.* Vol. 4 of Sources in Semiotics. Lanham, Md.: Univ. Press of America, 1985.

Segre, Cesare. *Semiotics and Literary Criticism.* The Hague and Paris: Mouton, 1973.

———. *Structures and Time.* Chicago: Univ. of Chicago Press, 1979.

Senn, Werner. The Labyrinth Image in Verbal Art: Sign, Symbol, Icon? *Word and Image,* 1986 (2:3), 219-30.

Shukman, Ann. *Literature and Semiotics: A Study of the Writings of Yu. M. Lotman.* Amsterdam: North-Holland, 1977.

Sicher, Efraim. *Style and Structure in the Prose of Isaak Babel'.* Columbus: Slavica Publishers, 1986.

Silbajoris, Rimvydas. The Poetic Texture of *Doctor Zhivago. Slavic and East European Journal,* 1965 (9:1), 19-28.

Stankiewicz, Edward. Structural Poetics and Linguistics. In *Linguistics and Adjacent Arts and Sciences.* Vol. 12 of Current Trends in Linguistics. Ed. Thomas A. Sebeok, 629-59. The Hague: Mouton, 1974.

———. Poetics and Verbal Art. In *A Perfusion of Signs.* Ed. Thomas A. Sebeok, 54-76. Bloomington: Indiana Univ. Press, 1977.

Steiner, Peter, ed. *The Prague School: Selected Writings, 1929-1946.* Austin: Univ. of Texas Press, 1982.

Sternberg, Meir. *Expositional Modes and Temporal Ordering in Fiction.* Baltimore: Johns Hopkins Univ. Press, 1978.

Struve, Gleb. Monologue Intérieur: The Origins of the Formula and the First Statement of Its Possibilities. *PMLA*, 1954 (69), 1101-11.

———. The Hippodrome of Life: The Problem of Coincidences in *Doctor Zhivago. Books Abroad,* 1970 (44:2), 231-36.

Terras, Victor. Line and Color: The Structure of I. Babel's Short Stories in *Red Cavalry. Studies in Short Fiction,* 1965 (3:1), 141-56.

Tolstoy, Leo. *Resurrection.* Trans. Vera Traill. New York: New American Library, 1961.

———. *Anna Karenina.* Trans. Constance Garnett. New York: Modern Library. 1965.

———. *War and Peace.* Trans. Constance Garnett. New York: Modern Library, [1972].

Tomashevsky, Boris. *Teoriya literatury: poetika* (Theory of Literature: Poetics). Ann Arbor: Ardis, 1928.

Toporov, V. N. O strukture romana Dostoevskogo v svjazi s arxaichnymi sxemami mifologicheskogo myshlenija (The Structure of a Novel by Dostoevsky in Relation to Archaic Schemes of Mythological Thought). In *Structure of Texts and Semiotics of Culture.* Eds. Jan van der Eng and Mojmir Grygar, 225-302. The Hague: Mouton, 1973.

Trilling, Lionel. Introduction. In Isaac Babel, *The Collected Stories,* 9-37. New York: Meridian Books, 1960.

Uspensky, Boris. *A Poetics of Composition: The Structure of the Artistic Text and Typology of a Compositional Form.* Trans. Valentina Zavarin and Susan Wittig. Berkeley: Univ. of California Press, 1977.

Vargas Llosa, Mario. *The Storyteller.* Trans. Helen Lane. New York: Penguin, 1990.

Veltruský, Jiří. Semiotic Notes on Dialogue in Literature. *Language and Literary Theory.* Papers in Slavic Philology no. 5. Eds. Benjamin A. Stoltz, I. R. Titunik, and Lubomír Doležel, 595-607. Ann Arbor: University of Michigan Press, 1984.

Vološinov, V. N. *Marxism and the Philosophy of Language.* Trans. Ladislav Matejka and I. R. Titunik. New York: Seminar Press, 1973.

Wiesel, Elie. *The Gates of the Forest.* Trans. Frances Frenaye. New York: Avon, 1967.

Wilson, Edmund. Doctor Life and His Guardian Angel. *New Yorker,* November 15, 1958, 201-26.

———. Legend and Symbol in *Doctor Zhivago. Encounter,* 1959 (12:6), 5-16.

INDEX

A

Allende, Isabel 15-16, 17
Appelfeld, Aharon 17, 20, 21
Aristotle 181, 185
Asturias, Angel 78
Auerbach, Eric 6-8
Augustine, 185

B

Babel, Isaac 133-51, 190-92
Bachelard, Gaston 78, 80, 85, 86,
    87, 94, 95, 96, 185
Bakhtin, Mikhail 6-8, 9, 10-11, 23,
    25, 37, 81, 116, 156-59, 167,
    170, 180, 182, 191, 192
Barthes, Roland 9, 24, 30, 37, 181,
    182, 183
Bergson, Henri 15, 22, 57-58, 60-63,
    67, 182-83, 185
Borges, Jorge Luis 15, 16
Brown, Norman O. 187
Buber, Martin 190
Bulgakov, Mikhail 77-89, 185-86

C

Carpentier, Alejo 16
Chatman, Seymour 37, 187
Comenius 101
Conrad, Joseph 97
Culler, Joseph 26-27, 158

D

Dostoevsky, F. M. 22, 24, 25, 30-31,
    33-34, 47, 119-23, 125-26, 127,
    128, 182, 186, 187-88

E

Ehrenburg, Ilya 191
Eichenbaum, Boris 175-76
Endo, Shusaku 120, 121, 126-31,
    189-90

F

Formalists 4, 9, 26-27
Forster, E. M. 25, 78
Frank, Joseph 185-86
Frye, Northrop 19, 102, 187

G

García Márquez, Gabriel 16, 17-18,
    21-22, 57-67, 101-11, 185, 186-87
Genette, Gérard 27, 29, 181, 182
Gogol, Nikolai 71

H

Hawthorne, Nathaniel 71-74, 91-99,
    186
Heidegger, Martin 62, 185

I

Ivanov, Viach. Vs. 23, 35

J

Joyce, James 8, 20-21

L

Leach, Edmund 15, 17, 78
Lotman, Yury 8, 78, 82, 86, 87, 91,
    98, 173, 180, 186, 190
Lubbock, Percy 30
Lukács, Georg 23, 27

M

Mendilow, A. A. 24, 63, 181, 182, 183
Meyerhof, Hans 183
Mukařovský, Jan 36, 156, 183

N

Neher, André 187, 188, 189

O

O'Connor, Flannery 120-26, 127,
    128, 187-88

Olesha, Yury 81
Ong, Walter 131, 187, 188, 189

P

Pasternak, Boris 8, 21, 39-55, 153-71,
    183-84, 186, 192-93
Patterson, David 186
Paz, Octavio 102
Peirce, Charles Sanders 93, 94-95,
    116, 163, 174, 190
Picard, Max 187, 189-90
Platonov, Andrei 71, 74-75
Poe, Edgar Allan 186
Prague School 156, 157, 192

S

Sebeok, Thomas A. 186
Segre, Cesare 26, 180, 181
Shklovsky, Victor 83
Sicher, Efraim 190, 191
Stankiewicz, Edward 28, 36
Sternberg, Meir 36, 181, 182
Struve, Gleb 183, 184

T

Terras, Victor 190-91
Todorov, Tzvetan 2
Tolstoy, Leo 22, 24, 30, 31-33, 34, 35,
    78, 126, 182, 183
Tomashevsky, Boris 27, 29, 183
Toporov, V. N. 82, 186
Trilling, Lionel 190

U

Uspensky, Boris 79, 83

V

Vargas Llosa, Mario 18-19
Vološinov, V. N. 116, 192, 193

W

Wiesel, Elie 17
Wilson, Edmund 184